# SIGNS for COMPUTING TERMINOLOGY

Steven L. Jamison

-1983-

---

Illustrated by Paul M. Setzer

---

A PUBLICATION OF
THE NATIONAL ASSOCIATION OF THE DEAF
814 Thayer Avenue
Silver Spring, Maryland 20910

SIGNS FOR COMPUTING TERMINOLOGY

STEVEN L. JAMISON



ISBN 0-913072-63-X

Printed in the United States of America

*Dedicated to*

*my son, Matthew,*
*for the marvelous ways*
*he has extended my horizons*
*and heightened my understanding.*

# Preface

This book of **Signs for Computing Terminology** is the result of the combined efforts of many people. To indicate adequately the nature and extent of these efforts, it is necessary to describe the procedures used in arriving at this final product.

The book's editor made the initial selection of the computing terms to be included, and developed a survey form to illustrate and/or describe alternative ways of signing the selected terms. The form also provided a means for reviewers to indicate: (1) which of the alternative signs they prefer, (2) how they sign the term (if different from any of the alternatives shown), (3) that they prefer to fingerspell the term, or (4) that they never use the term.

The editor made a selection of alternative signs for each of the computing terms that begin with the letter "A" and recorded them on the survey forms. This material was then sent to professionals in the computing field who are also skilled signers. They were asked if they would be willing to serve as project reviewers and if they could recommend other qualified individuals who should be contacted. A few were not able to participate because of work commitments, but reactions to the project were unanimously enthusiastic.

When reviewers returned these survey forms, they were mailed additional packets covering terms that begin with "B", "C" and "D". When these were returned, they received "E", "F" and "G", etc., until all terms had been reviewed. This process extended over a period of many months. Analysis of the completed forms showed that consensus had been reached on signs for about forty percent of the terms.

New survey forms were prepared for each term where agreement had not been reached. These forms included the signs from the first survey that received a significant level of support plus those additional signs that were recommended by one or more reviewers. These forms were again sent to all reviewers, first for all terms beginning with "A", "B" and "C" and progressing, as before, through the alphabet. This second iteration of the review process required many additional months of effort. The results now showed basic agreement on the signs for approximately seventy percent of the terms. For most of the remaining thirty percent, two alternative signs for each term received significant support. New survey forms were again prepared for these unresolved terms and sent to each reviewer.

All reviewers were then invited to attend a three-day workshop in the hope that consensus could be reached on the signs for these unresolved terms. All but four of the twenty-three reviewers were able to attend. The ability of reviewers to interact directly provided additional insight and led, for most terms, to a clear preference for one of the alternative signs. In other cases, agreement was given for the adoption of two separate signs for the same term. The editor anticipated the likelihood of including three distinct signs for the term "COMPUTER", but was surprised and pleased that one sign received essentially unanimous support. At this workshop, several new terms were introduced and agreement was reached on their signs.

Videotapes were then prepared by personnel at the National Technical Institute for the Deaf (NTID) at the Rochester Institute of Technology (RIT) to demonstrate the production of each sign selected. These tapes were made available to the reviewers to ensure that the sign (or signs) for each of the terms was produced properly; that is, the handshape(s), position(s), orientation(s), and movement(s) of each sign were correctly shown. Feedback from this review process resulted in a final set of three videotapes demonstrating these signs for computing terminology. These tapes have become an end product in themselves.

The artist used these tapes, as well as other project documentation, to create the illustrations contained in this book. All of these drawings were reviewed by the editor.

Although the procedures outlined here have been lengthy, involving the time and talent of so many capable people, it is hoped that the users of this book will feel that the results have been worth the effort.

# Acknowledgements

The development of this book, as described in the Preface, depended heavily on the cooperative participation of many dedicated individuals.

First and foremost, the author is keenly aware of the critically important role played by the many capable reviewers. Without their involvement, this book would not have been possible. Furthermore, their expertise, time, and effort were provided on a purely volunteer basis without remuneration. These reviewers, most of them deaf, represent a wide variety of backgrounds and professional affiliations from across the United States. Their commitment and dedication to the project were continuous throughout the development of the book, but were perhaps most evident at the three-day workshop where they contributed not only as individuals but also as parts of a well-functioning whole. Sincere appreciation is extended to each of them:

Karen K. Anderson, Computer Consultant and Chairman, Special Interest Group on Computers and the Physically Handicapped, Association for Computing Machinery, Rochester, New York.

Donald H. Beil, Associate Professor, Data Processing Department, National Technical Institute for the Deaf at RIT, Rochester, New York.

Philip W. Bravin, Advisory Systems Requirements Analyst, Information Systems Group, IBM Corporation, White Plains, New York.

Ronald C. Burdett, Associate Professor, Program for the Hearing Impaired, Ohlone College, Fremont, California.

Kevin B. Casey, Director, Computer Services, Gallaudet College, Washington, DC.

James A. Chmura, Assistant Professor, School of Computer Science and Technology, Rochester Institute of Technology, Rochester, New York.

David D. Custer, Member of the Technical Staff, Bell Laboratories, Denver, Colorado.

Kendall R. Doane, Technical Staff Member, Rocketdyne Division, Rockwell International, Canoga Park, California.

Robert J. Herbold, Assistant Director, Computer Services, Gallaudet College, Washington, DC.

Jack C. Lamberton, Staff Programmer, General Products Division, IBM Corporation, San Jose, California.

Paul Levenson, Advisory Systems Analyst/Programmer, European & Internal Business Division, Xerox Computer Services, Marina Del Rey, California.

Edward M. Li, Associate Programmer, General Products Division, IBM Corporation, Tucson, Arizona.

John Loos, President and Systems/Applications Software Designer, DairySoft™ Systems, Ltd., San Jose, California.

David M. Martin, Student, University of California, Berkeley, California.

David J. McGuinness, Assistant to the Vice President for Academic Affairs and Professor of Mathematics, Gallaudet College, Washington, DC.

Michael A. Miller, Applications Systems Manager, Management Information Services, Sykes Datatronics, Inc., Rochester, New York.

Marilyn K. Mitchell-Caccamise, Coordinator, Sign Language/Interpreting Services, Louisiana School for the Deaf, Baton Rouge, Louisiana.

Jadine Murello, Staff Interpreter, CIL Computer Training Program, Berkeley, California.

Chuzo Okuda, Associate Professor, Department of Mathematics, Gallaudet College, Washington, DC.

Diana Pryntz, Educational Specialist, Computer Science Support Team, National Technical Institute for the Deaf at RIT, Rochester, New York.

Joseph S. Slotnick, Computer Scientist, Abacus Programming Corporation, Van Nuys, California.

Sandra L. Sparks, Computer Scientist/Math Programmer, Computation Dept., Lawrence Livermore National Laboratory, Livermore, California.

E. Marshall Wick, Associate Professor, Business Administration Dept., Gallaudet College, Washington, DC.

Special recognition is given to Frank Caccamise, Senior Research Associate, Communication Program, NTID, Rochester Institute of Technology, Rochester, New York. In the early stages, his input served as a basic endorsement of the methodology being used and provided the book's editor with valuable insights and suggestions relating to the collection, evaluation, and documentation of technical signs. Dr. Caccamise also participated in the workshop, contributing much to the decision making process based on his rich background in the linguistics of sign language. And most significantly, he and Research Assistant Laurie Outermans directed the preparation of the videotapes. Others at NTID who should be recognized for their parts in the production of the tapes are Pattie Steele-Perkins, Mary Enders, Margie Grande-Ender, Jackie Montione, Mary Lou Basile, Jennie Ryan, and Diana Pryntz. In addition, appreciation is extended to Marshall Wick, Gallaudet College, for his consulting services during the initial taping.

Of course, the most visible aspect of the book is that provided by Paul M. Setzer, the artist responsible for the drawings that illustrate all of the included signs. Mr. Setzer has been remarkably successful at the difficult task of reducing live, three-dimensional figures and movements to still, two-dimensional drawings. His work is clean and uncluttered, realistically lifelike without extraneous detail. Robert and Patricia Herbold served as models for the artist; their involvement is greatly appreciated.

S. Melvin Carter, Jr., Director of the NAD Communicative Skills Program, deserves much thanks for his encouragement in the development of this book and for the interest and efforts of the NAD in coordinating all aspects of its publication.

And finally, the editor is deeply grateful to his employer, International Business Machines Corporation, for making the necessary time and other resources available to him to carry out his responsibilities in bringing this book to completion.

Steven L. Jamison
Editor

# Introduction

This sign language book is intended for use by: (1) deaf students preparing for careers in the computing field itself or in fields which have a significant interface with computing; (2) deaf employees currently in such careers; (3) teachers and instructors, both for pre-employment education and training and for similar activities on the job; (4) interpreters, both for educational and employment environments; and (5) managers and other work associates of deaf persons. This last category not only represents the largest number of potential users, but is also the group that will benefit most from the book's use. By facilitating communication with the people with whom they work, deaf employees are better able to interact and to contribute, thus increasing the productivity of the departments in which they work.

This book assumes that the user has some familiarity with conversational sign language. Only those terms that are commonly used in a computing context are included here. In fact, the vocabulary is heavily slanted toward computer programming and systems analysis, with less emphasis on computer engineering, computer operations, etc.

Furthermore, this is a sign language book, not a dictionary. Those who are interested in definitions of the terms or in diacritical markings to aid in their pronunciation are referred elsewhere. Also, the part of speech (noun, verb, adjective, etc.) is not given when it is either obvious or irrelevant.

This listing of computer-related terms is certainly not exhaustive and will become progressively less so as new terminology is introduced to meet the needs of this rapidly developing field. Similarly, some of the terms may become more or less obsolete with the passage of time. Nevertheless, the terms included here should provide a significant vocabulary base not only for the technical communication requirements of the computing field today but also well into the future. Terms are listed alphabetically to facilitate the use of the book as a reference manual.

A relatively high proportion (about 15%) of the entries are signed by fingerspelling the word (e.g., BAUD, FONT, PARITY), a shortened form of the word (e.g., AUX for AUXILIARY, EXEC for EXECUTIVE, SPEC for SPECIFICATION), or an acronym or abbreviation (ASCII for AMERICAN NATIONAL STANDARDS CODE FOR INFORMATION INTERCHANGE, MIPS for MILLION INSTRUCTIONS PER SECOND, RJE for REMOTE JOB ENTRY). About two thirds of all the fingerspelled entries are of this last type, reflecting the heavy use of acronyms and other abbreviations in the computing field. The names of all programming languages (e.g., APL, FORTRAN, PASCAL) are also fingerspelled. Although fingerspelling is an acceptable sign for any term, it is only referenced for those terms where it is the preferred sign.

Affixes (both prefixes and suffixes) are grouped together at the beginning of the list of entries. In addition, prefixes are also incorporated alphabetically in the main body of the text. This will facilitate the lookup of such terms as INCOMPATIBLE, MEGABYTE, and PREPROCESSOR. Although the signs for suffixes are given only in the special section on affixes, the need for an appropriate suffix is flagged by an asterisk(*) in many of the entries. In some instances, the appropriate suffix may be quite obvious from the word itself (e.g., DEVELOPMENT*, ERASABLE*, SENSOR*, USER*). But frequently the choice of suffix depends on the context of the word. In particular, does the word refer to a person and therefore require the personal suffix, or to a device, machine or program and therefore require the impersonal suffix? Many words can refer to either (e.g., EDITOR*, SCHEDULER*, SUPERVISOR*).

An entry may be for a single term (e.g., BUFFER) or for two or more closely related terms (e.g., INTEGRATE, INTEGRATED, INTEGRATION). In the latter case, the associated sign is correct for each of the related terms. If one of the terms has an added asterisk (e.g., PROGRAM, PROGRAMMER*, PROGRAMMING), then the sign for that term is the sign given plus the sign for the appropriate suffix. When the same sign is used for more than one term or one family of closely related terms, the corresponding entries are cross-referenced. For example, the entry: INSTALL, INSTALLATION (cf. INITIALIZE, SETUP) indicates that both INITIALIZE and SETUP are separate entries in this book and that they are signed in the same way as INSTALL.

If both a term and its abbreviation are commonly used in computer-related communication, then each is a separate entry in the alphabetical listing. In all such cases, the entry for the abbreviation directs the reader to the full expression (e.g., CAI (see COMPUTER ASSISTED INSTRUCTION)), and the associated sign is made by fingerspelling the abbreviation. If the abbreviation of a multi-word term has become an acronym (e.g., ASCII, DASD, MIPS, ROM), an indication is given as to its pronunciation.

Many of the entries include one of the following designations:

(fs) the term is signed by fingerspelling it.
(abbr) the term is signed by fingerspelling its abbreviation.
(acronym) the term is signed by fingerspelling the acronym.
(sm) single movement—the movement indicated in the drawing is done only once.
(dm) duplicated movement—the movement is done two or more times.

If no such designation is made, the movement indicated in the drawing may be done one or more times. Hands that are lightly outlined indicate initial or intermediate positions; bold outlines indicate final positions.

For each entry, phrases are included which illustrate the use of the term in a computing context (**Usage:**). For some entries, additional information is provided to relate the sign to other terms which are not entries in this book (**Same sign for:** or **Initialized form of:**) or as a clarifying adjunct to the drawing (**Note:**). When the note indicates a combination of two terms (BREAKPOINT: "break" + POINT), a term is capitalized (POINT) if that term is a separate entry in the book.

During the past three decades, computers have become increasingly pervasive. Nearly everyone's life is directly or indirectly affected on almost a daily basis by their use in business, industry and government. Furthermore, they are now vital elements in space programs, research efforts, and military preparedness. And small personal-sized computers are now more and more common in individual offices, classrooms, and homes. Computer literacy is fast becoming a necessity for all.

It is hoped that this book will spur improved communication with and among deaf persons who are involved, either directly or indirectly, in this exciting and dynamic field, as well as facilitate the entrance of many more.

# Fingerspelling

Why discuss something as elementary as fingerspelling in a book that focuses on the vocabulary of a highly technical field? Firstly, many users of this book, although perhaps advanced in their knowledge and skills in computing, are beginners in their knowledge and skills in signing. Secondly, the more technical the field the greater the number of terms that need to be fingerspelled. This book contains hundreds of signs for computing-related terms, but there is still a significant portion of entries where fingerspelling is recommended. Of course, there are many terms in the computing field which are not included in this book. For many of these, there is no generally agreed upon sign. And even if a standardized sign exists, the person wishing to use that term may never have learned the sign or may have forgotten it. Fingerspelling is always a viable alternative.

There are four major aspects of any sign, including those for the individual letters of the manual alphabet: handshape, position, orientation, and movement.

*Handshape.* Most of the letters of the alphabet have distinctive handshapes, as shown on the alphabet chart that follows. The exceptions are: G-Q, H-U, I-J, and K-P. In each of these cases, the handshape for the second letter of each pair is the same as that used for the first letter in the pair.

*Position.* Right-handed persons position their right hand a few inches in front of the right shoulder, the upper arm hanging at the side in the most comfortable position possible. Left-handed persons, of course, position the left hand similarly but in front of the left shoulder. The hand should not be too far to the side and should definitely not obscure the face.

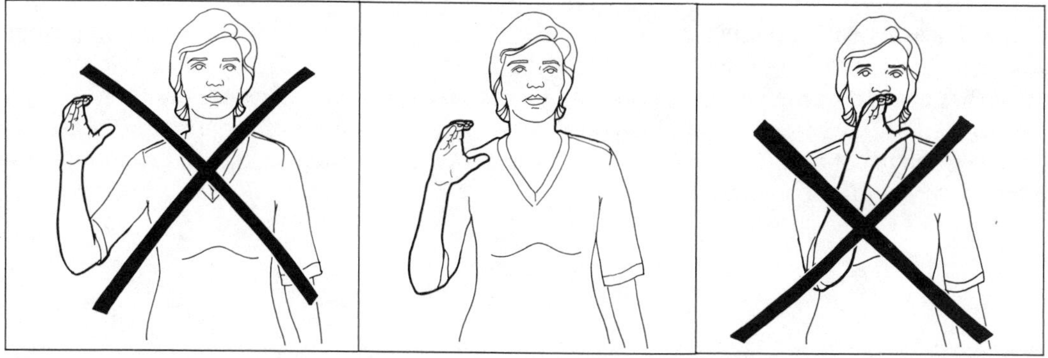

*Orientation.* Although most of the letters have different handshapes, most have the same orientation, namely having the palm facing forward in the general direction of the person reading the fingerspelled word. The exceptions: H (palm faces to signer's left), P and Q (palm faces downward). G can be made either with the palm forward or facing left, and J moves from palm facing forward to palm facing left (or even all the way around to facing inward).

*Movement.* Only two letters require movement, J and Z.

Of course, in spelling words there must be movement, but this is mostly finger movement as the speller changes handshapes from one letter to the next. Each change is made in the easiest and most direct way possible, applying the ''conservation of energy'' principle. Novice fingerspellers should resist the apparently natural tendency to emphasize each letter with a short, quick forward movement. ''Twiddling'' the fingers between letters or words should also be avoided.

The conservation of energy principle also applies in fingerspelling words that have a repeated letter. In spelling the word BOOLEAN, for example, the hand moves in the most direct way from B to O, but how does one move from the first O to the second O? Some movement is necessary or otherwise the word comes out BOLEAN. This can be done by very slightly opening the O handshape (perhaps a quarter of an inch) and then closing it again. If the O is opened too far, the word becomes BOCOLEAN. In general, any double letter (MM, TT, EE, etc) is made by forming the letter, then *slightly* relaxing the handshape, and then forming it again. Double L, as in SPELL, is usually an exception to this procedure. In this case, the first L is made in the usual way and then the L-hand is shifted to the right (for right-handers) a short distance (perhaps an inch). Some signers use this method for double letters other than just LL.

A slight pause is all that is needed to signal the end of a word. For example, in spelling ''. . . BAUD LINE . . .'', the D handshape is sustained briefly before changing into the L handshape. This pause can be a little longer at the end of a phrase or sentence, but punctuation marks (, ; : etc.) are usually not signed. A frequent exception to this is the question mark, but even here a slight forward tilt to the body and a questioning expression on the face is usually adequate.

A good maxim is: Clarity Before Speed. The speed of fingerspelling will gradually increase with time and practice but, if the early emphasis is on forming the letters with the correct handshapes, position, orientations and movements, a person will more likely develop into a good communicator.

And finally, if hearing people speak as they sign, they give the other person additional input which may facilitate the conversation. The signs for ENTRY and ACCESS, for example, are the same. The context of the sentence can sometimes make the meaning clear but, if the word is also spoken, the recipient can take additional advantage of whatever hearing or lipreading ability he/she may have. On fingerspelled words, however, the person should pronounce the word, not the individual letters.

# AMERICAN MANUAL ALPHABET

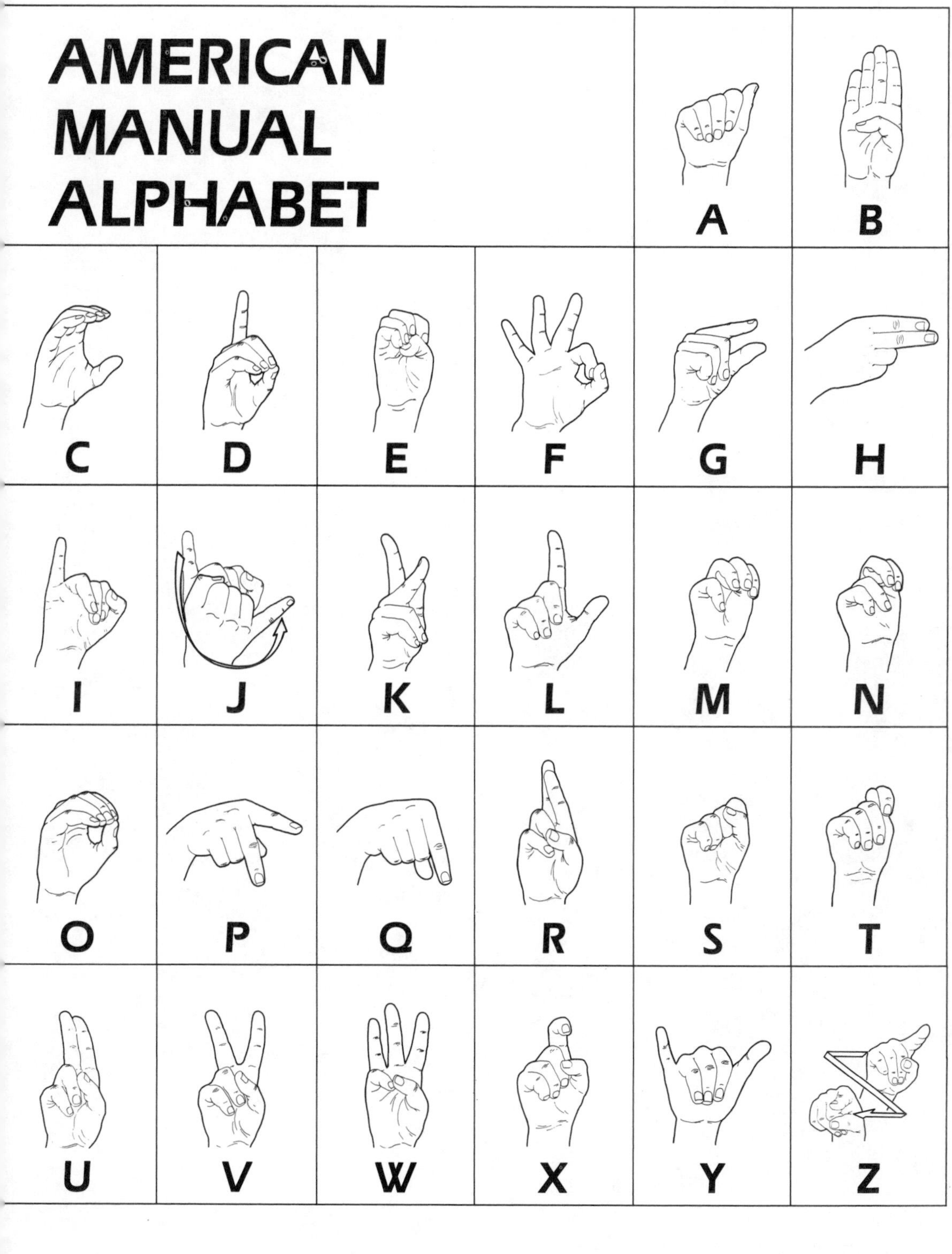

A B

C D E F G H

I J K L M N

O P Q R S T

U V W X Y Z

# PREFIXES AND SUFFIXES

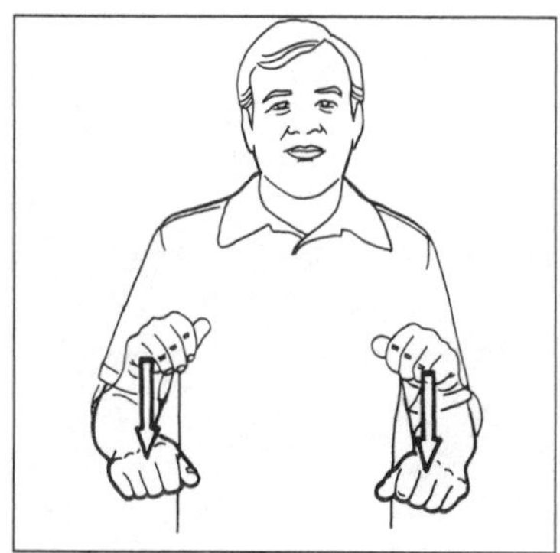

## -ABILITY, -ABLE

(sm)

**Same sign for:** ability, able, can, capable, possible.
**Usage:** addressable; relocatable; switchable; accessibility; reliability; transferability.

## -ER

(cf. -OR) (impersonal suffix) (abbr)

**Usage:** adapter; compiler; header; interpreter (referring to a device, machine, program, etc., but not a person).
**Note:** Simply add "R" to the sign for the verb.

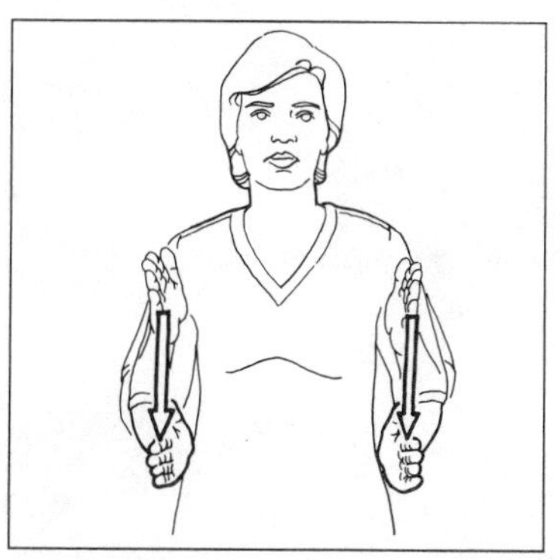

## -ER

(cf. -IAN, -IST, -OR) (personal suffix) (sm)

**Usage:** coder; manager; programmer; user (referring to a person).

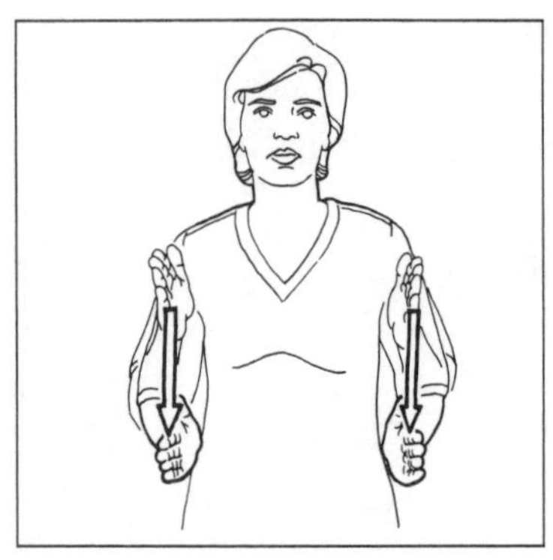

## -IAN

(cf. -ER, -IST, -OR) (personal suffix) (sm)

**Usage:** librarian; mathematician (referring to a person).

## IN-

(cf. NON-, UN-) (sm)

**Same sign for:** doesn't, don't, not.
**Usage:** inaccurate; inactive; incompatible; independent; indirect.
**Note:** Thumb pushes out from under chin.

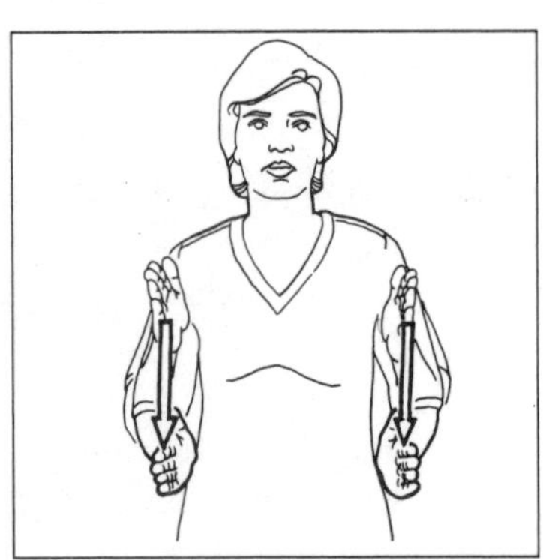

## -IST

(cf. -ER, -IAN, -OR) (personal suffix) (sm)

**Usage:** analyst; scientist; specialist; theorist (referring to a person).

## KILO-

(abbr)

**Usage:** kilobits; kilobytes; kilohertz.
**Note:** The single letter "K" is the sign for this prefix.

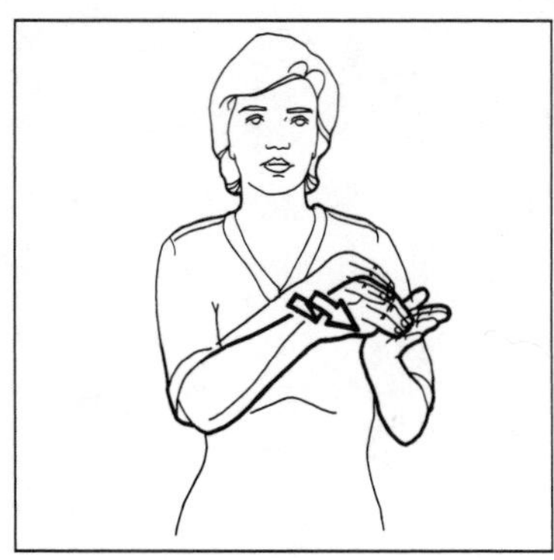

## MEGA-

(dm)

**Same sign for:** million.
**Usage:** megabytes; megahertz.
**Note:** Right M-hand into left palm exactly twice.

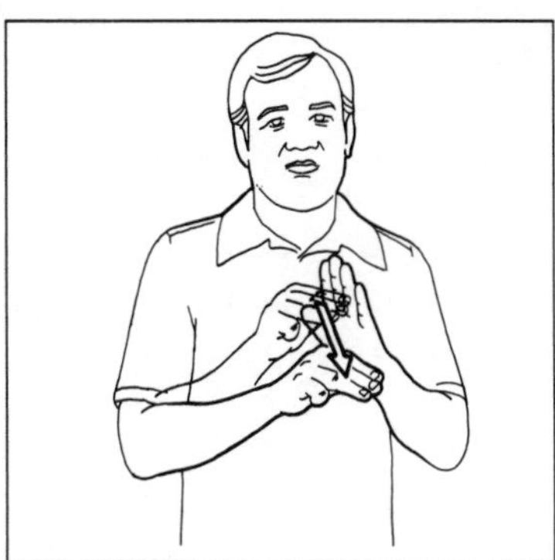

## -MENT

(sm)

**Usage:** development; management.
**Note:** Right M-hand slides down left palm.

M-I-C-R-O-

## MICRO-

(fs)

**Usage:** microcode; microprocessor; microprogram; microfiche.

M-I-L-L-I-

## MILLI-

(fs)

**Usage:** millisecond; millimeter; milligram.

# MINI-

(fs)

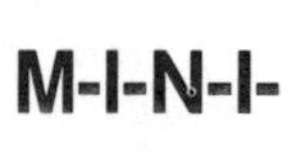


**Usage:** minicomputer; minidisk.

# MULTI-, MULTIPLE-

**Same sign for:** many, multiple, numerous.
**Usage:** multipass; multiprocessing; multitasking; multiple-precision; multiple-address.
**Note:** This movement is usually duplicated.

# NON-

(cf. IN-, UN-) (sm)

**Same sign for:** doesn't, don't, not.
**Usage:** nondestructive; nonresident; nonstandard; nonlinear.
**Note:** Thumb pushes out from under chin.

# -OR

(cf. -ER) (impersonal suffix) (abbr)

**Usage:** accumulator; generator; sensor; simulator (referring to a device, machine, program, etc., but not a person).
**Note:** Simply add "R" to the sign for the verb.

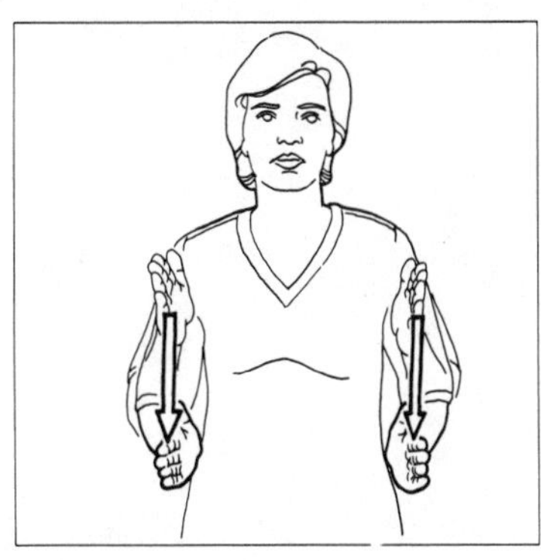

## -OR

(cf. -ER, -IAN, -IST) (personal suffix) (sm)

**Usage:** instructor; operator; supervisor (referring to a person).

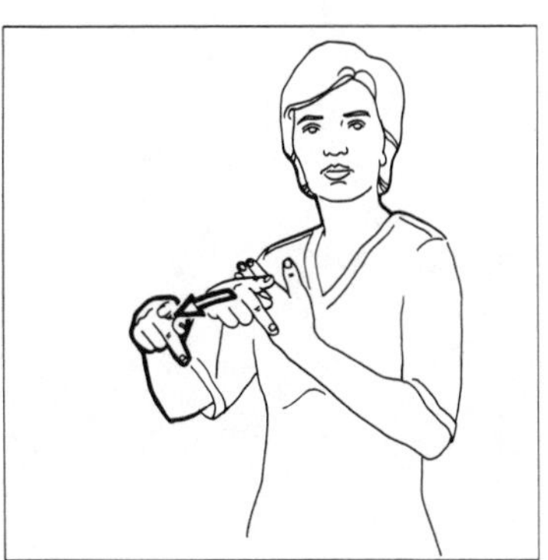

## POST-

(sm)

**Initialized form of:** after (P).
**Usage:** postprocessor; postinstallation; postrecovery.

## PRE-

(sm)

**Initialized form of:** before (P).
**Usage:** predefined; preprocessor; preset; presorted.

## PSEUDO-

(cf. ARTIFICIAL, DUMMY) (sm)

**Same sign for:** fake, false.
**Usage:** pseudo code; pseudo instruction; pseudo-random.
**Note:** Index finger passes in front of lips (perpendicular to direction used in signing REAL).

# RE-

(sm)

**Initialized form of:** again (R).
**Usage:** reentrant; restart; reread; reassign; reinitialize.

# SELF-

(sm)

**Usage:** self-adapting; self-checking; self-organizing.
**Note:** This sign can also be made without involving the left hand.

# SINGLE-

(sm)

**Usage:** single-address; single-precision; single-step.

# SUB-

**Usage:** subchannel; subfield; subset; subsystem; subtask.

## UN-

(cf. IN-, NON-) (sm)

**Same sign for:** doesn't, don't, not.
**Usage:** unassigned; unpacked; unprotected; unrecoverable; unscheduled.
**Note:** Thumb pushes out from under chin.

# COMPUTING TERMINOLOGY

## A

## ABEND

(sm)

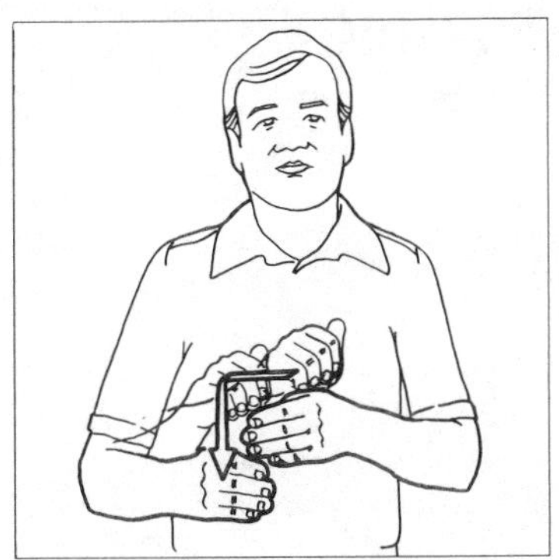

**Initialized form of:** END (A-B).
**Usage:** causing the program to abend;
and the associated abend code.
**Note:** The term ABEND is a contraction of ABnormal END.

## ABORT

(cf. DELETE) (sm)

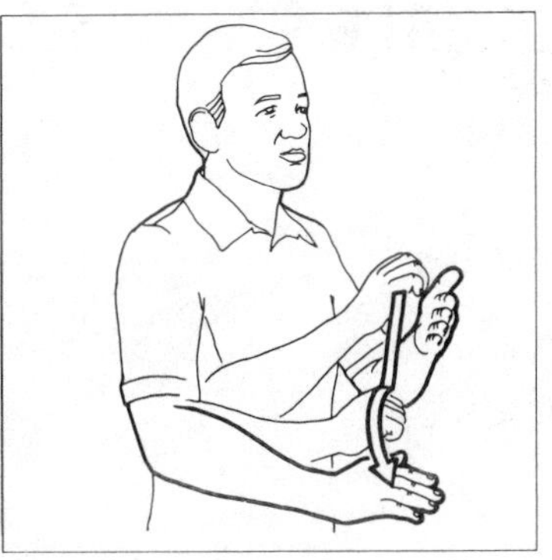

**Same sign for:** eliminate.
**Usage:** the operator's decision to abort the program;
the job was aborted by the supervisor program.

# A

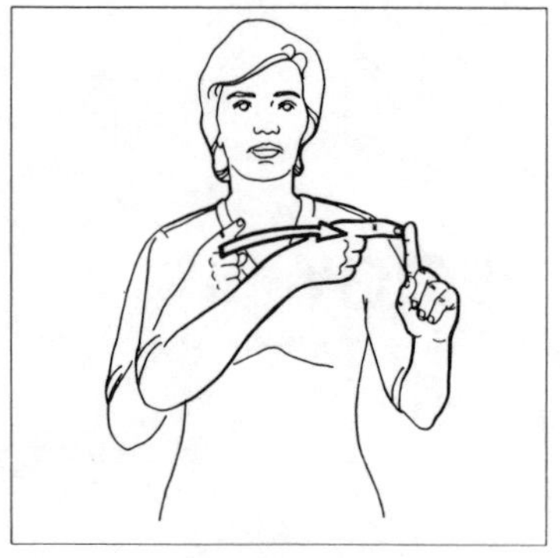

## ABSOLUTE
(cf. POINT) (sm)

**Usage:** absolute addressing; absolute error; absolute loader.

## ABSTRACT, ABSTRACTION
(sm)

**Initialized form of:** imagine (A).
**Usage:** abstract data; an abstract symbol; a procedural abstraction.

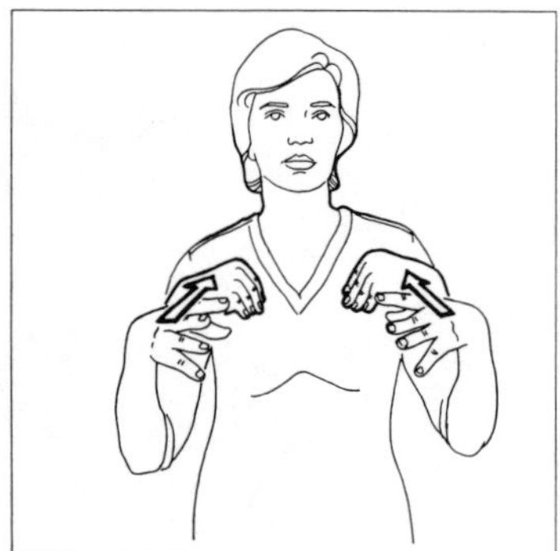

## ACCEPT, ACCEPTANCE
(sm)

**Usage:** a routine that does not accept negative numbers; a station that accepts messages; a system that passed its acceptance tests.

## ACCESS, ACCESSIBLE*, ACCESSIBILITY*
(cf. ENTER) (sm)

**Same sign for:** entrance, into.
**Usage:** an access mechanism; file access method; access time; direct access; sequential access; private files accessible only to; data accessibility.

## ACCOUNT, ACCOUNTING

(dm)

**Usage:** to each customer's account; an accounting machine; accounting applications.
**Note:** Right F-hand slides up left palm twice.

## ACCUMULATE, ACCUMULATOR*

(cf. COLLECT)

**Same sign for:** gather.
**Usage:** to accumulate the sum of the products; add to the contents of the accumulator; to clear the accumulator.
**Note:** This movement is usually duplicated.

## ACCURACY, ACCURATE

(cf. PRECISE) (sm)

**Same sign for:** exact, exactly.
**Usage:** if more accuracy is desired; a result accurate to the nearest thousandth.
**Note:** The small circular motion of the right hand is optional.

## ACRONYM

(sm)

**Same sign for:** abbreviate, condense, summarize, summary.
**Usage:** DASD is the acronym for; many acronyms used in the computing field.

## ACTION, ACTIVE, ACTIVITY

(cf. PERFORMANCE)

**Same sign for:** do.
**Usage:** requires some action by the operator; the active file; an active page; the high activity records in the file.
**Note:** Palm-down C-hands move to the right and return.

## ACTUAL

(cf. REAL) (sm)

**Same sign for:** really, sure, true.
**Usage:** actual memory size; an actual disk drive; the actual memory location.
**Note:** ACTUAL as opposed to VIRTUAL.

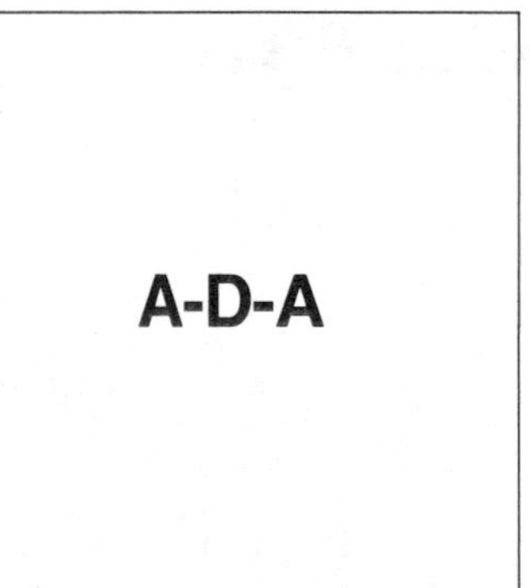


## ADA

(fs)

**Usage:** government endorsement of the Ada programming language; program designs expressed in Ada.

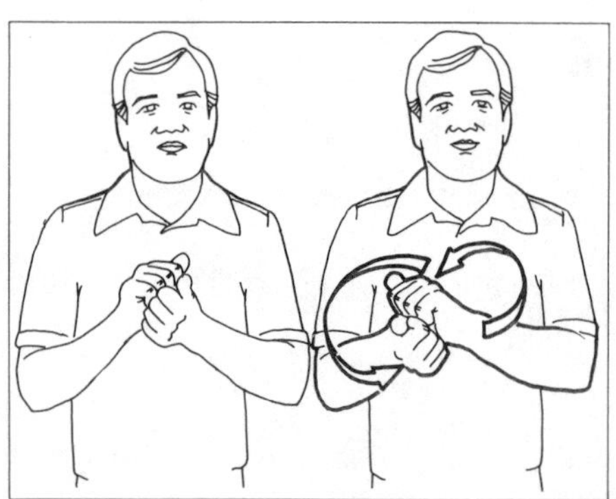

## ADAPT, ADAPTER*

(sm)

**Initialized form of:** change (A).
**Usage:** to adapt the program to run on the new system; a line adapter; a channel-to-channel adapter.

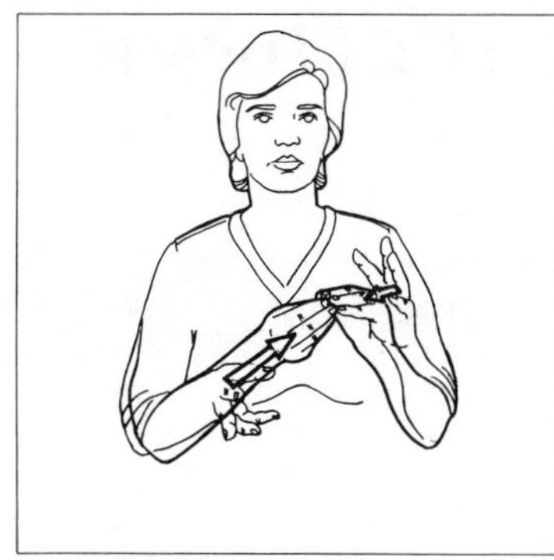

## ADD, ADDER*, ADDITION

(cf. TOTAL) (sm)

**Same sign for:** sum.
**Usage:** the ADD operation; the add time; a full adder; a serial adder; parallel addition.

## ADDRESS, ADDRESSABLE*, ADDRESSING

(sm)

**Usage:** the effective address; the address part of the instruction; address modification; indirect addressing; symbolic addressing; addressable storage.
**Note:** A-hands move upward on chest.

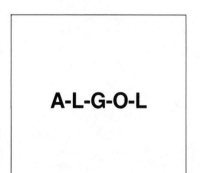

## ADVANCED (adj.)

(sm)

**Same sign for:** promote, promotion.
**Usage:** a course in advanced COBOL; providing advanced function for communication.

A-L-G-O-L

## ALGOL

(fs)

**Usage:** the ALGOL language; use of ALGOL at many universities.
**Note:** The term ALGOL is a contraction of ALGOrithmic Language; rhymes with "gal-gall."

## ALGORITHM, ALGORITHMIC
(sm)

**Initialized form of:** law (A-M).
**Usage:** a paging algorithm; an algorithm for determining priorities; an algorithmic language.

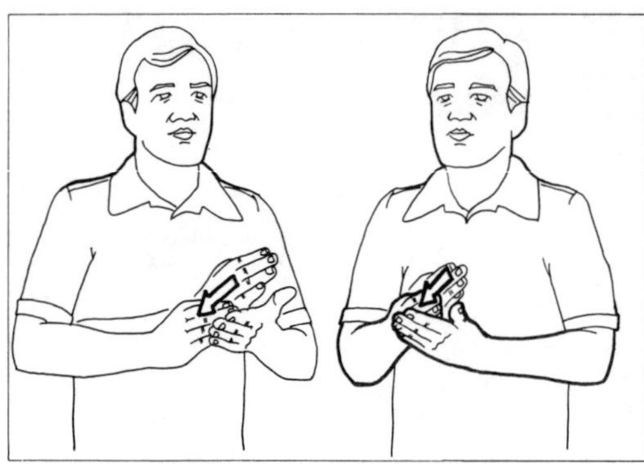

## ALLOCATE, ALLOCATED, ALLOCATION
(sm)

**Usage:** to allocate resources; space allocation; dynamic storage allocation.
**Note:** Sign for "part" or PARTITION is made two or three times, each time farther to the right.

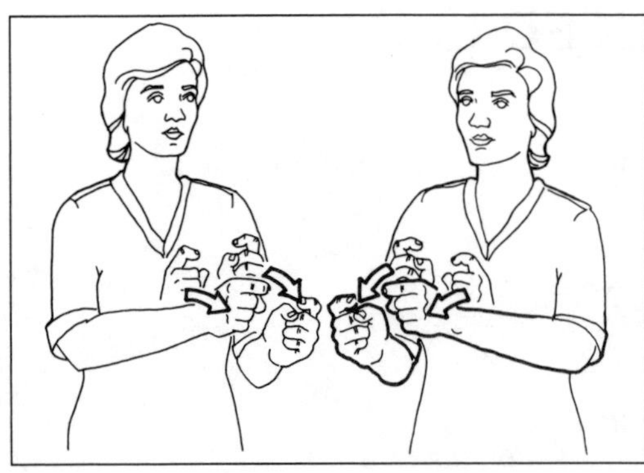

## ALLOCATE, ALLOCATED, ALLOCATION
(sm)

**Usage:** to allocate resources; space allocation; dynamic storage allocation.
**Note:** Sign for "donate" or "award" is made two or three times, each time farther to the right.

**A-B-C**

## ALPHABET, ALPHABETIC, ALPHABETICALLY
(sm)

**Usage:** for each letter of the alphabet; an alphabetic character; an alphabetic field; arranged alphabetically by name.

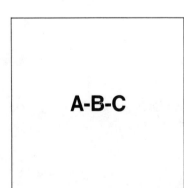

A-L-P-H-A

## ALPHABET, ALPHABETIC, ALPHABETICALLY

(abbr)

**Usage:** for each letter of the alphabet; an alphabetic character; an alphabetic field; arranged alphabetically by name.

A-N

## ALPHAMERIC, ALPHANUMERIC

(abbr)

**Usage:** alphameric part numbers; alphanumeric data; an alphanumeric keyboard.

## ALTERNATE (adj.)

(sm)

**Same sign for:** another, other, else.
**Usage:** using an alternate code; on an alternate track; the alternate route.

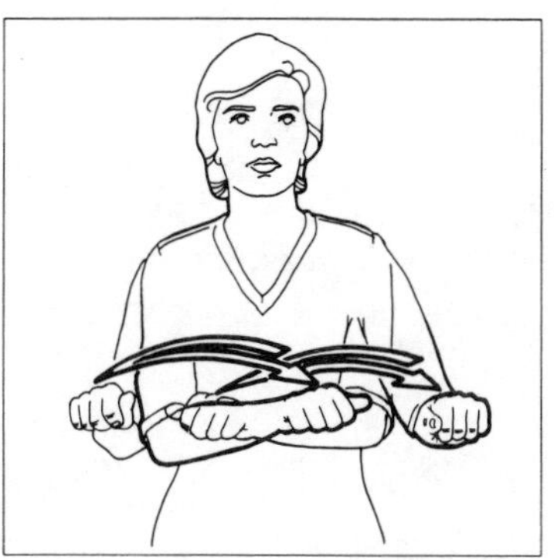

## ANALOG

(sm)

**Usage:** an analog computer; analog inputs; analog simulation.
**Note:** Palm-down A-hands move to the right and return.

## ANALOG-TO-DIGITAL, A-TO-D
(sm)

**Initialized form of:** then (A-D).
**Usage:** an analog-to-digital converter; requiring analog-to-digital conversion; A-TO-D devices.

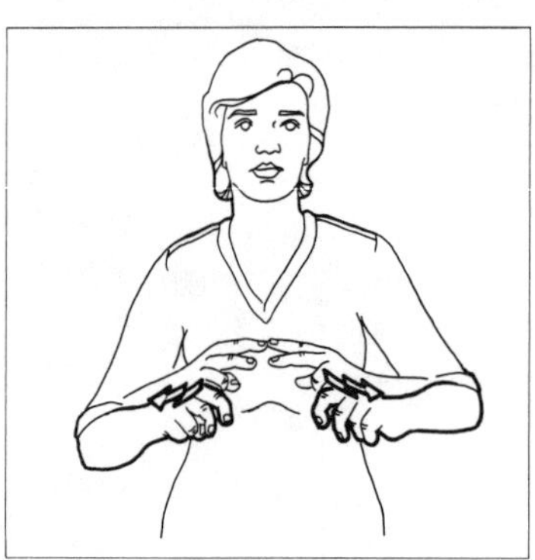

## ANALYSIS, ANALYST*, ANALYZE, ANALYZER*
(dm)

**Usage:** a flow analysis; numerical analysis; a systems analyst; to analyze the results; a network analyzer.
**Note:** Hands separate to the sides, Vs changing to bent Vs; repeat.

## ANSI
(fs)

**Usage:** a compiler for ANSI COBOL; an ANSI standard.
**Note:** ANSI is the acronym for American National Standards Institute; rhymes with "fancy."

## APL
(fs)

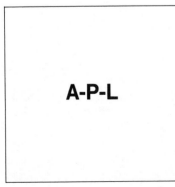

**Usage:** the APL language; the APL character set.
**Note:** APL is the abbreviation for A Programming Language.

## APPLICATION, APPLY
(cf. ASSIGN) (sm)

**Usage:** application programs; scientific applications; a business applications programmer; if any limitations apply; can be applied to networks.

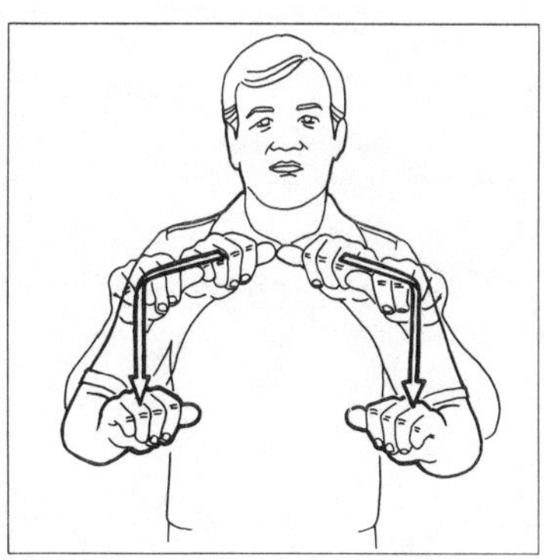

## ARCHITECT*, ARCHITECTURAL, ARCHITECTURE
(sm)

**Usage:** a presentation by the principal architect of the system; the architectural design features of the program; system network architecture.
**Note:** ARCHITECT requires the personal suffix (-ER).

## AREA
(sm)

**Usage:** the output area; a common area; a main storage area.
**Note:** Thumbs of A-hands touch, circle back, and touch again.

## ARITHMETIC
(cf. CALCULATE, COMPUTE) (dm)

**Same sign for:** figure, multiply.
**Usage:** binary arithmetic; the arithmetic and logic unit; an arithmetic operation.
**Note:** Palm-in V-hands brush past each other; repeat.

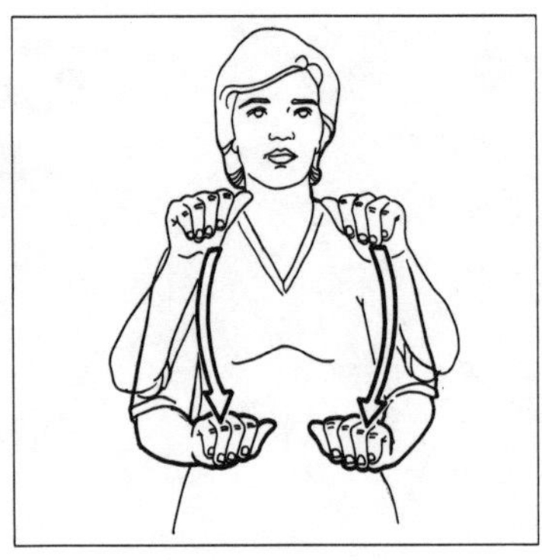

## ARRAY
(sm)

**Usage:** algorithms for array processing; a rectangular array; a three-dimensional array.

## ARTIFICIAL
(cf. DUMMY, PSEUDO-) (sm)

**Same sign for:** fake, false.
**Usage:** artificial intelligence.
**Note:** Index finger passes in front of lips (perpendicular to direction used in signing REAL).

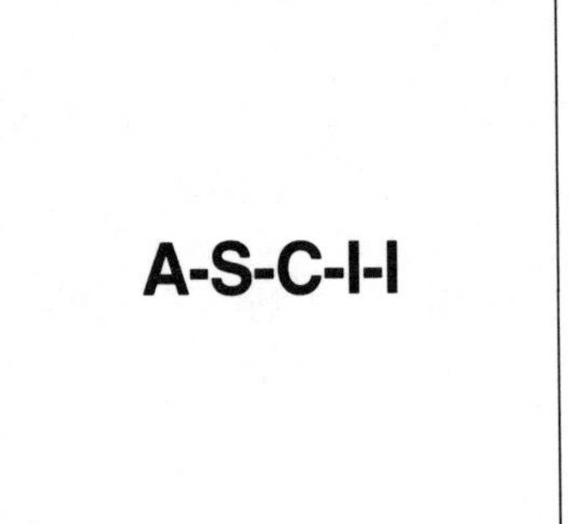


## ASCII
(fs)

**Usage:** the eight bit ASCII code; internal representation in ASCII.
**Note:** ASCII is the acronym for American National Standard Code for Information Interchange; rhymes with "pass key."

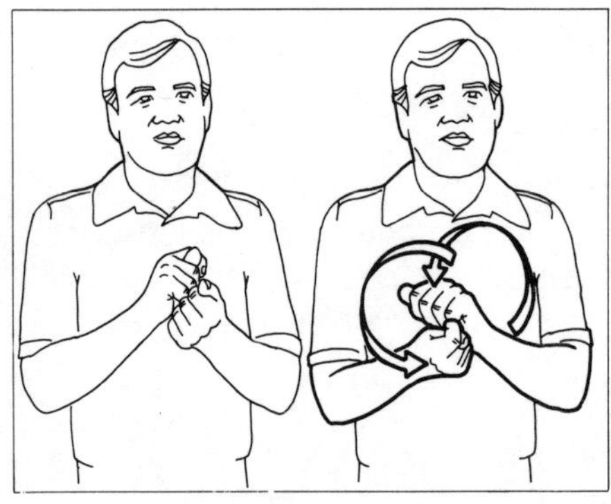

## ASSEMBLE, ASSEMBLER*, ASSEMBLY
(sm)

**Initialized form of:** change (left A-hand, right T-hand).
**Usage:** assemble-and-go mode; the assembler converts symbolic to virtual addresses;
the assembly language; the assembly listing.

## ASSIGN, ASSIGNMENT

(cf. APPLICATION) (sm)

**Usage:** to assign values to the parameters; the assignment of disk drives to channels.

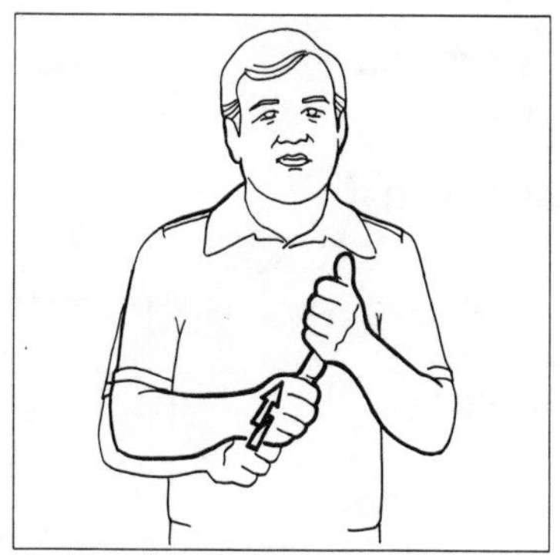

## ASSIST, ASSISTED

(dm)

**Usage:** to assist with the documentation; computer assisted diagnosis; computer assisted design.

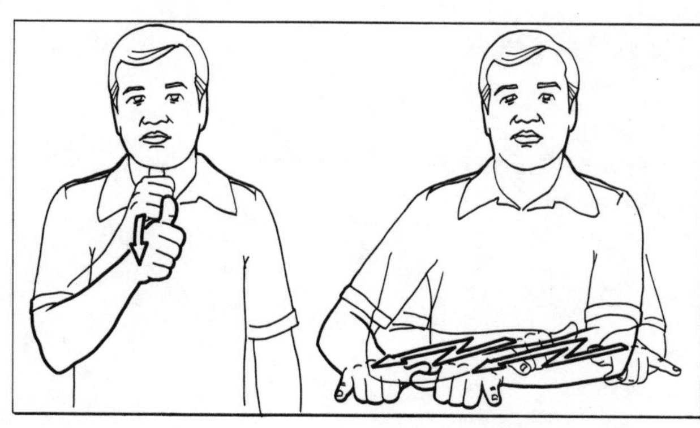

## ASYNCHRONOUS

(sm)

**Usage:** asynchronous operation; asynchronous data transmission.
**Note:** UN- SYNCHRONOUS. Palm-down Y-hands move out and to the right in a Z pattern.

## A-TO-D

(see ANALOG-TO-DIGITAL)

## ATTENTION

**Same sign for:** concentrate.
**Usage:** the ATTENTION key; an attention interrupt.

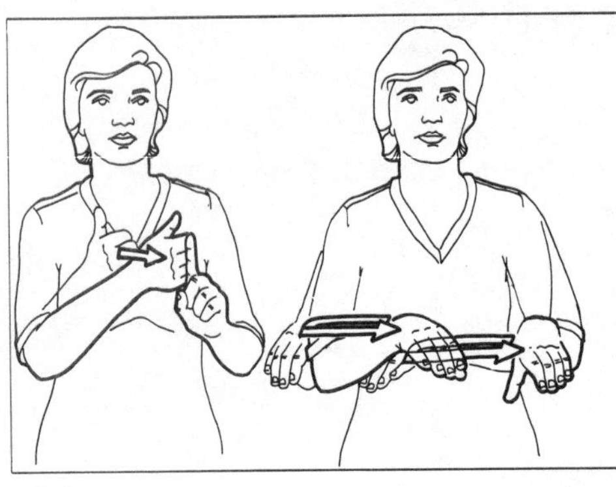

## AUTOMATA, AUTOMATIC, AUTOMATION

**Usage:** automata theory; automatic machine tool control; design automation.
**Note:** SELF- ACTION.

## AUXILIARY

(abbr)

**Usage:** auxiliary storage; an auxiliary operation; auxiliary equipment.

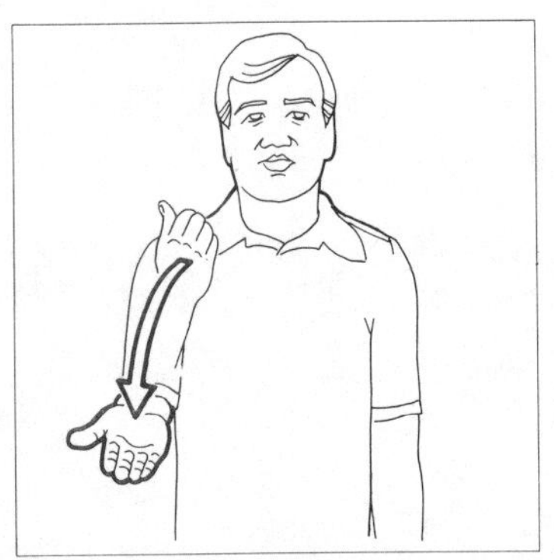

## AVAILABLE, AVAILABILITY

(sm)

**Same sign for:** there.
**Usage:** available resources; system availability.

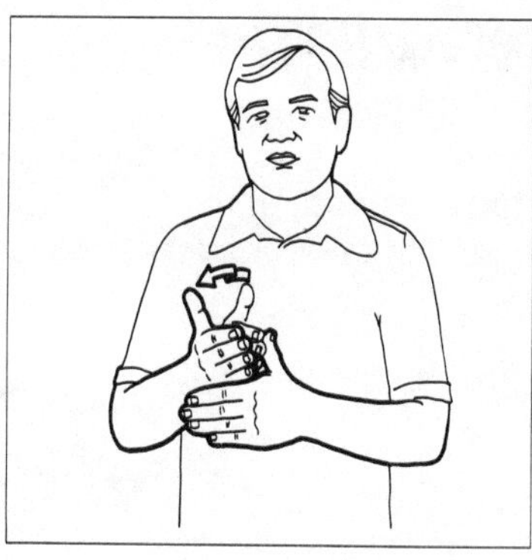

## AVERAGE

**Usage:** average access time; average run time; average queue length.
**Note:** Flat hands cross at right angles; right teeters on left.

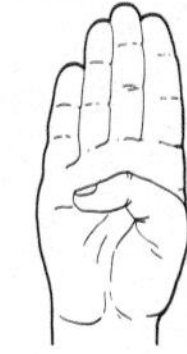

# B

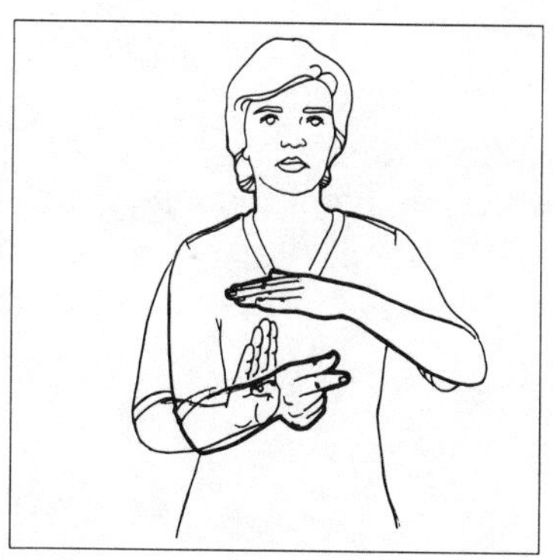

## BACKGROUND
(sm)

**Usage:** a low-priority background job; background processing.

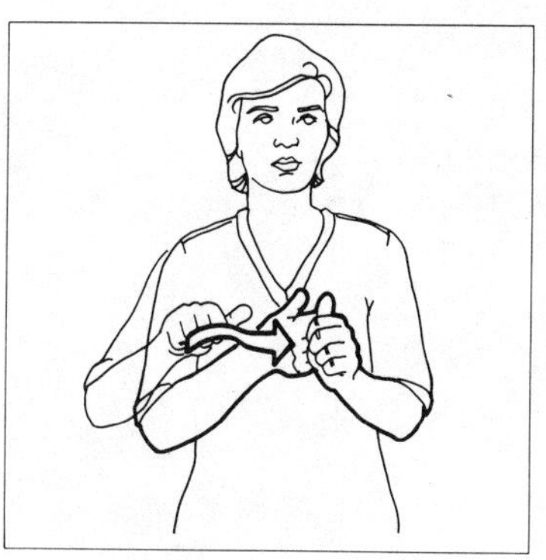

## BACKUP
(sm)

**Usage:** a file backup and recovery procedure; the backup file.

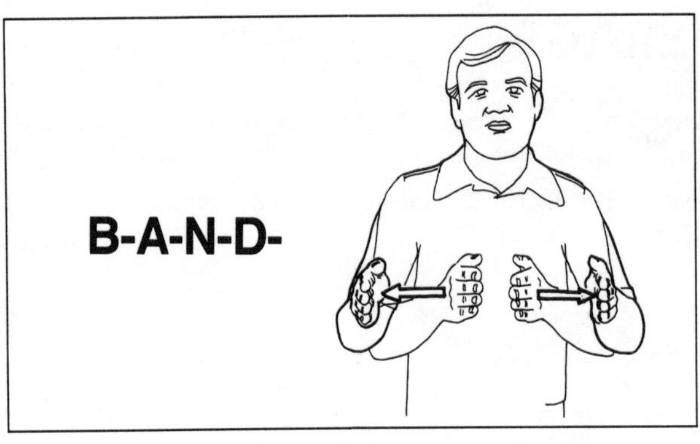


## BANDWIDTH

(fs/sm)

**Usage:** the bandwidth of transmission frequencies; of limited bandwidth.

## BANK

(cf. STORE) (dm)

**Usage:** a data bank; a bank teller's terminal.

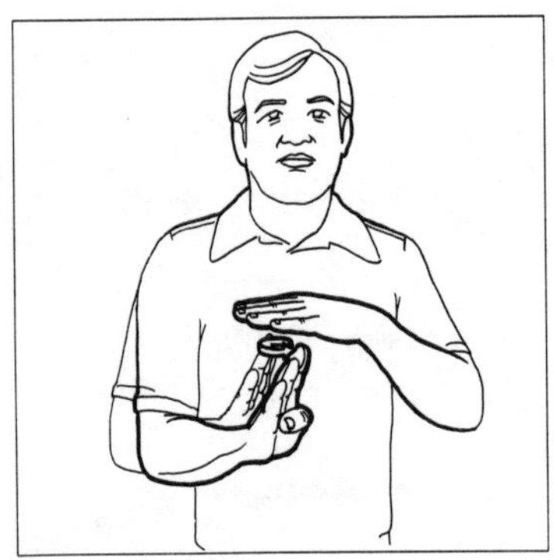

## BASE

**Usage:** by adding the relative address to the base address; the base address register; base-two arithmetic.

## BASED, BASIC

**Same sign for:** below, underlying.
**Usage:** a computer-based system; computer-based instruction; a basic course in computer concepts.

B-A-S-I-C

## BASIC
(fs)

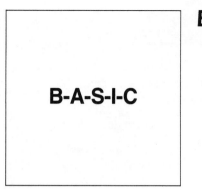

**Usage:** to program in BASIC; using the BASIC language.
**Note:** BASIC is the acronym for Beginner's All-Purpose Symbolic Instruction Code.

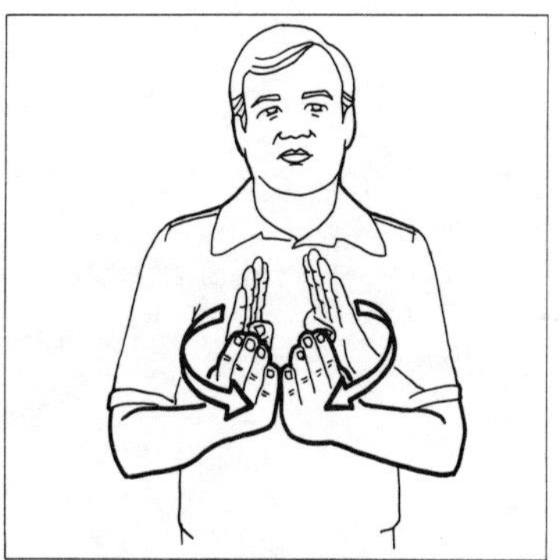

## BATCH, BATCHED
(sm)

**Initialized form of:** class (B).
**Usage:** batch jobs on second shift; batch processing; a batch region; batched communication.

## BAUD
(fs)

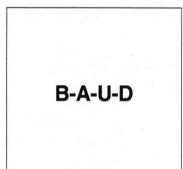

**Usage:** a 9600 baud line.

## BENCHMARK
(dm)

**Same sign for:** measure.
**Usage:** system performance on the benchmark tests; selecting the benchmark programs.
**Note:** Thumbs of palm-down Y-hands touch twice.

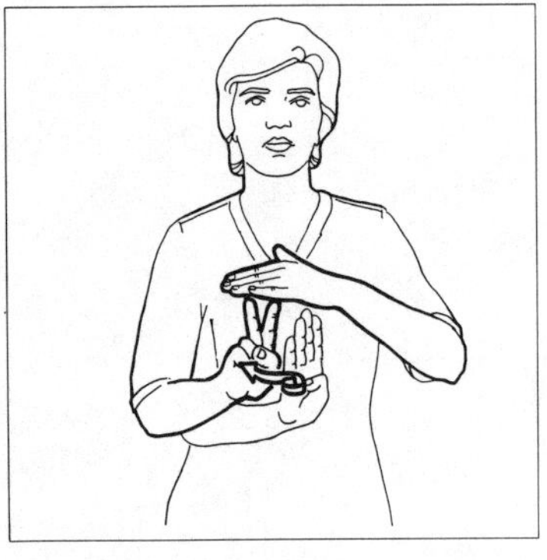

## BINARY

(sm)

**Same sign for:** base two.
**Usage:** binary-to-decimal conversion; binary notation; a binary operator; binary search.

## BIT

(sm)

**Usage:** an 8-bit byte; each bit position; the bit density on tape.
**Note:** Right B-hand bumps down left palm; BIT is a contraction of Binary digIT.

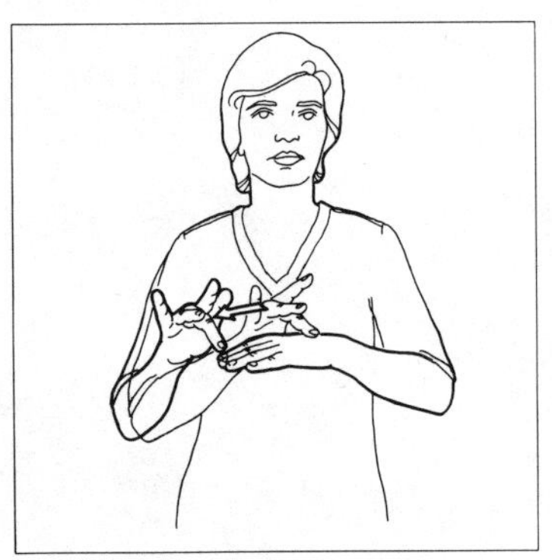

## BLANK

(cf. NULL, SPACE) (sm)

**Same sign for:** bare, empty, vacant.
**Usage:** a blank field; eliminating blank characters.

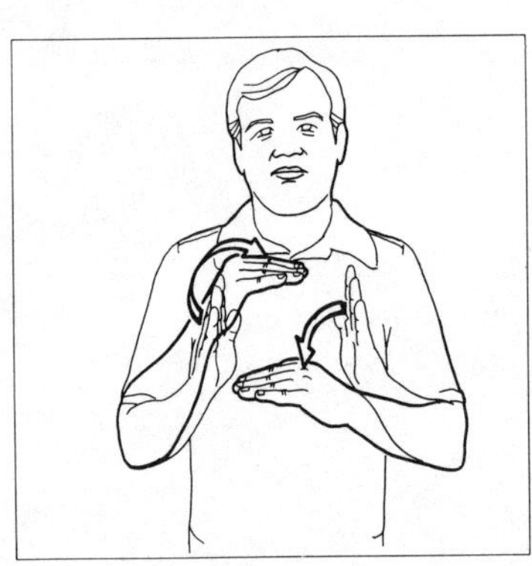

## BLOCK, BLOCKING

(sm)

**Usage:** block transfer of data; with a blocking factor of; a block diagram of the system; block size.

## BOARD
(sm)

**Usage:** a circuit board; a plug board.
**Note:** Like plugging a circuit board into a slot.

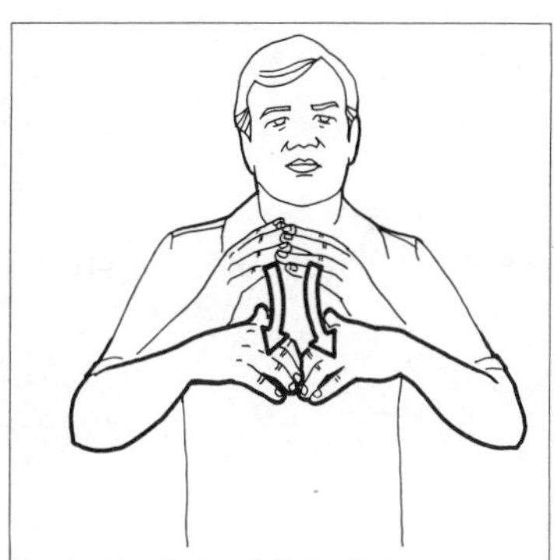

## BOMB
(sm)

**Same sign for:** breakdown, cave in, collapse.
**Usage:** the program bombed (slang expression).

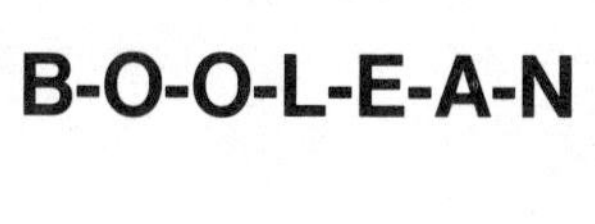


## BOOLEAN
(fs)

**Usage:** A boolean operation; boolean algebra.

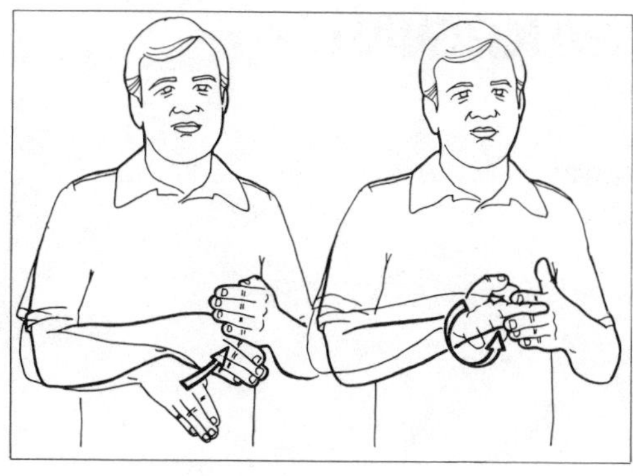

## BOOT, BOOTSTRAP
(sm)

**Usage:** to boot the system; a bootstrap procedure; a bootstrap loader; bootstrapping techniques.
**Note:** "kick" + START.

# B

## BOUNDARY

**Usage:** a word boundary; a page boundary; boundary alignment.
**Note:** Little finger of right B-hand along index of left B-hand; right teeters on left.

## BRANCH
(sm)

**Same sign for:** deviate, divert, stray.
**Usage:** a conditional branch instruction; to branch to the error routine.

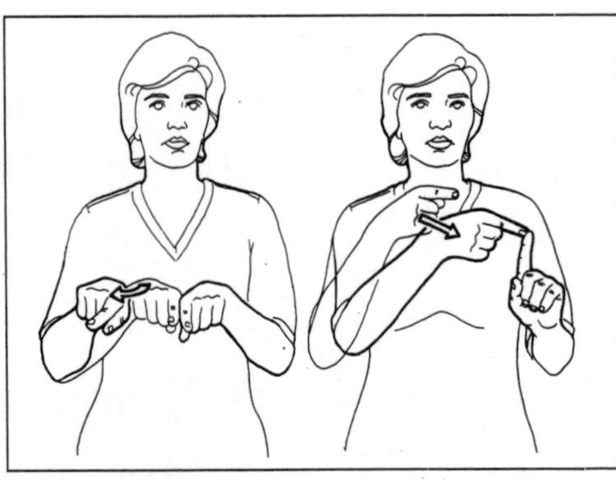

## BRANCHPOINT
(sm)

**Usage:** the address of each branchpoint; performs a test at each program branchpoint.
**Note:** BRANCH + POINT.

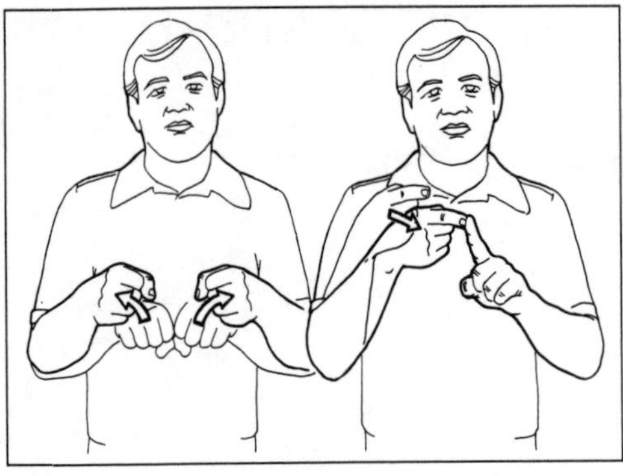

## BREAKPOINT
(sm)

**Usage:** a breakpoint in the program; allowing monitor program intervention at the breakpoint.
**Note:** "break" + POINT.

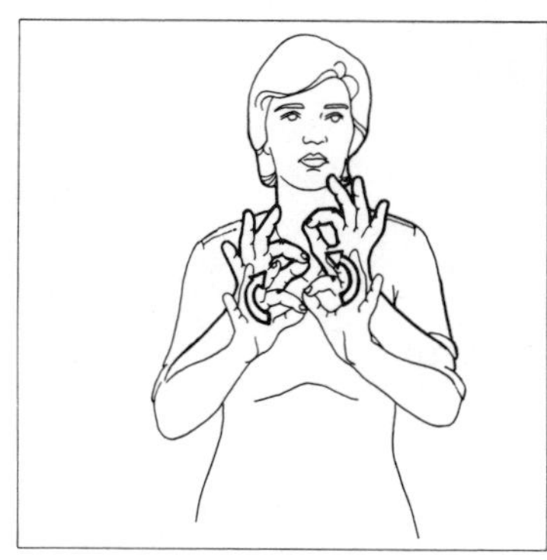

## BUBBLE
(sm)

**Usage:** a bubble sort; magnetic bubble memory.
**Note:** Hands move up alternately; right above left, then left above right, then right above left, etc.

## BUFFER
(dm)

**Usage:** buffer storage; an input buffer area; a buffered device; the buffer pool.

## BUG

**Same sign for:** insect.
**Usage:** a hardware bug; another bug in my program.
**Note:** Thumb of 3-hand on nose; bend the fingers down. This movement is usually duplicated.

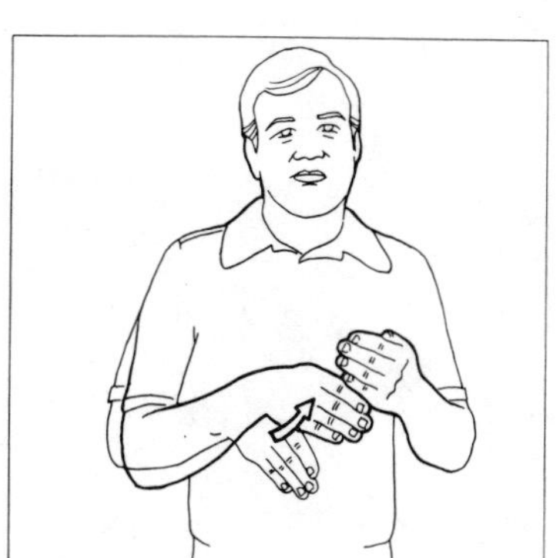

## BUMP (verb)
(sm)

**Same sign for:** kick.
**Usage:** was bumped off the system.

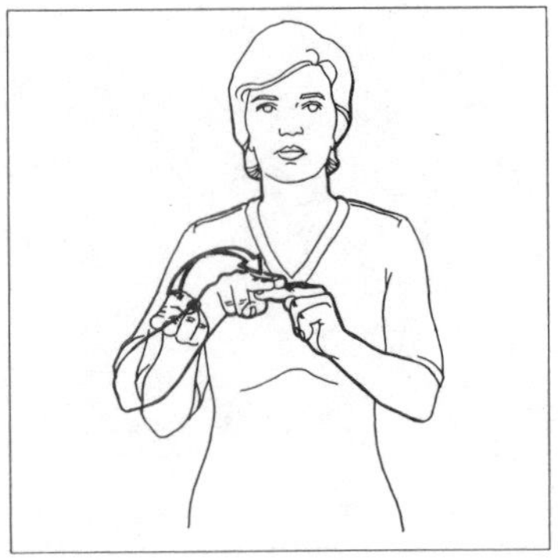

## BUMP

(cf. INCREMENT) (sm)

**Same sign for:** increase.
**Usage:** to bump the counter by 1; and the address register is bumped.
**Note:** Right-H turns over onto left-H.

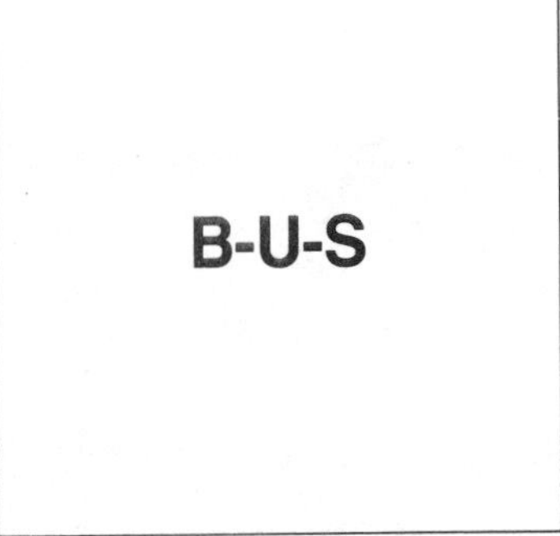


## BUS

(fs)

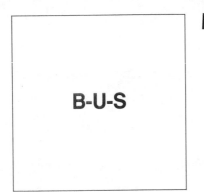

**Usage:** the memory bus; minimizing the bus length.

## BUSINESS

(dm)

**Usage:** business data processing; a business application programmer.

## BUSINESS

**Initialized form of:** work (B).
**Usage:** business data processing; a business application programmer.

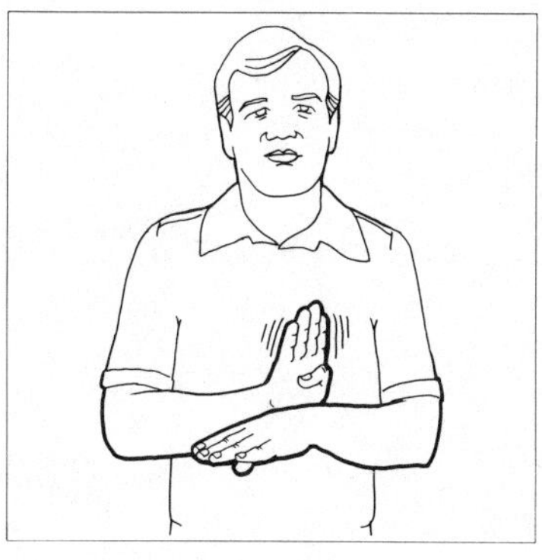

# BUSY
(dm)

**Usage:** a busy signal; whenever the channel is busy.

# BYTE
(sm)

**Usage:** an 8-bit byte; a 4-byte field; each addressable byte; a byte multiplexer channel.
**Note:** Right B-hand slides down left palm.

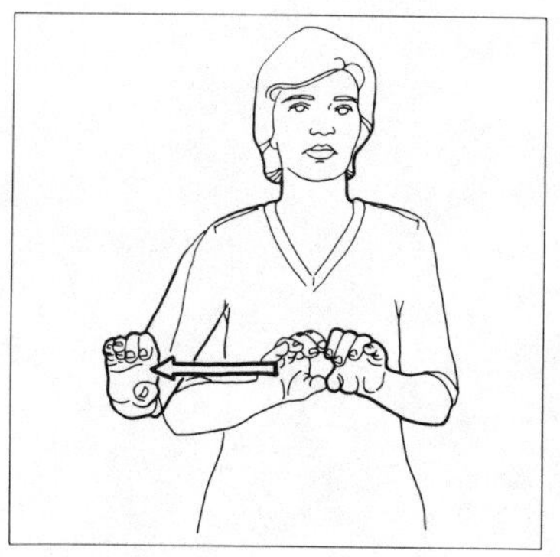

# CABLE
(sm)

**Usage:** the maximum cable length; coaxial cable.

# C

## CAI

(see COMPUTER ASSISTED INSTRUCTION)

## CALCULATE, CALCULATION, CALCULATOR*

(cf. ARITHMETIC, COMPUTE) (dm)

**Same sign for:** figure, multiply.
**Usage:** to calculate the square root; the results of the calculation; a hand-held calculator.
**Note:** Palm-in V-hands brush past each other; repeat.

## CALL, CALLING

(sm)

**Same sign for:** summon.
**Usage:** a subroutine call; the calling sequence; each time the main program calls a subroutine.

## CAPACITY

(sm)

**Initialized form of:** maximum (C).
**Usage:** channel capacity; storage capacity; memory capacity; capacity planning.

## CARD
(sm)

**Usage:** a card reader; the card image; an 80-column card; a header card.
**Note:** This sign indicates the approximate size of the card.

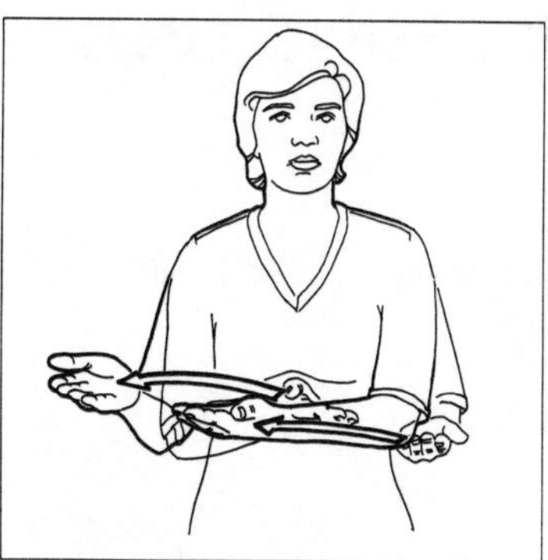

## CARRIER*, CARRY
(sm)

**Usage:** addition without carry; carrier frequency; high speed carrier.

## CATALOG, CATALOGED
(cf. INDEX, LIST) (sm)

**Usage:** a data set catalog; a cataloged procedure; the master catalog.
**Note:** Bent right hand bumps down left palm.

## CATHODE RAY TUBE, CRT
(abbr)

**Usage:** a cathode ray tube display; on the face of the CRT.

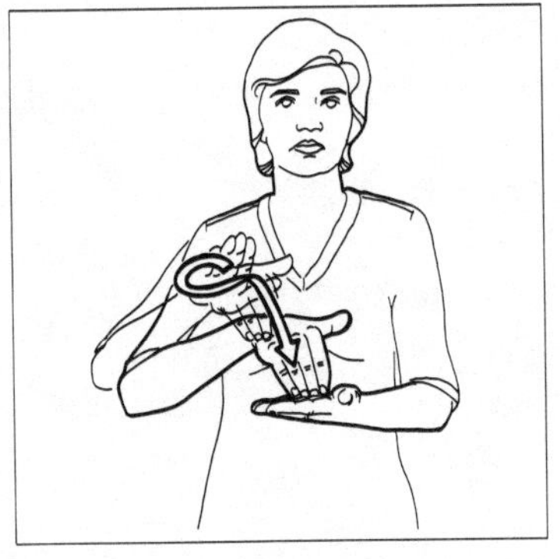

## CENTER, CENTRAL

(sm)

**Same sign for:** middle.
**Usage:** the data processing center; switching center; the central computer.

C-P-U

## CENTRAL PROCESSING UNIT, CPU

(abbr)

**Usage:** attached to each central processing unit; for each minute of CPU time.

## CHAIN, CHAINED, CHAINING

(sm)

**Usage:** a Markov chain; a chained list; a chaining search; a chain printer.
**Note:** Represents successive links of a chain.

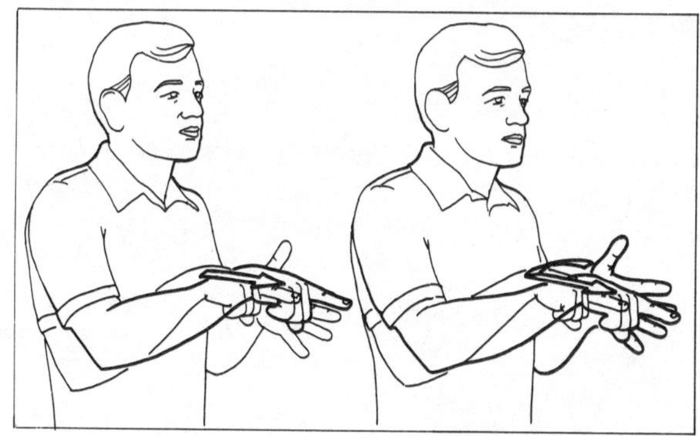

## CHANNEL
(sm)

**Usage:** a channel adapter; channel capacity; channel commands; an output channel.
**Note:** The right index finger slides out successively along two or more fingers of the left hand.

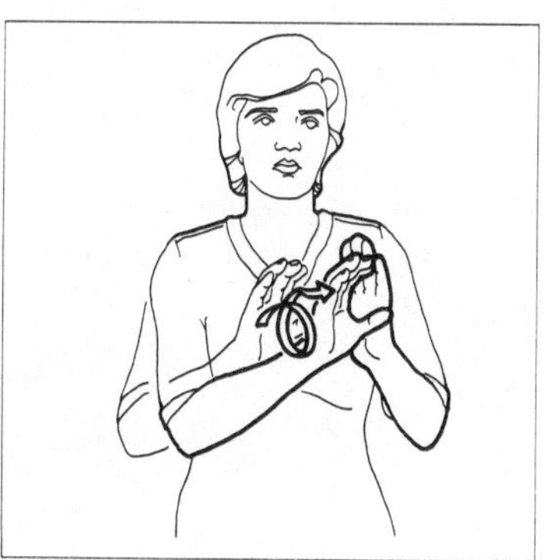

## CHARACTER
(sm)

**Usage:** character recognition devices; the APL character set; a character string; the data type is "character."
**Note:** C-hand circles in front of left palm, then is placed against it.

## CHECK
(sm)

**Usage:** a check bit or check character; to desk-check a program; completeness check; consistency check.
**Note:** Right index finger makes a check mark on left palm.

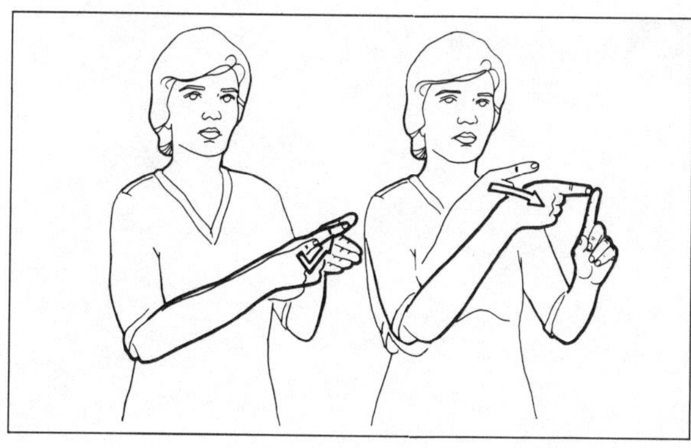

## CHECKPOINT
(sm)

**Usage:** including checkpoint/restart procedures; the checkpoint record.
**Note:** CHECK + POINT.

## CHIP
(sm)

**Usage:** thousands of circuit elements on a quarter-inch chip; an LSI chip.
**Note:** The sign should emphasize the small size of a chip.

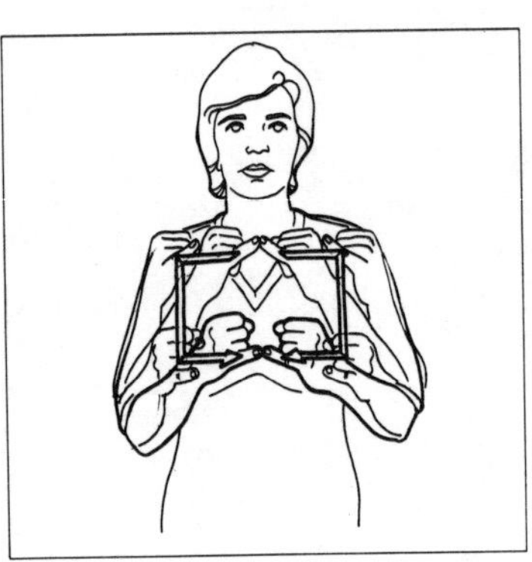

## CIRCUIT
(sm)

**Usage:** circuit design; circuit switching; printed circuits; integrated circuits.
**Note:** Little fingers outline a rectangle.

## CLEAR
(sm)

**Same sign for:** clean, nice.
**Usage:** clear the register; clear the display; the CLEAR key.
**Note:** Right palm brushes out across, and off the end of, left hand.

## CLOCK
(sm)

**Usage:** the master clock; the clock rate; an elapsed-time clock; a clock signal.

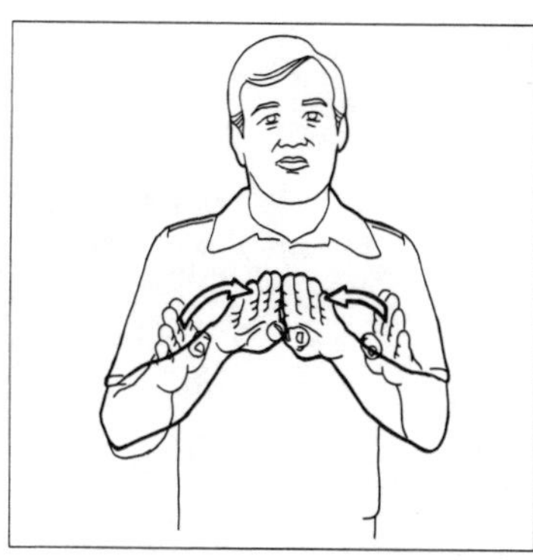

## CLOSE, CLOSED
(sm)

**Same sign for:** shut.
**Usage:** to close a file; a closed shop; a closed subroutine.

## CMS
(see CONVERSATIONAL MONITOR SYSTEM)

**C-O-B-O-L**

## COBOL
(fs)

**Usage:** a COBOL compiler; to program in COBOL; the COBOL language.
**Note:** The term COBOL is a contraction of COmmon Business-Oriented Language; rhymes with "snow ball."

**C-O-D-A-S-Y-L**

## CODASYL
(fs)

**Usage:** the CODASYL COBOL committee.
**Note:** The term CODASYL is a contraction of Conference On DAta SYstems Languages; pronounced "codicil."

## CODE, CODING
(cf. WRITE)

**Usage:** a program ready to code; coded in FORTRAN; a coding sheet; straight-line coding.
**Note:** Right hand "writes" on left hand.

C-O-D-E

## CODE
(fs)

**Usage:** code conversion; an 8-level code; an error-detecting code.

## COLD
(dm)

**Same sign for:** chilly, shiver, winter.
**Usage:** a cold start; requiring the system to be cold started.
**Note:** Shivering movement.

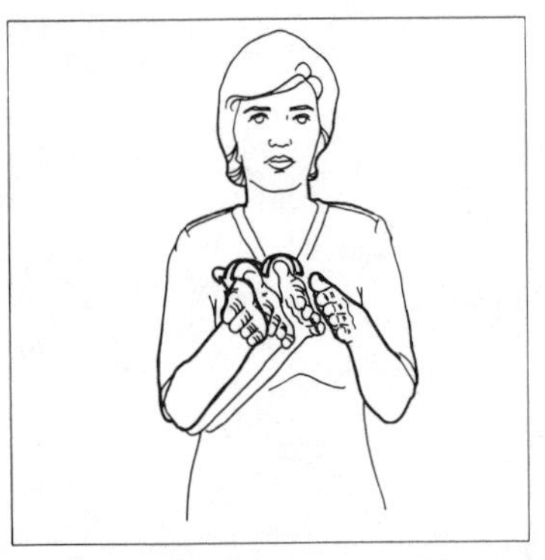

## COLLATE, COLLATING
(sm)

**Usage:** to collate the transaction and master files; the collating sequence.
**Note:** Left hand does not move.

## COLLECT, COLLECTION

(cf. ACCUMULATE)

**Same sign for:** gather.
**Usage:** to collect and record temperature readings; data collection equipment.
**Note:** This movement is usually duplicated.

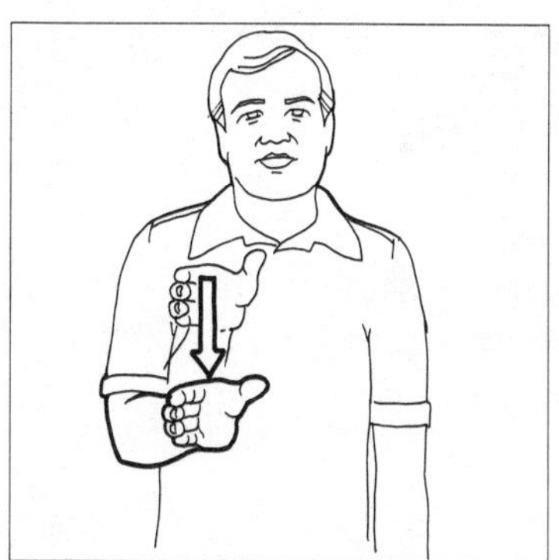

## COLUMN

(sm)

**Usage:** an 80-column card; punched out in column binary; columns of data on the output form.

## COMMAND

(sm)

**Same sign for:** order.
**Usage:** executes the channel commands; a powerful command language; the command name followed by the operands.

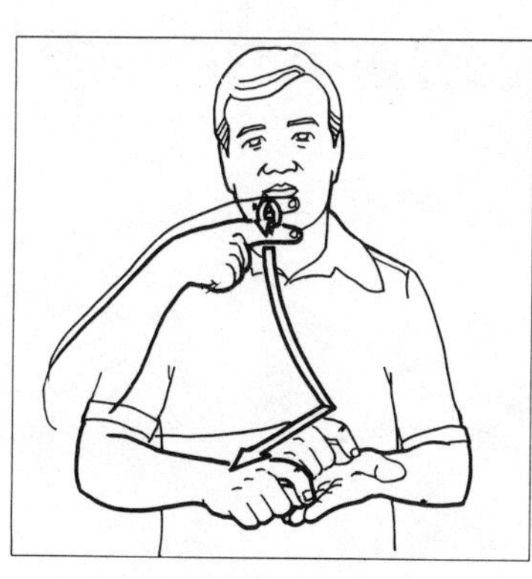

## COMMENT

**Usage:** a comment statement; comments that aid debugging.
**Note:** "say" + WRITE.

## COMMON
(cf. SHARE)

**Usage:** several programs accessing the common area; common block; common field; common carrier.
**Note:** Lower edge of right hand sweeps back and forth in angle formed by left thumb and fingers.

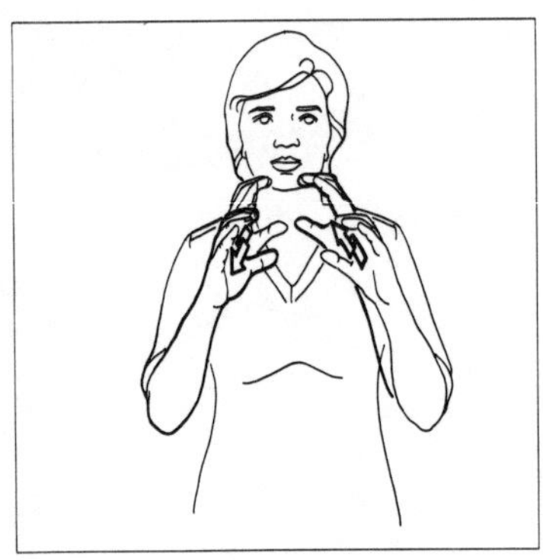

## COMMUNICATE, COMMUNICATION

**Initialized form of:** talk (C).
**Usage:** the user communicates with the system; a communication network; a data communication channel.

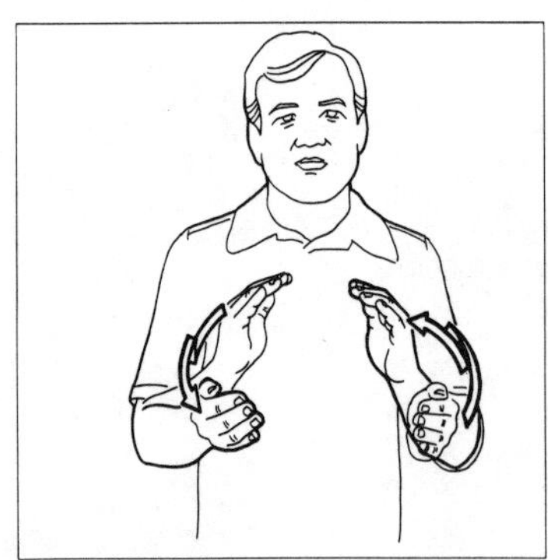

## COMPARE, COMPARISON

**Usage:** to compare character strings; the comparison operators; a comparison test.

## COMPATIBLE, COMPATIBILITY
(sm)

**Usage:** to be plug-compatible; upward compatible; use of the compatibility feature.

## COMPILATION, COMPILE, COMPILER*

(sm)

**Usage:** during the compile phase; compiler options; compilation time.

## COMPLEX

(sm)

**Usage:** complex systems; a complex algorithm.
**Note:** Index fingers change from 1 to X to 1, etc. as hands move in from sides, crossing in front of chin.

## COMPUTATION, COMPUTE

(cf. ARITHMETIC, CALCULATE) (dm)

**Same sign for:** figure, multiply.
**Usage:** a time-consuming computation; to compute the trigonometric functions.
**Note:** Palm-in V-hands brush past each other; repeat.

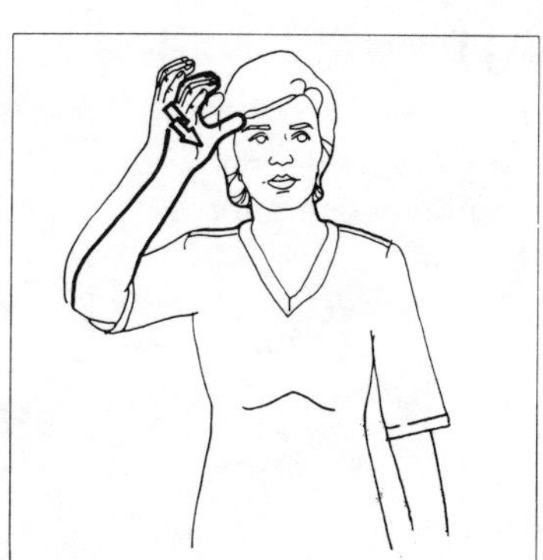

## COMPUTER

(dm)

**Usage:** a computer program; a computer operator; the computer room; computer architecture.
**Note:** Thumbnail of right C-hand taps forehead two or more times.

C-A-I

## COMPUTER ASSISTED INSTRUCTION, CAI

(abbr)

**Usage:** individual use of computer assisted instruction; authored several CAI courses.

## CONCATENATE, CONCATENATION

(sm)

**Usage:** concatenate the two strings; concatenated messages; the concatenation procedure.
**Note:** Left hand does not move.

## CONCEPT

(sm)

**Initialized form of:** imagine (C).
**Usage:** programming concepts; basic concepts in data structures.

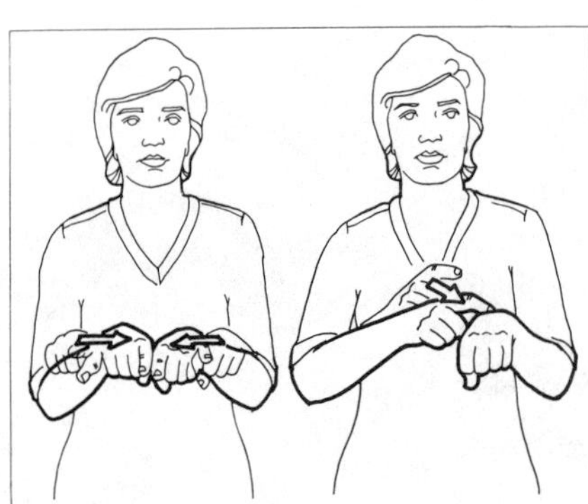

## CONCURRENT

(cf. SIMULTANEOUS) (sm)

**Usage:** concurrent peripheral operations; concurrent processing.
**Note:** "same" + TIME. Also see next entry.

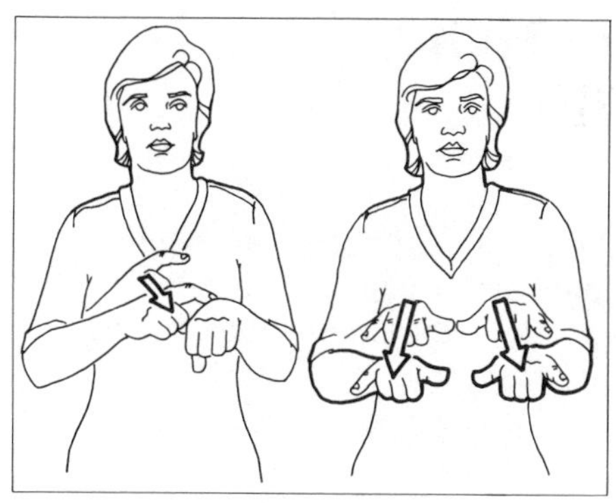

## CONCURRENT

(cf. SIMULTANEOUS) (sm)

**Usage:** concurrent peripheral operations; concurrent processing.
**Note:** After signing TIME, Y-hands move downward and separate slightly to the sides. Also see previous entry.

## CONDITION

(sm)

**Same sign for:** circumstance.
**Usage:** an error condition; a restart condition; the I/O condition code.
**Note:** Palm of right C-hand faces left index finger as it makes semicircular arc around it.

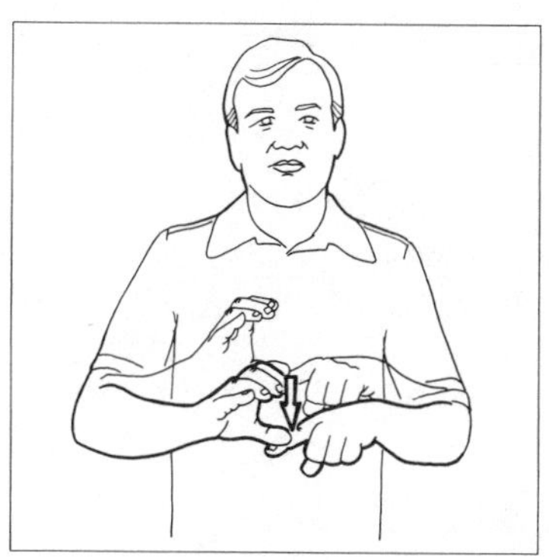

## CONDITIONAL

**Initialized form of:** depend (C).
**Usage:** a conditional branch instruction; IF-THEN is a conditional statement.

C-O-N-F-I-G

## CONFIGURATION, CONFIGURE

(abbr)

**Usage:** system configuration; the target configuration; to configure a system based on requirements.
**Note:** Also see next entry.

## CONFIGURATION, CONFIGURE

(sm)

**Usage:** system configuration; the target configuration; to configure a system based on requirements.
**Note:** C-hands separate to the sides and then move downward. Also see previous entry.

## CONNECT, CONNECTED

(cf. LINK) (sm)

**Same sign for:** attach, belong, join, unite.
**Usage:** to connect additional terminals to the system; disk drives connected to the system.

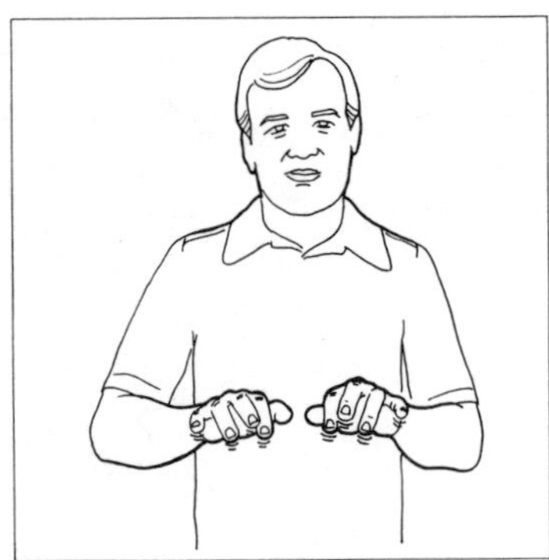

## CONSOLE

(cf. TYPE)

**Usage:** the CPU console; a console operator; console lights and buttons; a display console.
**Note:** Imitate typing movements.

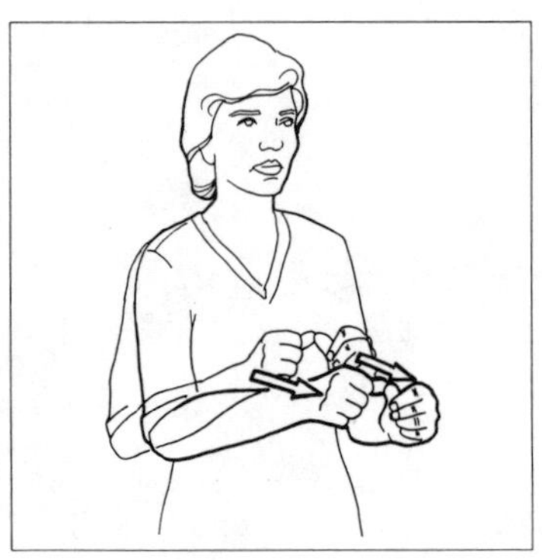

## CONSTANT

(cf. PERMANENT) (sm)

**Same sign for:** continue, persist.
**Usage:** a numeric constant; at a constant rate.

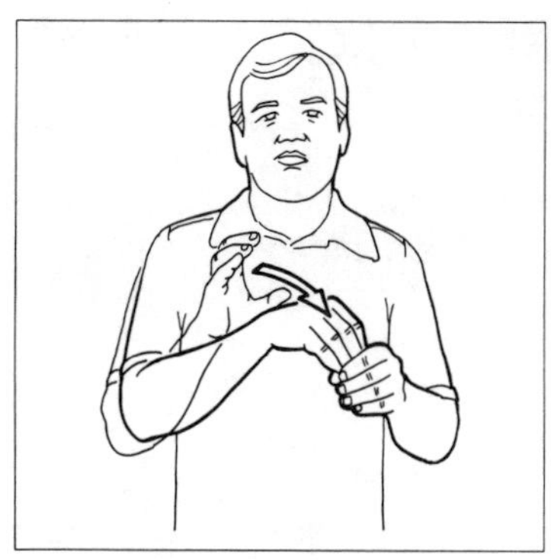

## CONTENT
(sm)

**Initialized form of:** in (C).
**Usage:** the contents of the register; the information content.

## CONTROL, CONTROLLER*
(cf. MANAGE)

**Same sign for:** govern, regulate.
**Usage:** process control applications; realtime control; the control panel; the communications controller; the various controller functions.
**Note:** Like holding the reins.

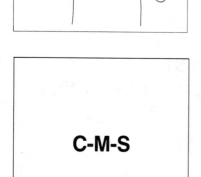

## CONVERSATIONAL

**Same sign for:** converse, talk.
**Usage:** CAI operates in a conversational mode; provides a conversational interface.

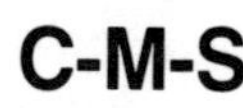


## CONVERSATIONAL MONITOR SYSTEM, CMS
(abbr)

**Usage:** the system disk for the Conversational Monitor System; a CMS user; the CMS editor.

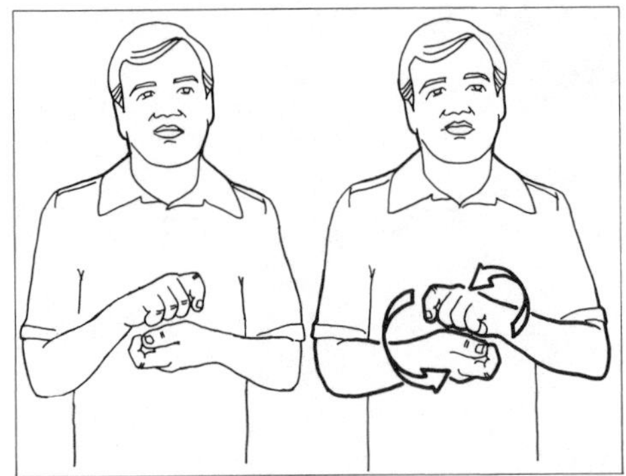

## CONVERSION, CONVERT

(cf. UPDATE) (sm)

**Same sign for:** change.
**Usage:** code conversion; binary-to-decimal conversion; to convert from analog to digital.

## COPY

**Usage:** to copy a tape; to copy a file onto an output tape; an extra copy of the output.
**Note:** Copying something onto the left palm.

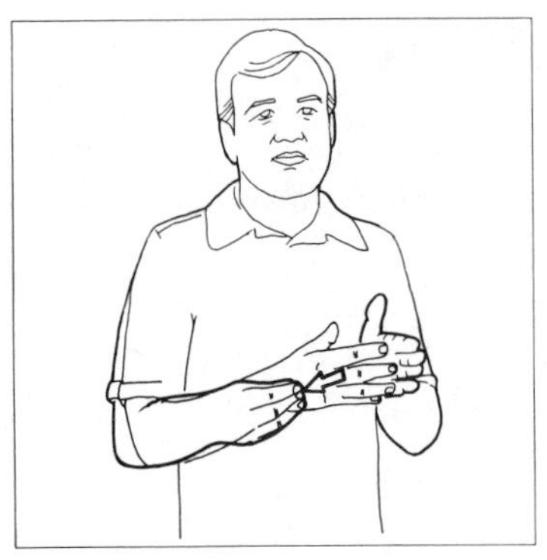

## COPY

**Usage:** to copy a tape, to copy a file onto an output tape; an extra copy of the output.
**Note:** Copying something from the left palm.

## CORRECT (verb), CORRECTING, CORRECTION

**Same sign for:** cancel, criticize.
**Usage:** to correct any errors; automatic error correction; a self-correcting code.
**Note:** Right index draws a large X in left palm.

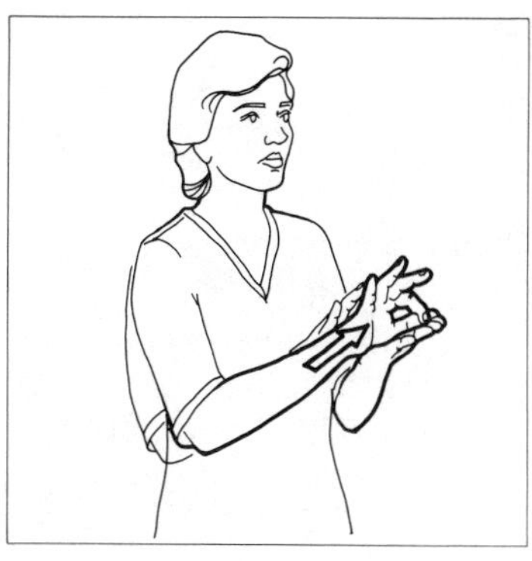

## COUNT, COUNTER*
(sm)

**Usage:** a record count; to count the number of loop executions; the instruction counter.
**Note:** Right F-hand slides up left palm once.

## CPU
(see CENTRAL PROCESSING UNIT)

## CRT
(see CATHODE RAY TUBE)

C-R-Y-P-T

## CRYPTOGRAPHIC, CRYPTOGRAPHY
(abbr)

**Usage:** a cryptographic algorithm; a cryptographic device; data transmission protected by cryptography.

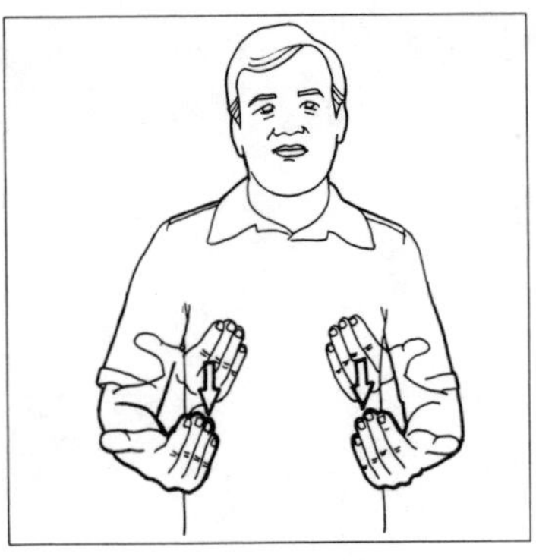

## CURRENT (adj.)

(sm)

**Same sign for:** now.
**Usage:** the current line pointer; the current record; the current priority level; the current status.
**Note:** Fingers bend up as hands are lowered.

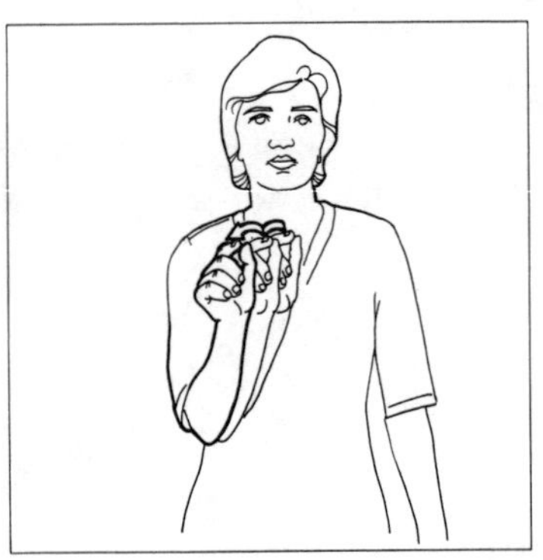

## CURSOR

(sm)

**Usage:** move the cursor to the desired position; cursor control keys.
**Note:** Indicates small cursor moving across display screen.

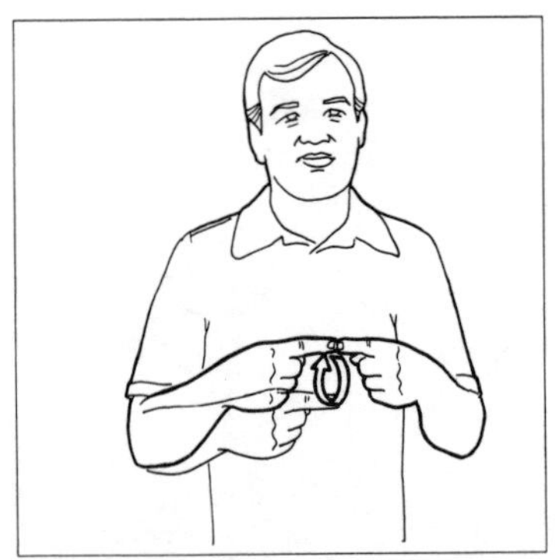

## CYCLE

(sm)

**Usage:** the internal cycle time; the read cycle; cycle sharing.

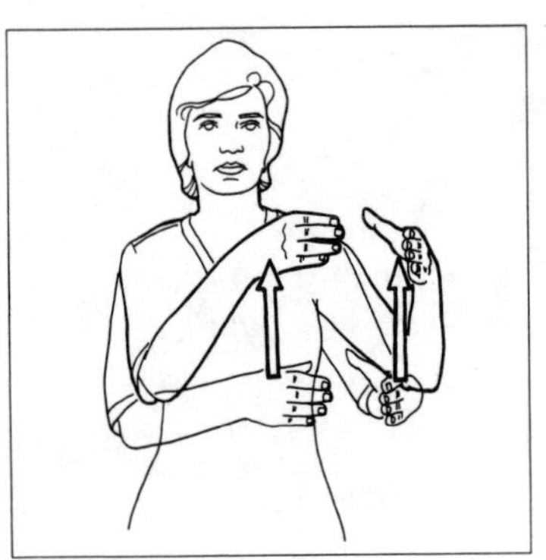

## CYLINDER

(cf. DRUM) (sm)

**Usage:** cylinders per disk pack; tracks in a cylinder.
**Note:** Hands move up an imaginary cylinder.

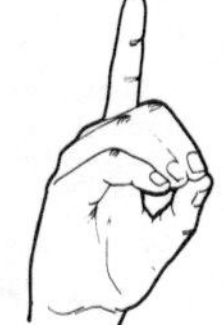

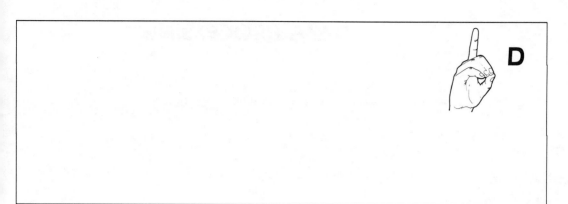

# D

## DASD

(see DIRECT ACCESS STORAGE DEVICE)

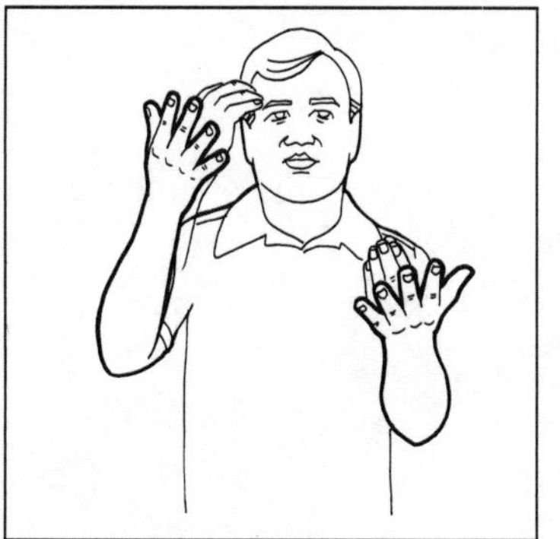

## DATA

(cf. INFORMATION) (sm)

**Same sign for:** inform, notify.
**Usage:** a data entry terminal; a data bank; data collection; data communication; data management; data reduction; abstract data.

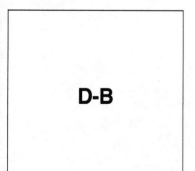

D-B

## DATA BASE

(abbr)

**Usage:** a data base system; the data base administrator; a relational data base.

D-P

## DATA PROCESSING
(abbr)

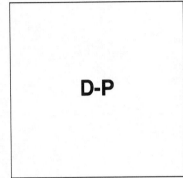

**Usage:** business data processing; a data processing system; distributed data processing.

D-S

## DATA SET
(abbr)

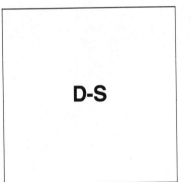

**Usage:** a partitioned data set; a sequential data set; data set organization.

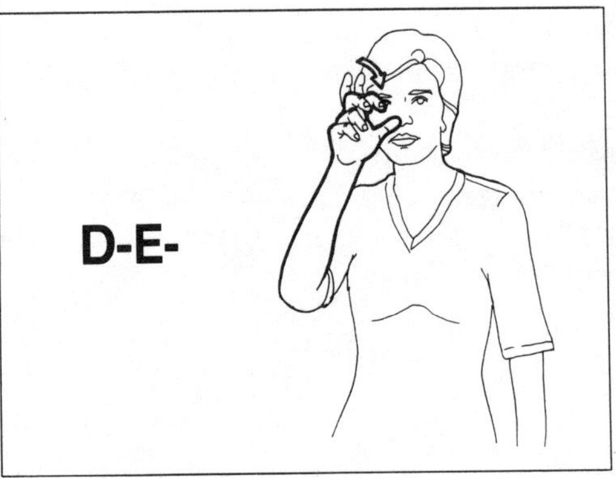


## DEBUG
(fs/sm)

**Usage:** to debug a program; documentation that aids debugging.

## DECIMAL
(sm)

**Same sign for:** base ten.
**Usage:** binary-coded decimal; a decimal digit; hexadecimal-to-decimal conversion.

## DECIMAL POINT (or POINT)
(sm)

**Same sign for:** period.
**Usage:** floating decimal point; an answer of 7.6 (seven point six).

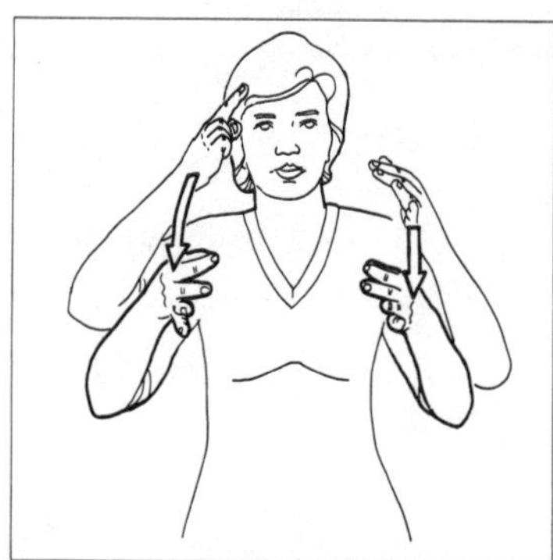

## DECIDE, DECISION
(sm)

**Usage:** to decide on the program parameters; to construct a decision table; a decision block in a flow chart.

## DECK
(sm)

**Usage:** a deck of cards; submission of input decks.
**Note:** Like holding a deck of punched cards.

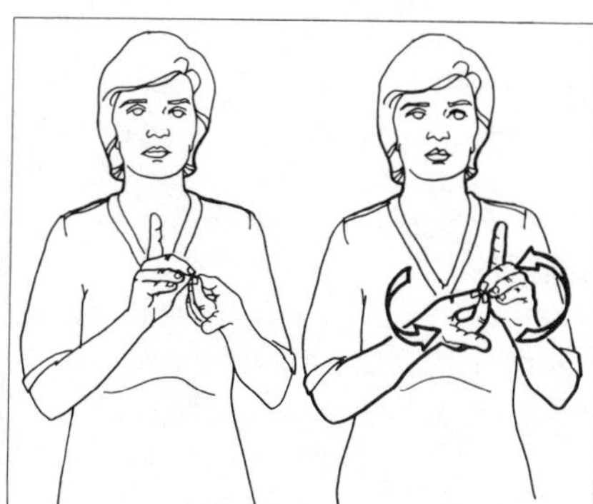

## DECODE, DECODER*
(sm)

**Initialized form of:** change (D).
**Usage:** to decode the instruction; the decoded message; the instruction decoder.

## DECREMENT
(sm)

**Usage:** to decrement the counter; a decrement of 1.
**Note:** Right-H on left-H; right turns over and goes down.

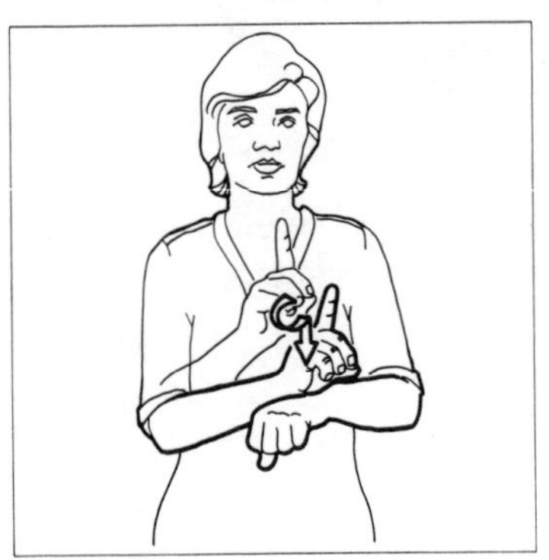

## DEDICATE, DEDICATED
(sm)

**Initialized form of:** establish (D).
**Usage:** to dedicate a resource to a particular function; a terminal dedicated to a single application; a dedicated channel.

## DEFAULT
(sm)

**Same sign for:** assume, take up.
**Usage:** the default values of the parameters; the default option; the default file attributes.

## DEFERRED
(cf. DELAY) (sm)

**Same sign for:** postpone, put off.
**Usage:** deferred addressing; deferred exit from a program; deferred maintenance.
**Note:** F-hands together; then right hand moves forward. Sign can also be made moving both hands forward.

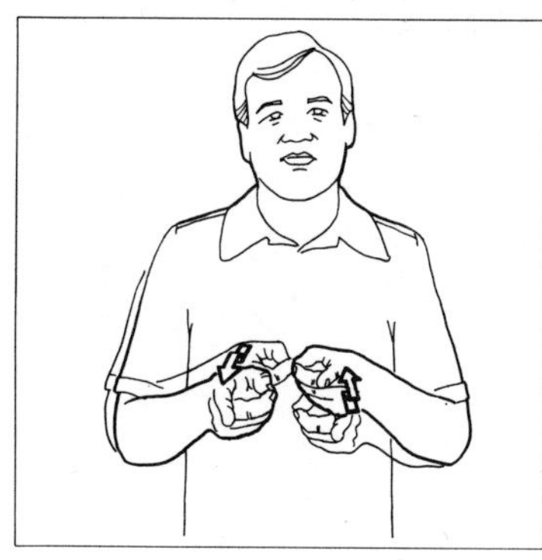

# DEFINE, DEFINITION
(cf. DESCRIBE)

**Usage:** to define the problem; data definition; macro definition.
**Note:** Right D-hand moves out as left moves in and vice versa. Sign can also be made as shown, but using F-hands.

# DEGRADATION, DEGRADE
(sm)

**Same sign for:** deteriorate.
**Usage:** performance degradation; graceful degradation; causing the response time to degrade.

# DELAY, DELAYED
(cf. DEFERRED) (sm)

**Same sign for:** postpone, put off.
**Usage:** a time delay; delayed response mode; rotational delays.
**Note:** F-hands together; then right hand moves forward. Sign can also be made by moving both hands forward.

# DELETE, DELETION
(sm)

**Usage:** to delete leading zeros; to delete the salary field; deletion of the # character.
**Note:** Like flicking something from the end of the finger. This sign usually used for small deletions.

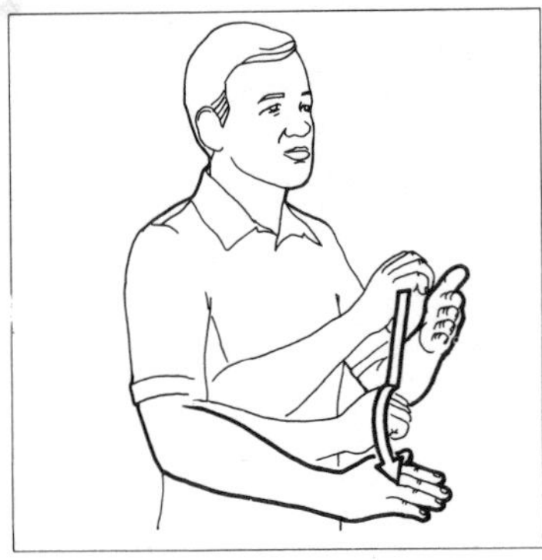

## DELETE, DELETION
(cf. ABORT) (sm)

**Same sign for:** eliminate.
**Usage:** to delete the whole file; to delete inactive records; file deletion.
**Note:** This sign usually used for larger deletions.

## DENSITY
(fs)

**Usage:** bit density; track density; packing density; recording density.

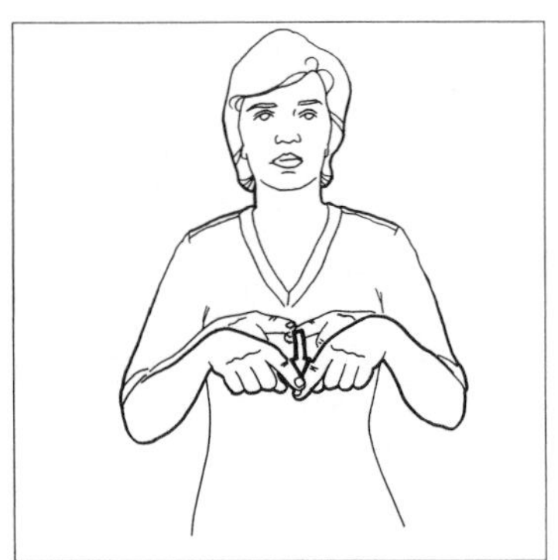

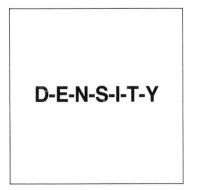

## DEPEND, DEPENDENT
(cf. RELY)

**Usage:** the branch that is taken depends on the computed value of; device-dependent code; a dependent segment.
**Note:** This movement is usually duplicated.

## DESCRIBE, DESCRIPTION
(cf. DEFINE)

**Usage:** to describe a procedure; the problem description; a data description language.
**Note:** Right D-hand moves out as left moves in and vice versa. Sign can also be made as shown, but using F-hands.

## DESIGN

(cf. DIAGRAM) (sm)

**Initialized form of:** art (D).
**Usage:** design automation; system design; functional design; the logic design; the design methodology.
**Note:** Right D-hand draws wavy line down left palm.

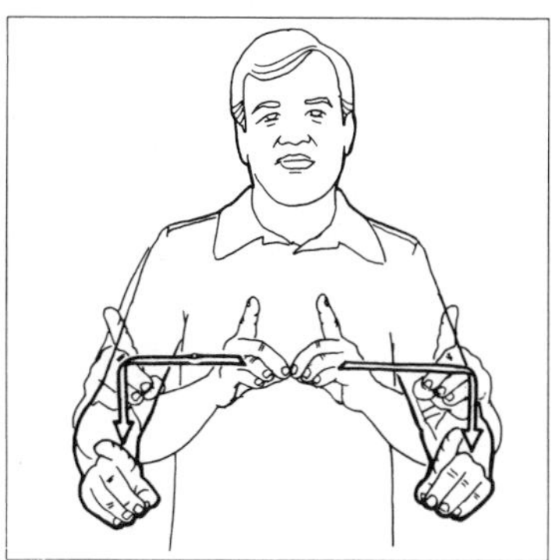

## DESK

(sm)

**Initialized form of:** table (D).
**Usage:** to desk-check a program; a desk-top calculator.
**Note:** D-hands separate to the sides and then move downward.

## DESTROY, DESTRUCTIVE

(sm)

**Usage:** destroyed most of the file; a non-destructive read.

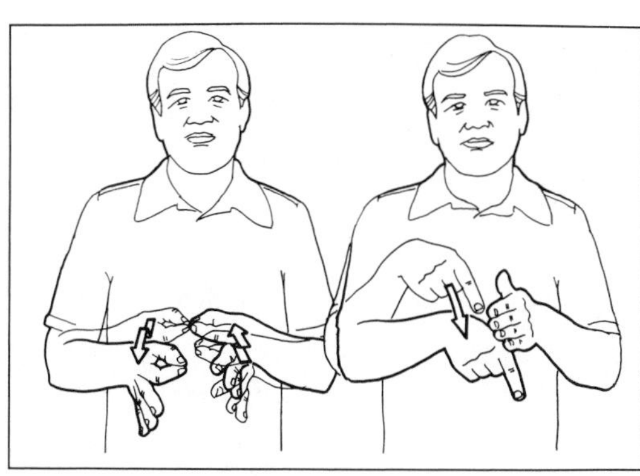

## DETAIL

**Usage:** each detail line on the report; the detail file used to prepare the summary report.
**Note:** "explain" + "deep."

## DEVELOP, DEVELOPMENT*

(sm)

**Usage:** to develop an implementation plan; program development and test; the development team.
**Note:** Right D-hand slides up left palm.

## DEVICE

(cf. DRIVE, MACHINE) (dm)

**Same sign for:** mechanism, motor.
**Usage:** the physical device address; a display device; a device-dependent program.
**Note:** Bent fingers mesh like gears; oscillate up and down.

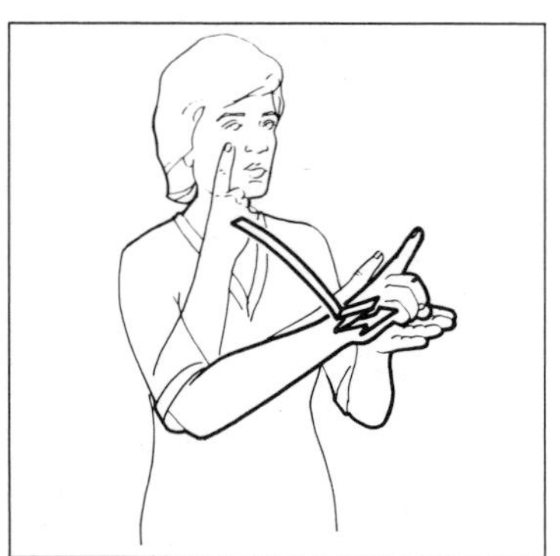

## DIAGNOSE, DIAGNOSTIC

**Initialized form of:** inspect, investigate (D).
**Usage:** to diagnose logic errors; a diagnostic program; diagnostic techniques.

## DIAGRAM

(cf. DESIGN) (sm)

**Initialized form of:** art (D).
**Usage:** a block diagram; the logic diagrams; a Venn diagram.
**Note:** Right D-hand draws wavy line down left palm.

## DICTIONARY

(cf. DIRECTORY) (dm)

**Usage:** relocation dictionary; data dictionary; external symbol dictionary.
**Note:** Right D-hand "turns pages" on left palm.

## DIGIT, DIGITAL

(cf. NUMBER) (sm)

**Usage:** number of significant digits; a binary digit; a digital computer; using digital techniques.

## DIGITAL-TO-ANALOG, D-TO-A

(sm)

**Initialized form of:** then (D-A).
**Usage:** a digital-to-analog converter; D-to-A control devices.

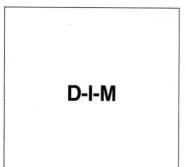

## DIMENSION

(abbr)

**Usage:** dimensions of the array; dimension declaration.

## DIRECT
(sm)

**Initialized form of:** straight (D).
**Usage:** direct addressing; direct access storage.
**Note:** Right D-hand slides outward on top of left D-hand.

D-A-S-D

## DIRECT ACCESS STORAGE DEVICE, DASD
(acronym)

**Usage:** direct access storage devices for on-line applications; a tape copy of the DASD file.
**Note:** The term DASD rhymes with "jazz-dee."

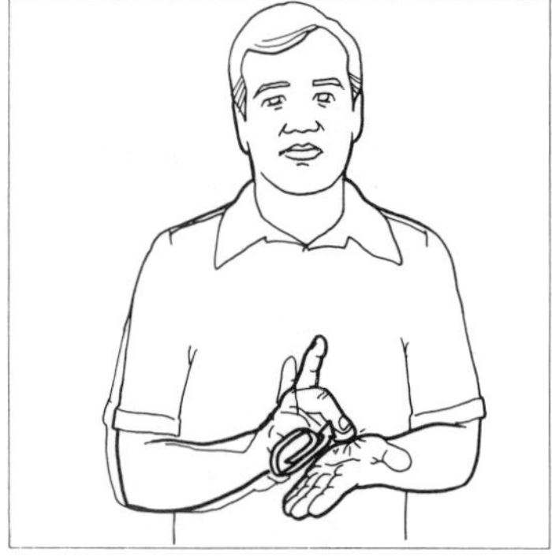

## DIRECTORY
(cf. DICTIONARY) (dm)

**Usage:** a file directory; a directory of currently active pages; to update the directory.
**Note:** Right D-hand "turns pages" on left palm.

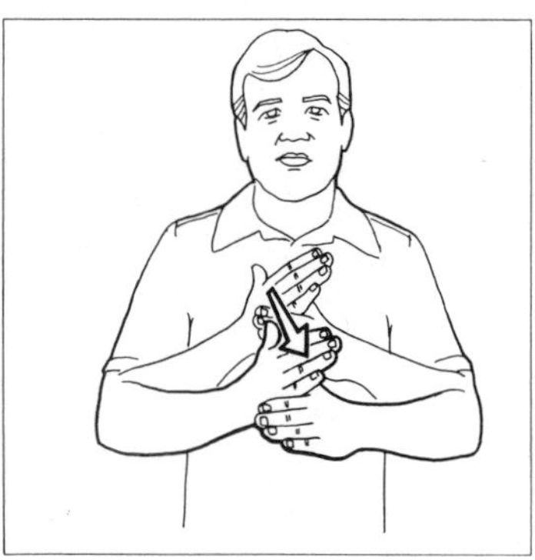

## DISABLE, DISABLED
(sm)

**Same sign for:** block, prevent.
**Usage:** instructions to enable and disable interrupts; in disabled mode.

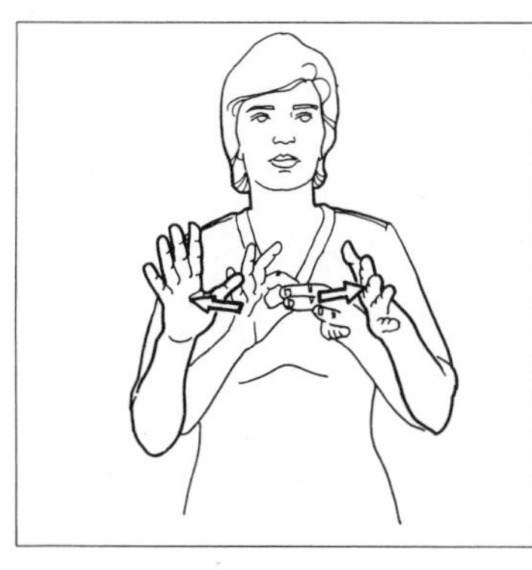

## DISCONNECT
(sm)

**Same sign for:** detach.
**Usage:** a disconnect signal; was disconnected from the host processor.

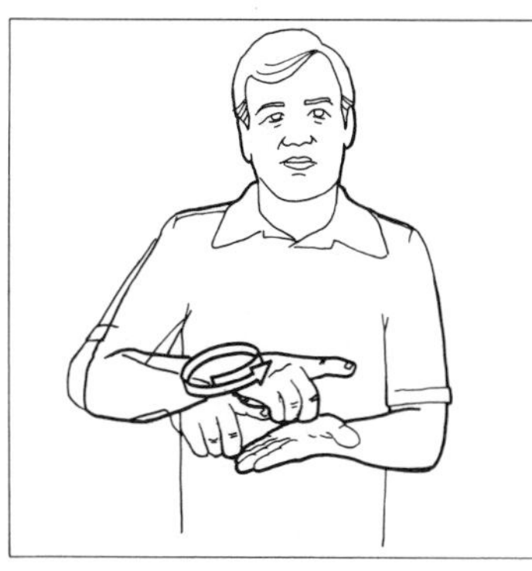

## DISK

**Usage:** a disk drive; a disk pack; disk storage; a floppy disk.
**Note:** Right D-hand circles over left palm.

D-O-S

## DISK OPERATING SYSTEM, DOS
(acronym)

**Usage:** using a disk operating system; operating under DOS.
**Note:** The term DOS rhymes with "boss."

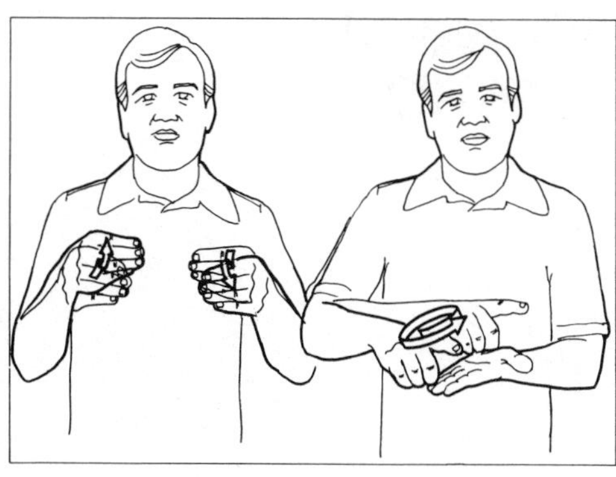

## DISKETTE

**Usage:** a formatted diskette; a diskette storage drive.
**Note:** FLOPPY + DISK.

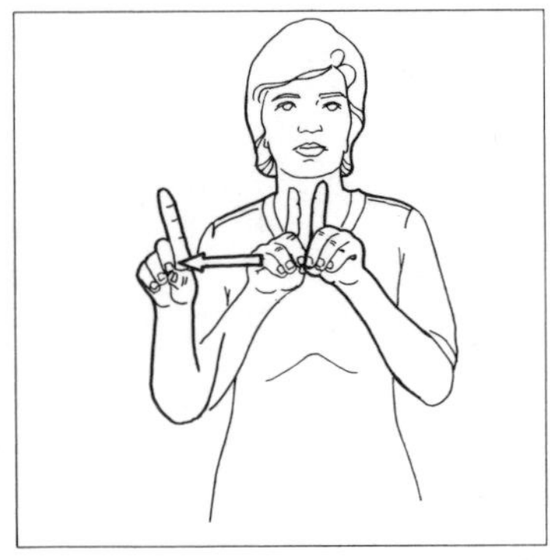

## DISPLACEMENT
(sm)

**Usage:** a displacement of 40 bytes; displacement within the record; displacement from the base address.
**Note:** Right D-hand moves to the right.

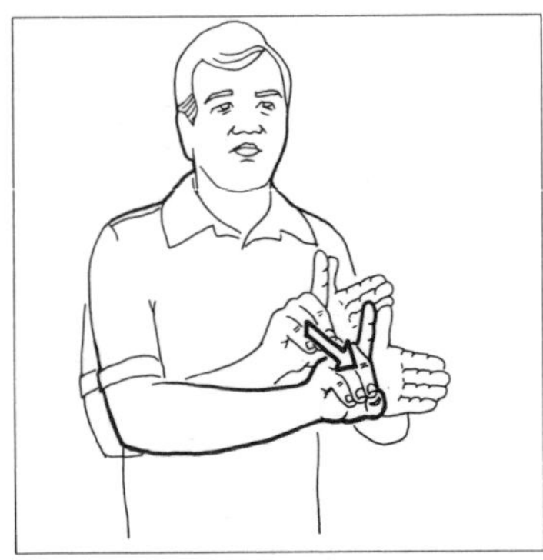

## DISPLAY
(sm)

**Initialized form of:** show (D).
**Usage:** a display console; hard-copy display; to display the contents.
**Note:** Right D-hand against left palm; both hands move forward.

## DISTRIBUTE, DISTRIBUTED
(sm)

**Same sign for:** scatter, spread.
**Usage:** to distribute printer output to the users; distributed data processing; distributed systems.

## DOCUMENT (verb), DOCUMENTATION
(sm)

**Usage:** using comments to document the program; standard documentation procedures; a documentation error.
**Note:** Right D-hand writes two or three lines on left palm. Also see next entry.

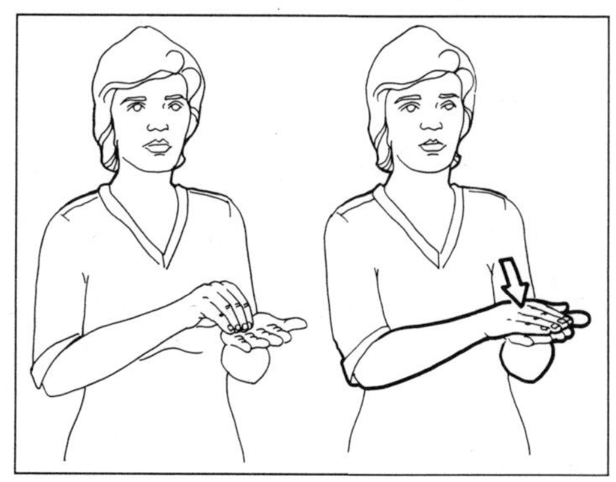

## DOCUMENT (verb), DOCUMENTATION

(cf. RECORD) (sm)

**Usage:** using comments to document the program; standard documentation procedures; a documentation error.
**Note:** Right thumb and fingertips in left palm; then fingers abruptly open as right hand flattens on left palm. Also see previous entry.

## DOS

(see DISK OPERATING SYSTEM)

## DOUBLE

(cf. DUPLEX) (sm)

**Same sign for:** twice.
**Usage:** double precision; a double word; double-density recording.

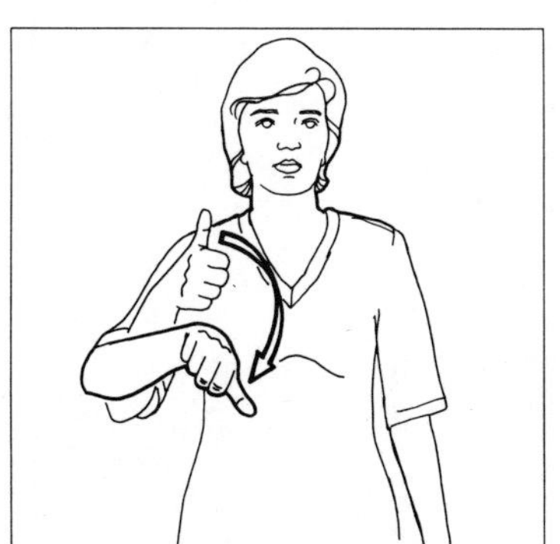

## DOWN

(sm)

**Usage:** brought the system down; amount of downtime.

## DRIVE
(cf. DEVICE, MACHINE) (dm)

**Same sign for:** mechanism, motor.
**Usage:** a disk drive; a tape drive; put the tape reel on the indicated drive.
**Note:** Bent fingers mesh like gears; oscillate up and down.

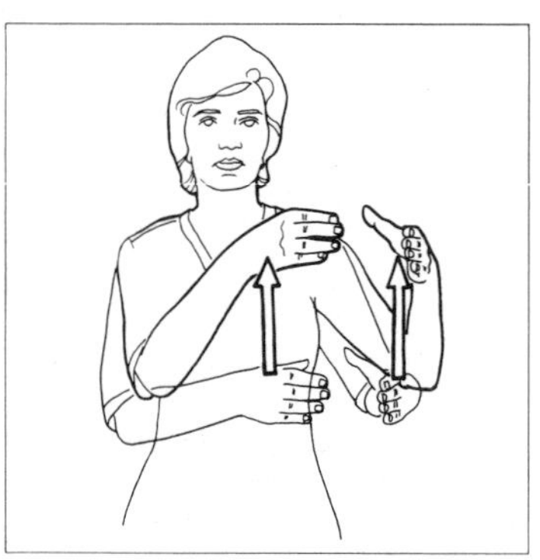

## DRUM
(cf. CYLINDER) (sm)

**Usage:** a magnetic drum; drum storage; a high-speed drum.
**Note:** Hands move up an imaginary drum.

## D-TO-A
(see DIGITAL-TO-ANALOG)

## DUMMY
(cf. ARTIFICIAL, PSEUDO-) (sm)

**Same sign for:** fake, false.
**Usage:** a dummy instruction; dummy terminal input; dummy test data.
**Note:** Index finger passes in front of lips (perpendicular to direction used in signing REAL).

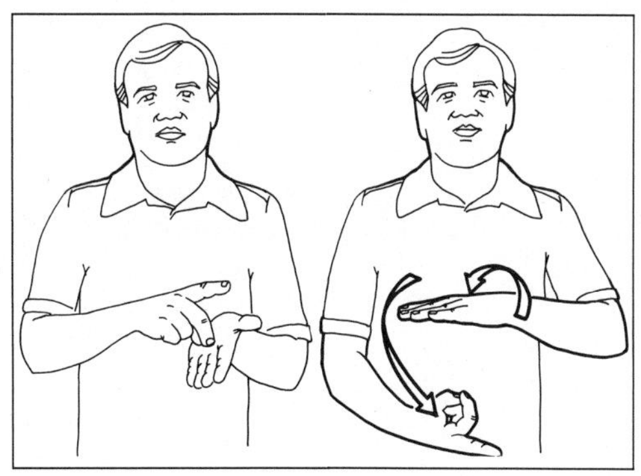

## DUMP
(sm)

**Usage:** a postmortem dump; a selective dump; a memory dump; a dump routine.
**Note:** Left palm turns over, dumping right D-hand.

## DUPLEX, DUPLEXED
(cf. DOUBLE) (sm)

**Same sign for:** twice.
**Usage:** duplex operation; a duplexed system; a half-duplexed line.

## DYNAMIC

**Initialized form of:** do (D).
**Usage:** dynamic address translation; dynamic storage allocation; dynamic programming.
**Note:** This sign is made with energy (i.e., dynamically).

E-D-I-T

## EDIT, EDITING, EDITOR*

(fs)

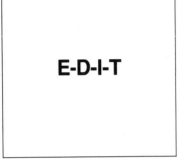

**Usage:** an edit check; in edit mode; a text editing system; the system editor.

## EDP

(see ELECTRONIC DATA PROCESSING)

## EFT

(see ELECTRONIC FUNDS TRANSFER)

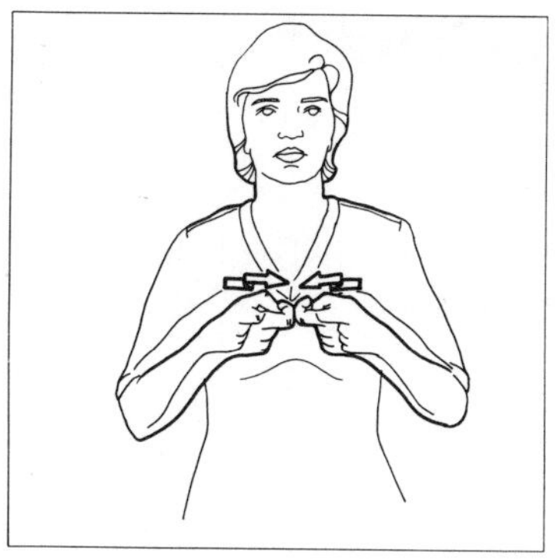

## ELECTRIC, ELECTRONIC
(dm)

**Usage:** an electric typewriter; the electronic circuitry; the electronics industry.
**Note:** Index fingers of X-hands bump together twice.

E-D-P

## ELECTRONIC DATA PROCESSING, EDP
(abbr)

**Usage:** impossible without electronic data processing; manager of the EDP department.

E-F-T

## ELECTRONIC FUNDS TRANSFER, EFT
(abbr)

**Usage:** considering electronic funds transfer as a step toward a cashless society; legal considerations of EFT.

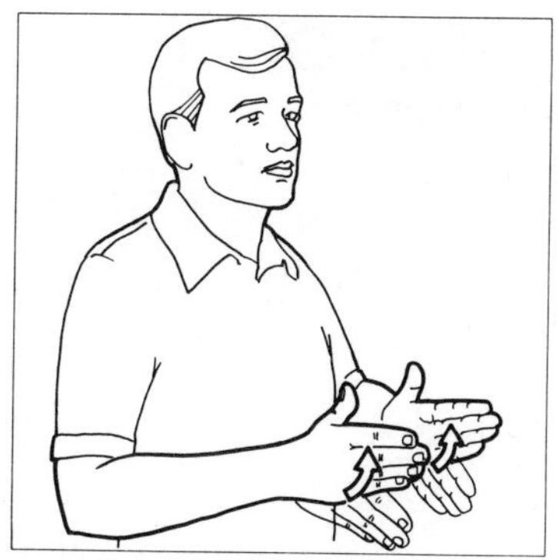

## ENABLE, ENABLED
(sm)

**Same sign for:** allow, let.
**Usage:** to enable the interrupts; running in the enabled mode.

## ENCODE, ENCODER*

(sm)

**Initialized form of:** change (E).
**Usage:** to encode the data before transmission; the encoded message; a hardware encoder.

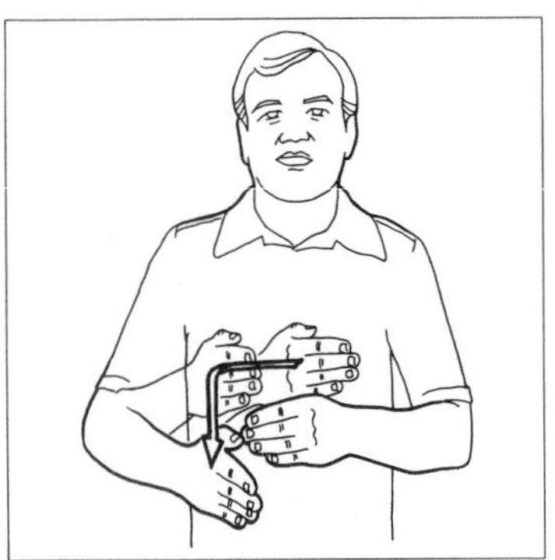

## END

(sm)

**Usage:** the end user; the END statement; the end of the program.

E-O-F

## END-OF-FILE, EOF

(abbr)

**Usage:** the end-of-file mark; an EOF condition.

E-O-T

## END-OF-TAPE, END-OF-TRANSMISSION, EOT

(abbr)

**Usage:** the end-of-tape mark; an EOT procedure.

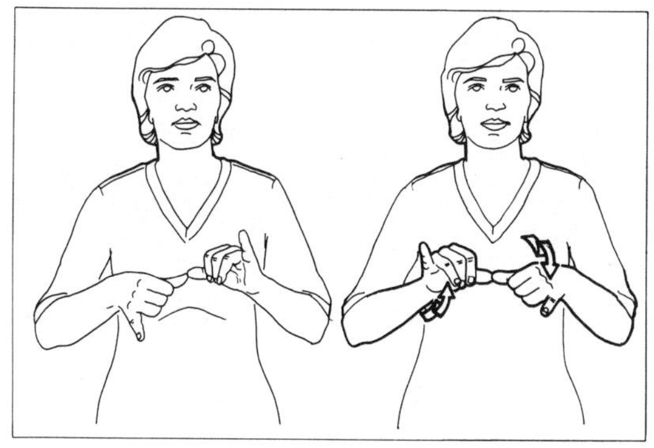

## ENGINEER*, ENGINEERING
(dm)

**Usage:** programs for engineering applications; software engineering; an engineering change to the equipment; the engineers are working on it.

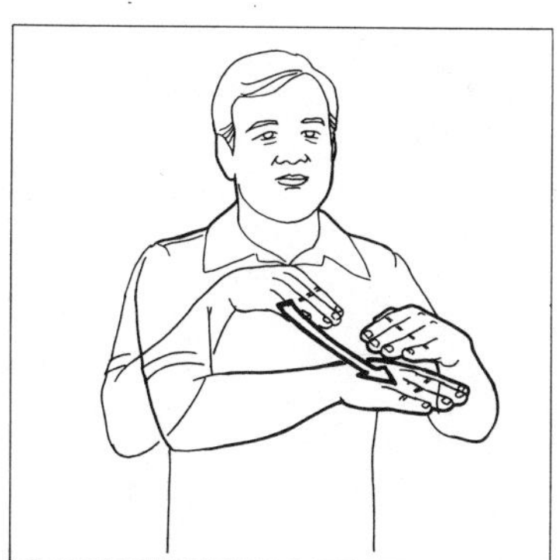

## ENTER, ENTRY
(cf. ACCESS) (sm)

**Same sign for:** entrance, into.
**Usage:** enter your password; enters the execution phase; data entry; the entry point of the routine; an entry-level programmer.

## ENVIRONMENT
(sm)

**Initialized form of:** CONDITION (E).
**Usage:** a batch environment; the environment division of the program; an interactive environment; the operating system environment.
**Note:** Palm of right E-hand faces left index finger as it makes a semicircular arc around it.

## EOF
(see END-OF-FILE)

## EOT
(see END-OF-TAPE)

## EPROM
(see ERASABLE PROGRAMMABLE READ-ONLY MEMORY)

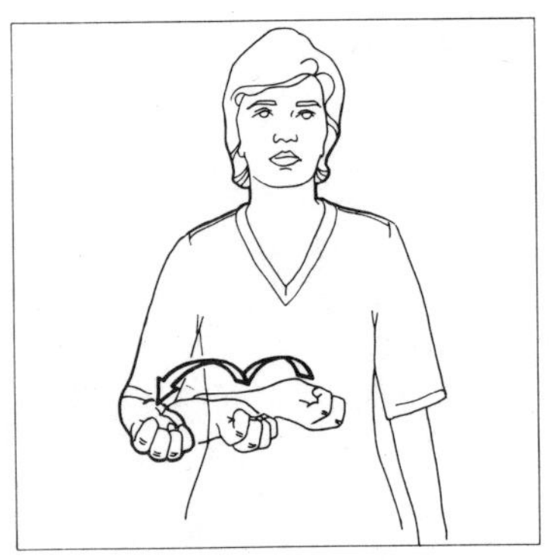

## EQUIPMENT
(sm)

**Initialized form of:** thing (E).
**Usage:** with various auxiliary equipment; a peripheral equipment operator.

## ERASE, ERASABLE*

**Usage:** the erase head on the tape drive; to erase the data from disk; erasable storage.
**Note:** Right A-hand scrubs left palm.

E-P-R-O-M

## ERASABLE PROGRAMMABLE READ-ONLY MEMORY, EPROM
(acronym)

**Usage:** with 16K of EPROM.
**Note:** The term EPROM is pronounced "ee-prom."

## ERROR
(cf. FAULT, INVALID) (sm)

**Same sign for:** mistake, wrong.
**Usage:** an error condition; error correcting code; an error message; error recovery procedures.
**Note:** Y-hand placed on chin.

## ESCAPE
(cf. EXIT) (sm)

**Usage:** the ESCAPE character; to escape from a loop; the escape sequence.

## EVALUATE, EVALUATION

**Initialized form of:** judge (E).
**Usage:** to evaluate alternative designs; performance evaluation; evaluation criteria.

## EXCEPT, EXCEPTION

(cf. SPECIAL) (sm)

**Usage:** all systems are running except that one; an overflow exception; an exception message; an exception report.

## EXEC

(see EXECUTIVE)

## EXECUTE, EXECUTION

(cf. RUN) (dm)

**Usage:** the time to execute the routine; executes each instruction; after the execution phase.
**Note:** Right hand brushes underside of left hand in two or more outward movements.

**E-X-E-C**

## EXECUTIVE, EXEC

(abbr)

**Usage:** an executive routine; through an individualized EXEC program.

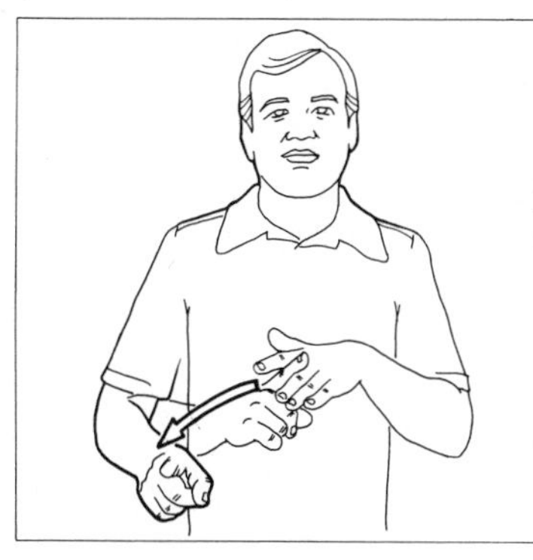

## EXIT

(cf. ESCAPE) (sm)

**Usage:** to exit from the subroutine; an exit routine; to provide program exits.

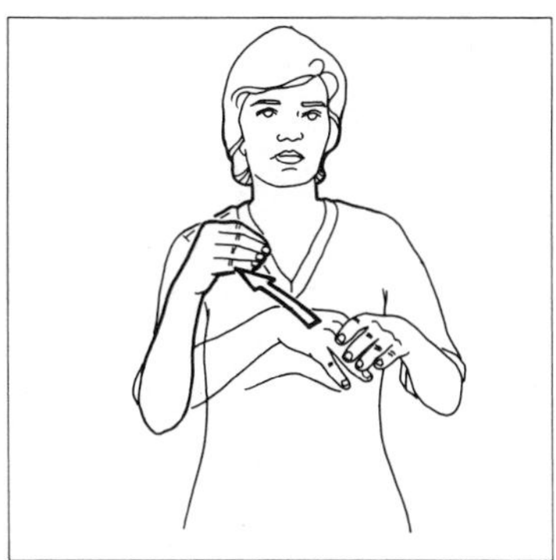

## EXTERNAL

(sm)

**Usage:** an external interrupt; external storage.

# F

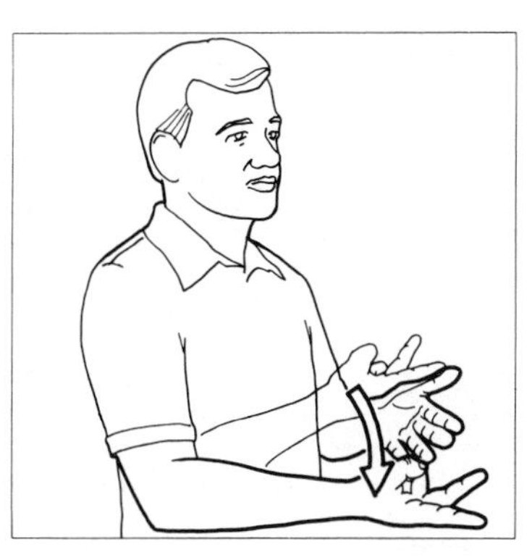

## FAIL, FAILURE

(sm)

**Usage:** causing the system to fail; having intermittent failures.
**Note:** Palm-up V-hand slides off left palm.

## FAULT

(cf. ERROR, INVALID) (sm)

**Same sign for:** mistake, wrong.
**Usage:** research on fault-tolerant systems; the fault rate.
**Note:** Y-hand placed on chin.

## FEEDBACK

(sm)

**Usage:** using a feedback loop; an information feedback system; feedback from the users.
**Note:** Palm-left right hand moves back, changing from F to B.

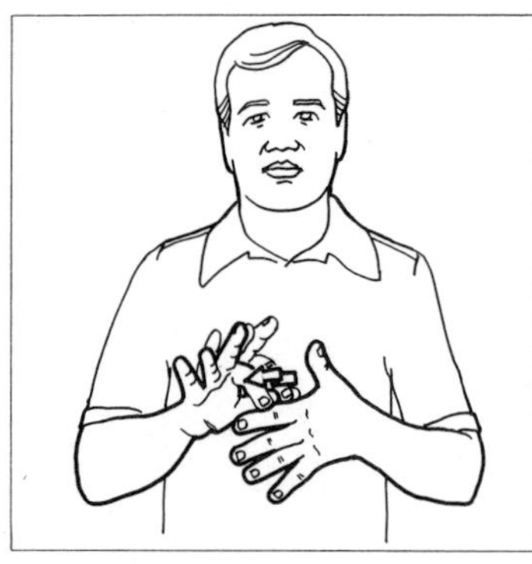

## FIELD

(dm)

**Usage:** a variable-length field; an alphabetic field; the key field.
**Note:** Right F-hand moves back and forth along a short portion of left index (the whole left index represents a record).

## FIFO

(see FIRST-IN-FIRST-OUT)

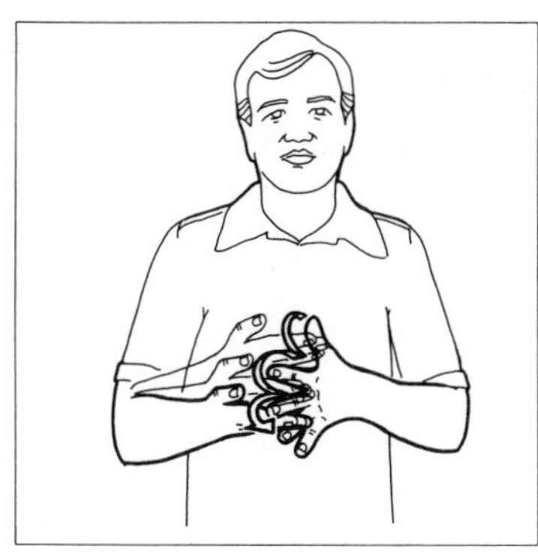

## FILE
(sm)

**Usage:** file access method; file maintenance; master file; backup file; file description.
**Note:** Right flat hand is inserted successively into gaps between fingers.

## FINAL
(sm)

**Same sign for:** last.
**Usage:** accumulate and print the final total; the final time through the loop.

## FIRST-IN-FIRST-OUT, FIFO
(acronym)

**Usage:** on a first-in-first-out basis; using a FIFO discipline.
**Note:** The term FIFO is pronounced "fife-o."

## FIXED
(sm)

**Usage:** fixed-length records; a fixed-point constant; a fixed word length computer.
**Note:** Right S-hand quivers on back of left wrist.

## FLOATING
(sm)

**Usage:** floating-point arithmetic; a floating-point register.

## FLOPPY
(dm)

**Same sign for:** flexible.
**Usage:** a floppy disk.
**Note:** Made with small rapid movements.

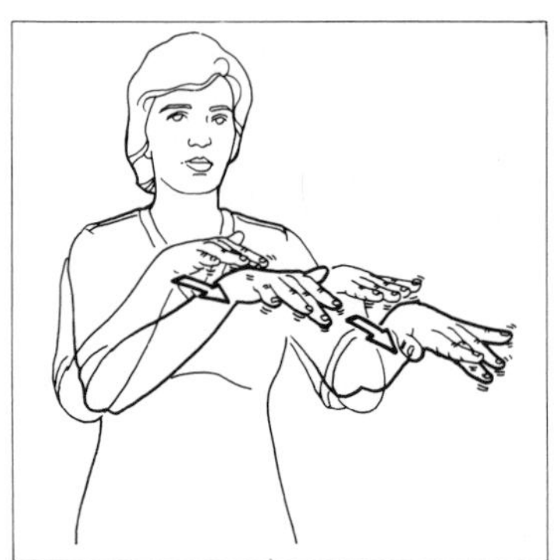

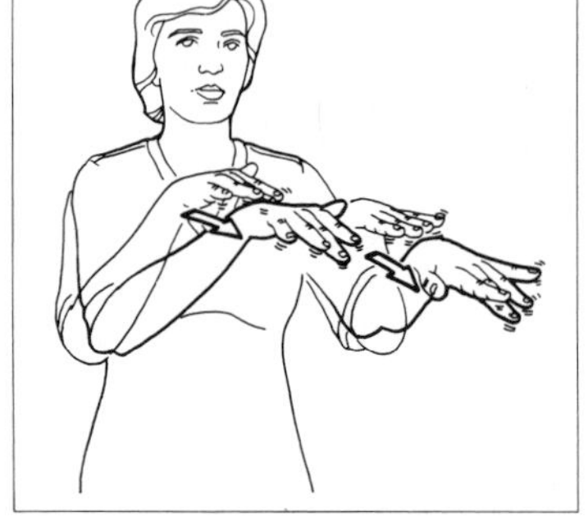

## FLOW
(sm)

**Usage:** a flow analysis of the program; to trace the flow of control.

F-C

## FLOWCHART
(abbr)

**Usage:** a programming flowchart; using standard flowchart symbols; to flowchart the logic.

F-O-N-T

## FONT
(fs)

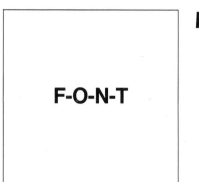

**Usage:** a printer with selectable fonts; which type font is used.

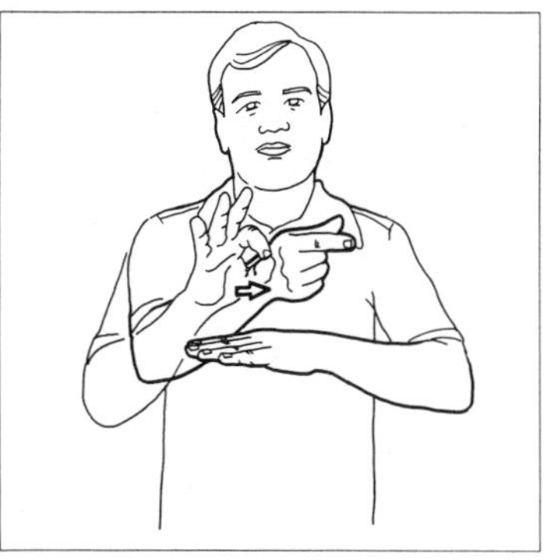

## FOREGROUND
(sm)

**Usage:** a foreground job; a foreground-initiated background job; foreground processing.

## FORM
(sm)

**Usage:** design of the output form; use of pre-printed forms.

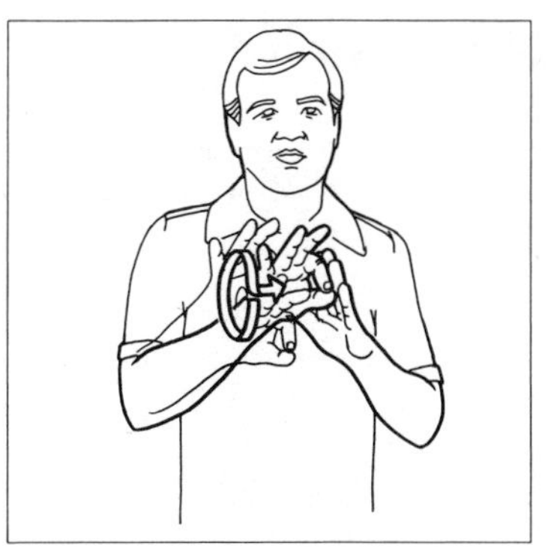

## FORMAT, FORMATTED
(sm)

**Usage:** the instruction format; the input format; a formatted dump.
**Note:** F-hand circles in front of left palm, then is placed against it.

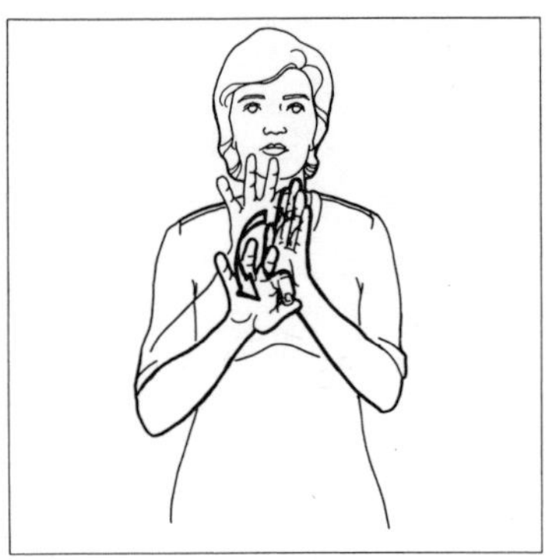

## FORMULA
(sm)

**Initialized form of:** law (F).
**Usage:** formula manipulation; a formula to calculate the values of.

F-O-R-T-R-A-N

## FORTRAN
(fs)

**Usage:** the FORTRAN language; a FORTRAN compiler; a skilled FORTRAN programmer.
**Note:** FORTRAN is a contraction of FORmula TRANslation.

## FULL
(sm)

**Usage:** a full duplex operation; a full adder; a full-screen editor; the queue is full.
**Note:** Right hand brushes inward across left S-hand.

## FUNCTION, FUNCTIONAL

**Usage:** the function keys; to meet the functional requirements; a recursive function; functional specs.

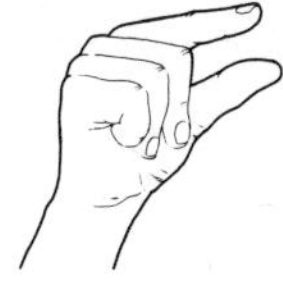

# GAME

**Usage:** computer games; game theory.

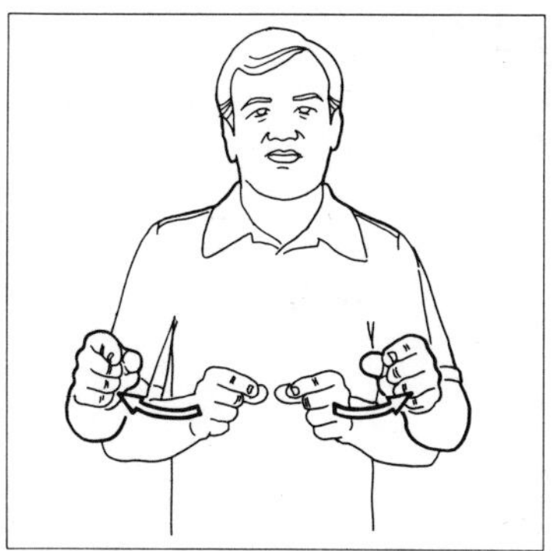

# GENERAL, GENERALIZED
(sm)

**Usage:** a general-purpose computer; a generalized sort/ merge program.
**Note:** G-hands separate as they move outward.

# GENERATE, GENERATOR*
(sm)

**Initialized form of:** make (G).
**Usage:** generates pseudo-random numbers; generates an interrupt; a character generator; a macro generator.

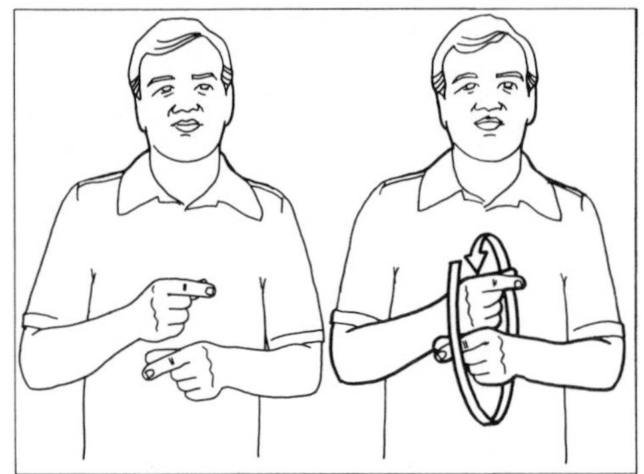

# GLOBAL
(sm)

**Initialized form of:** world (G).
**Usage:** a global search; global and local variables.

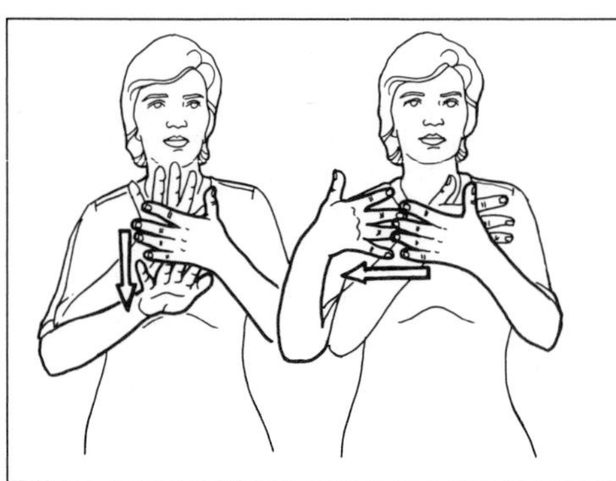

# GRAPH, GRAPHIC
(cf. SCHEDULE) (sm)

**Usage:** graph theory; to plot a graph; a graphic display program; a graphics language.

# GROUP, GROUPED
(sm)

**Initialized form of:** class (G).
**Usage:** a groupmark; group addressing; a group line in COBOL; grouped records.

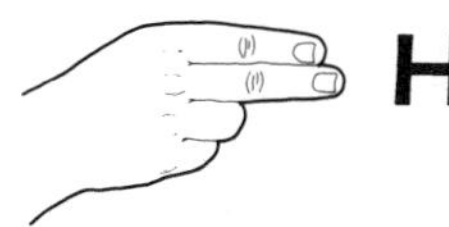


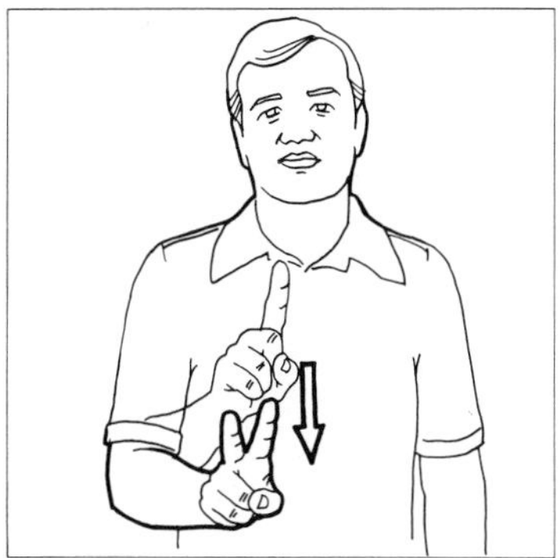

## HALF
(sm)

**Usage:** half duplex operation; a half word.
**Note:** "one" over "two."

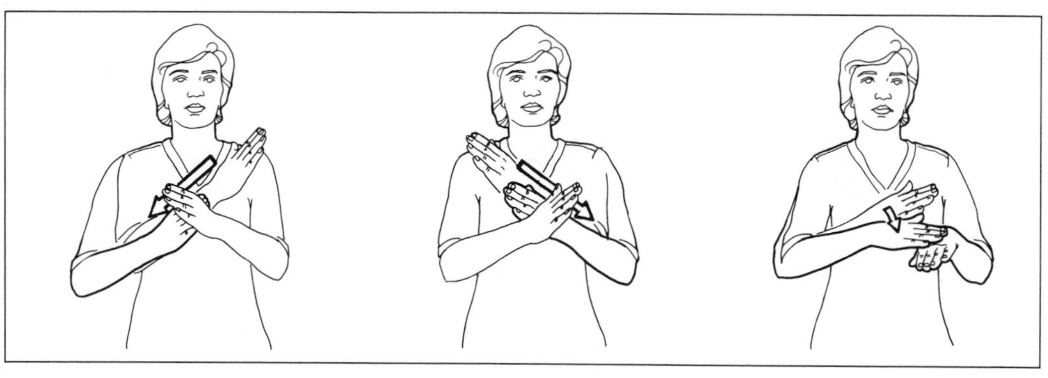

## HANDS-ON
(sm)

**Usage:** a lot of hands-on experience; to get some hands-on time.
**Note:** "hands" + "on."

# H

## HARD
(sm)

**Usage:** a hard-copy terminal; a terminal hardwired to the computer; a hard stop.

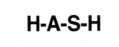

## HARDWARE
(abbr)

H-W

**Usage:** hardware diagnostics; a hardware check; hardware interfaces.

## HASH
(fs)

H-A-S-H

**Usage:** generate a hash total; hashing the record key to generate the record address.

## HEAD, HEADER*
(sm)

**Usage:** the read/write head; the message header; a header record.
**Note:** Fingertips of right hand touch side of forehead and chin.

H-E-U-R-I-S-T-I-C

## HEURISTIC
(fs)

**Usage:** heuristic methods used in artificial intelligence; heuristic problem solving; heuristic design.

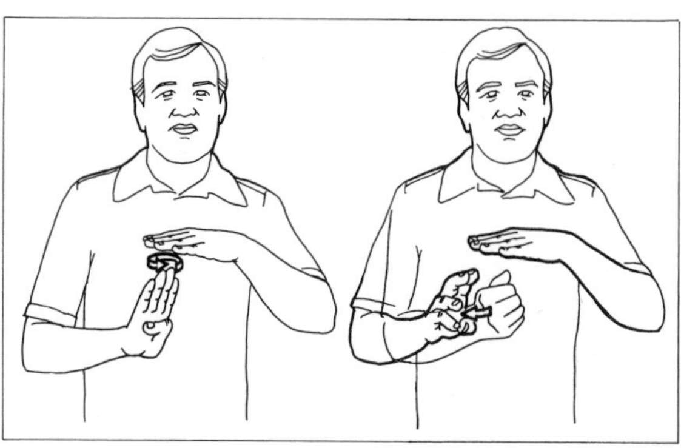

## HEXADECIMAL
(sm)

**Same sign for:** base sixteen.
**Usage:** a hexadecimal digit; convert to hexadecimal.

## HIERARCHIC, HIERARCHICAL, HIERARCHY
(sm)

**Usage:** a hierarchic sequence; hierarchical structures; hierarchical access method; levels in the hierarchy.

## HIGH-ORDER
(sm)

**Usage:** in the high-order position; if the high-order digit is not zero.

H-O-S-T

## HOST

(fs)

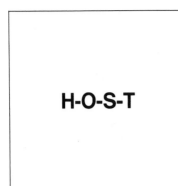

**Usage:** a program on the host computer; communication with a host processor; host system responses.

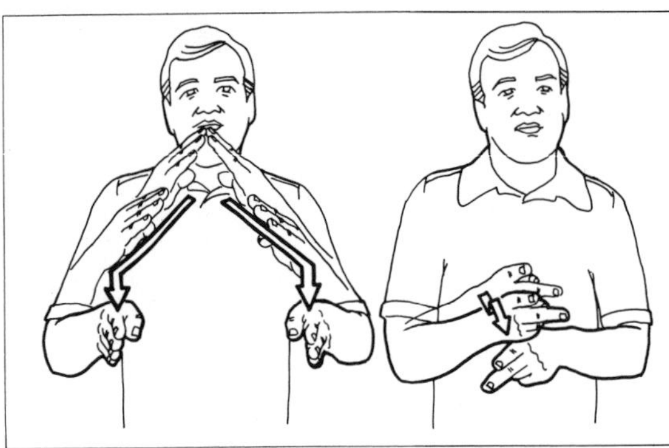

## HOUSEKEEPING

(sm)

**Usage:** good housekeeping procedures; as part of the initial housekeeping.
**Note:** "house" + "keep."

## HYBRID

(sm)

**Initialized form of:** cross, intersect (H).
**Usage:** a hybrid computer; a hybrid system for flight simulation.

I-D

## IDENTIFICATION, IDENTIFIER
(abbr)

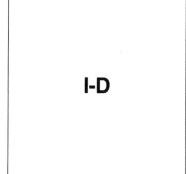

**Usage:** the unique identifier; the identification division of the COBOL program; the user identification number.

## IDENTIFY
(sm)

**Usage:** to identify each field of the record; the way the various files are identified.

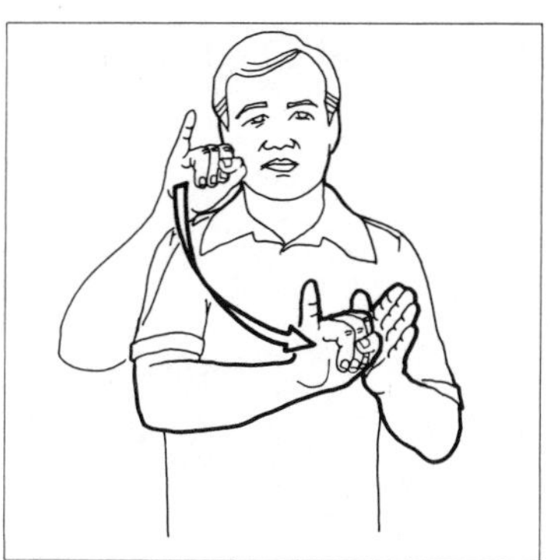

## IMAGE
(sm)

**Initialized form of:** picture (I).
**Usage:** image enhancement; a card image; the image area.

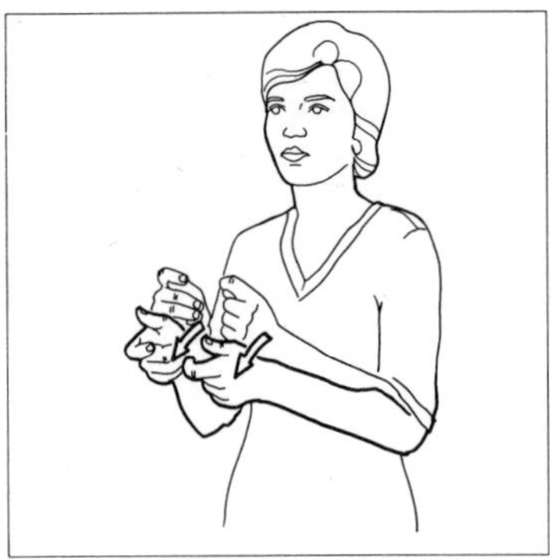

## IMMEDIATE

(sm)

**Same sign for:** fast, quick.
**Usage:** immediate access storage; immediate addressing; immediate response mode.
**Note:** Thumbs flick up from under bent indexes; sometimes done with only one hand.

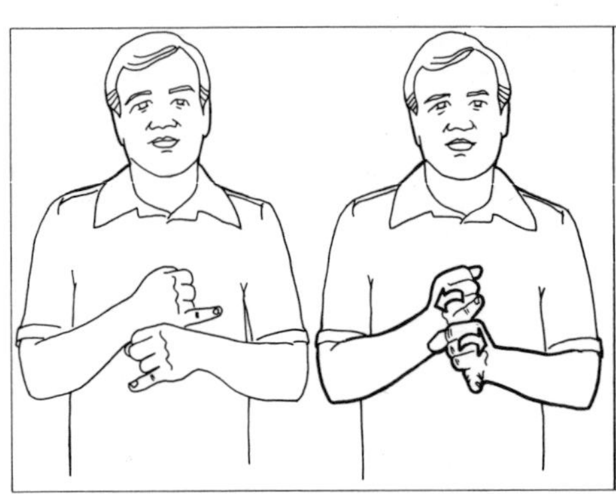

## IMPLEMENT, IMPLEMENTATION

(sm)

**Initialized form of:** make (I).
**Usage:** the computerized application is ready to implement; now in the implementation phase.

## IN-

(cf. NON-, UN-) (sm)

**Same sign for:** doesn't, don't, not.
**Usage:** inactive; inaccurate; incompatible; independent; indirect.
**Note:** Thumb pushes out from under chin.

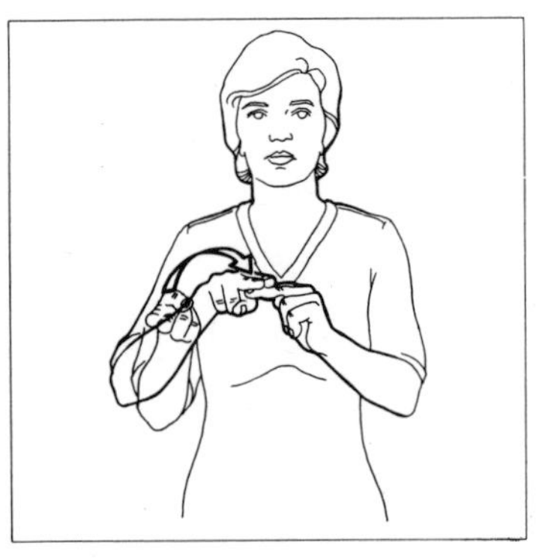

## INCREMENT, INCREMENTAL

(cf. BUMP) (sm)

**Same sign for:** increase.
**Usage:** to increment the counter; the increment size; incremental improvements.
**Note:** Right H-hand turns over onto left-H.

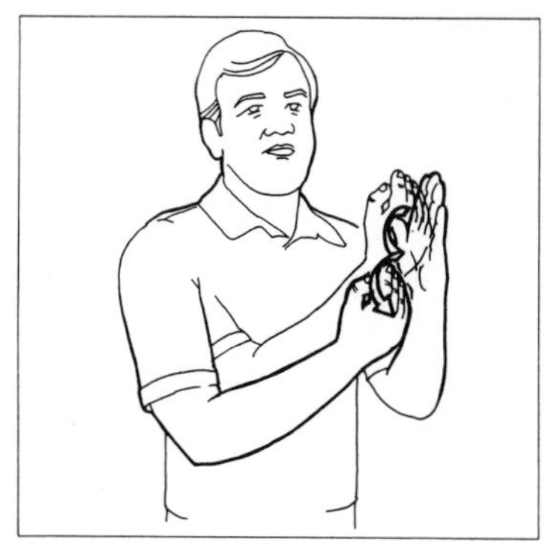

## INDEX, INDEXED

(cf. CATALOG, LIST) (sm)

**Usage:** contents of the index register; an indexed sequential data set; the index to the file.
**Note:** Bent right hand bumps down left palm.

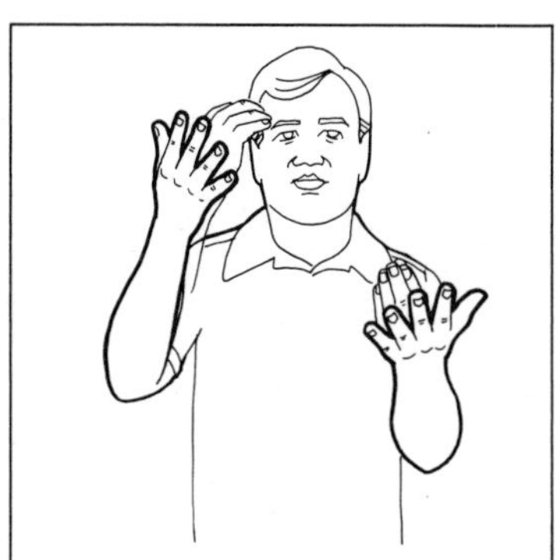

## INFORMATION

(cf. DATA) (sm)

**Same sign for:** inform, notify.
**Usage:** information storage and retrieval; information theory; the information content.

## INITIAL PROGRAM LOAD, IPL

(abbr)

**Usage:** an initial program load to bring the system up; to IPL the system.

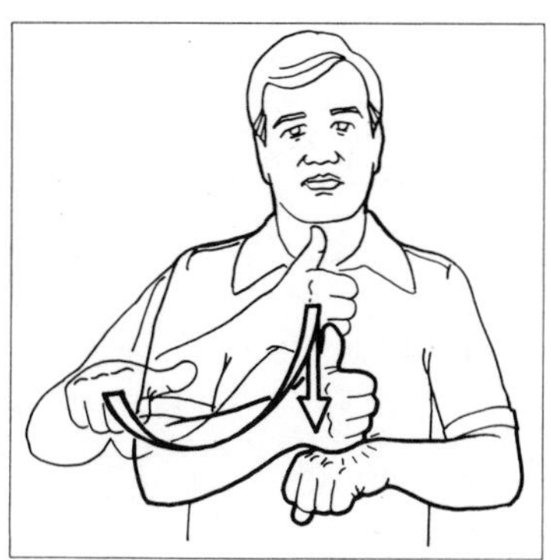

## INITIALIZATION, INITIALIZE

(cf. INSTALL, SETUP) (sm)

**Same sign for:** establish.
**Usage:** improper loop initialization; to initialize the counters to their starting values.

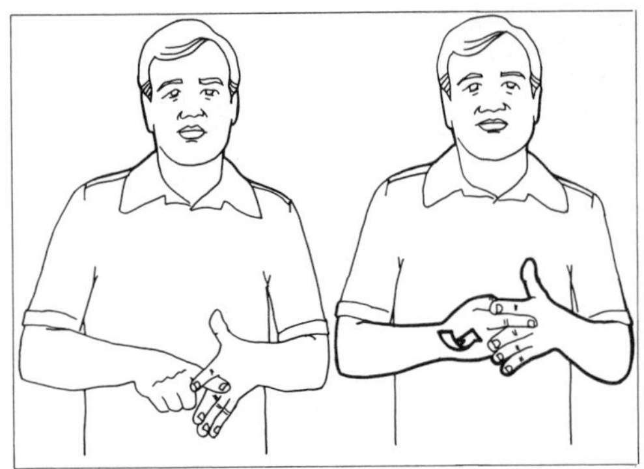

## INITIATE, INITIATOR*
(cf. SOURCE, START) (sm)

**Same sign for:** begin.
**Usage:** to initiate recovery procedures; the initiator function of the job scheduler.

## INPUT
(dm)

**Usage:** the input area; input data; an input device; an input routine; the input queue.

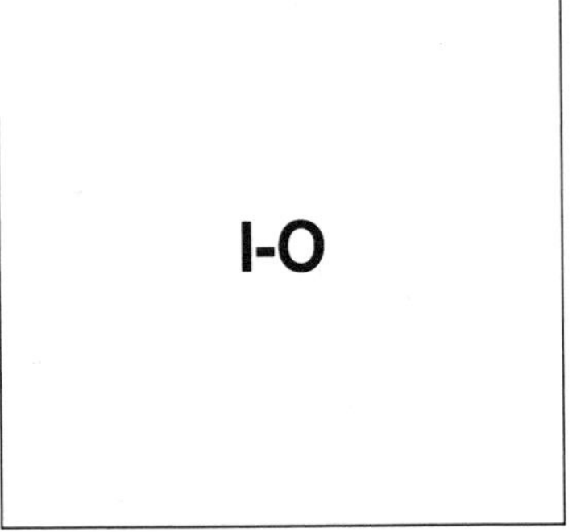


## INPUT/OUTPUT, I/O
(abbr)

**Usage:** an input/output channel; the input/output control system; an I/O interrupt.

## INQUIRY
(cf. QUERY) (sm)

**Same sign for:** question.
**Usage:** a data base inquiry; an inquiry station; inquiry/response operation.
**Note:** The straight index finger draws the upper part of the question mark; it then contracts to an X-shape and straightens out again, thus adding the dot at the bottom.

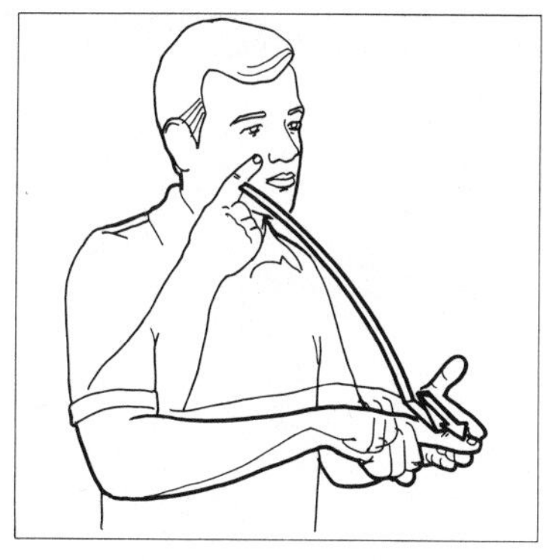

## INSPECTION

**Same sign for:** investigate.
**Usage:** to participate in a design walk-through and code inspection; arrange for code and test inspections; logic inspections.

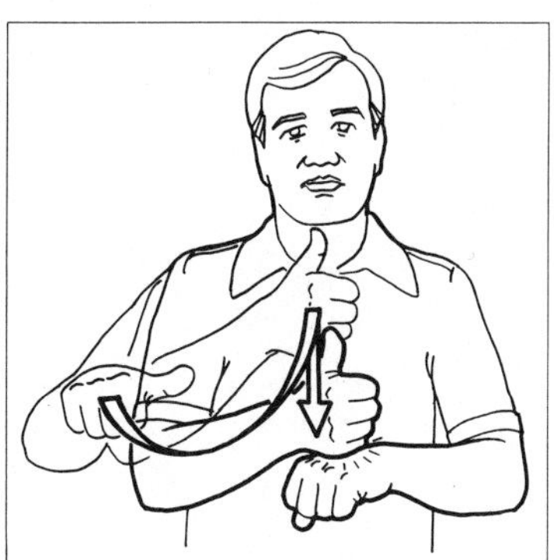

## INSTALL, INSTALLATION
(cf. INITIALIZE, SETUP) (sm)

**Same sign for:** establish.
**Usage:** when the new system is installed; to visit our installation; installation management.

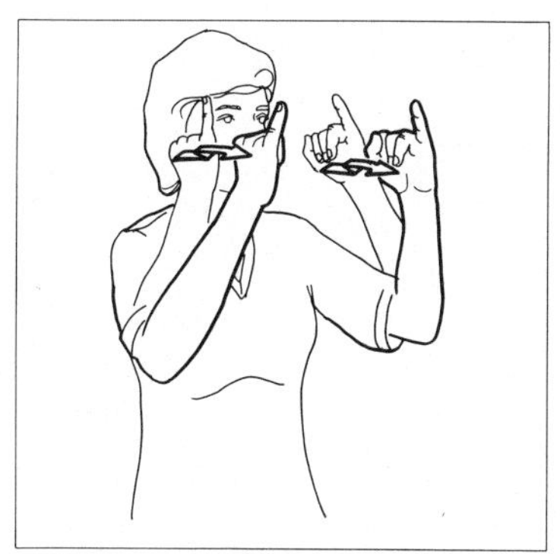

## INSTRUCTION
(dm)

**Initialized form of:** teach (I).
**Usage:** a privileged instruction; the instruction address; the instruction counter; the instruction set.

## INTEGRATE, INTEGRATED, INTEGRATION
(cf. MERGE) (sm)

**Usage:** to integrate related files into a single data base; an integrated circuit board; large-scale integration; an integrated data base; an integrated file adapter.

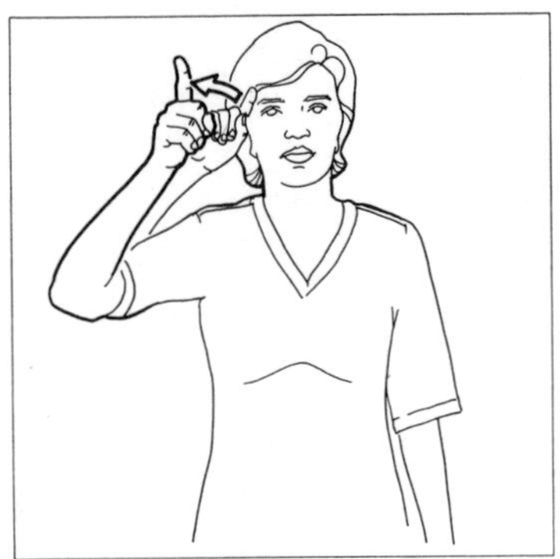

## INTELLIGENCE, INTELLIGENT
(sm)

**Same sign for:** brilliant, smart.
**Usage:** artificial intelligence; an intelligent terminal.
**Note:** Right index finger moves out quickly from forehead.

## INTERACTIVE

**Same sign for:** associate (verb), mingle.
**Usage:** an interactive reservation system; interactive graphics.

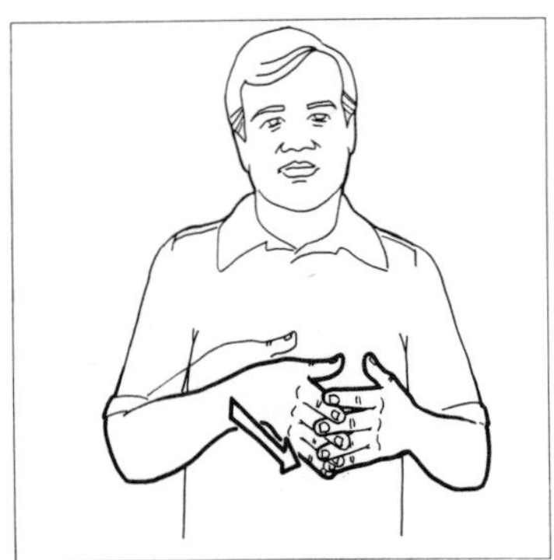

## INTERFACE
(sm)

**Usage:** a hardware interface; a software interface; data interface; a person to interface to the test group.

## INTERMEDIATE
(dm)

**Usage:** to calculate the intermediate totals; an intermediate-sized system.
**Note:** Little finger edge of right hand slices down twice between left index and middle fingers.

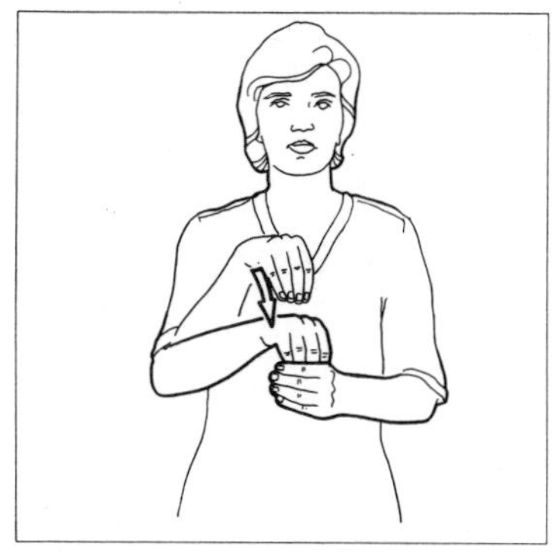

# INTERNAL, INTERNALS

**Same sign for:** in.
**Usage:** an internal sort; internal storage; internal representation; the internals of the operating system.

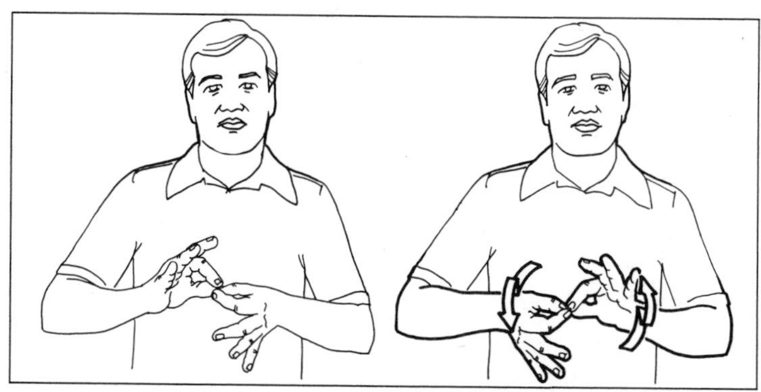

# INTERPRET, INTERPRETER*, INTERPRETIVE

**Usage:** to interpret the results; the interpreter interprets each instruction; interpretive execution.

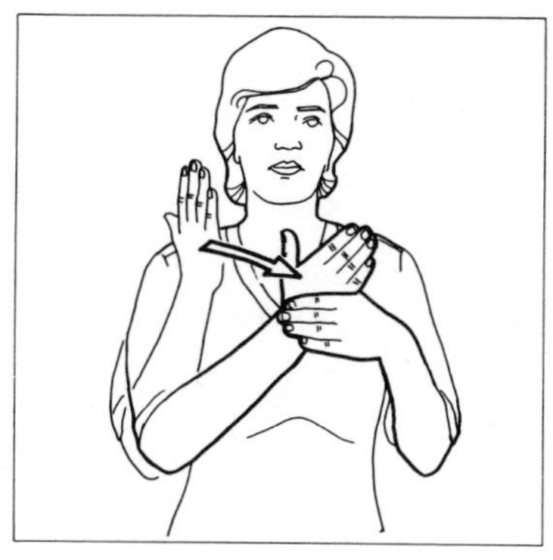

# INTERRUPT

(sm)

**Same sign for:** disrupt, impede, interfere.
**Usage:** an I/O interrupt; to disable the interrupts; an interrupt signal.
**Note:** Little finger edge of right hand slices down sharply between left thumb and index finger.

# INVALID

(cf. ERROR, FAULT) (sm)

**Same sign for:** mistake, wrong.
**Usage:** an invalid character; an invalid key; an invalid operation code.
**Note:** Y-hand placed on chin.

# I/O

(see INPUT/OUTPUT)

# IPL

(see INITIAL PROGRAM LOAD)

# ITERATE, ITERATION, ITERATIVE

**Same sign for:** again.
**Usage:** to iterate the inner loop; an iterative procedure; and continue the iteration until the condition is met.
**Note:** Movement is frequently duplicated.

# JCL
(see JOB CONTROL LANGUAGE)

# JES
(see JOB ENTRY SUBSYSTEM)

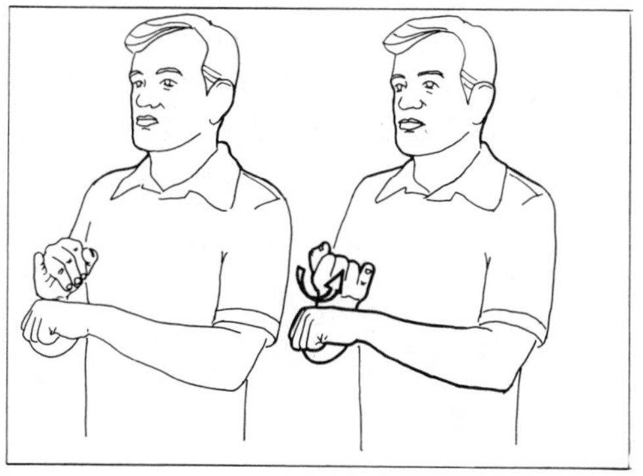

# JOB
(sm)

**Usage:** a batch job; a background job; the job stream; a job control statement.
**Note:** Little finger of J-hand brushes against back of left fist.

J-C-L

## JOB CONTROL LANGUAGE, JCL
(abbr)

**Usage:** using the Job Control Language to describe the job requirements to the operating system; a JCL error.

J-E-S

## JOB ENTRY SUBSYSTEM, JES
(acronym)

**Usage:** with the Job Entry Subsystem managing the job queues, I/O, etc; a function of JES.
**Note:** The term JES rhymes with "says."

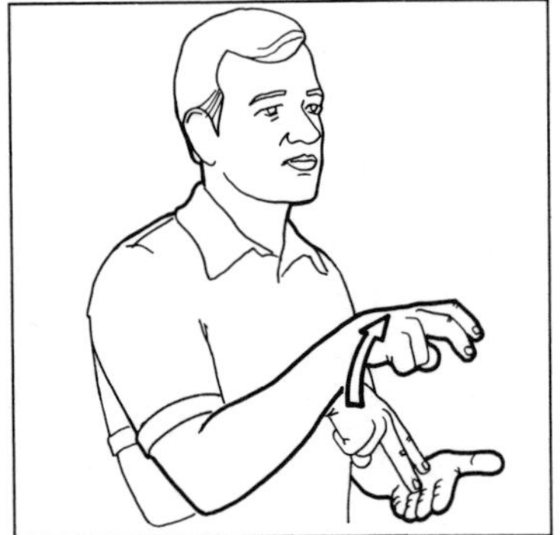

## JUMP
(sm)

**Usage:** a conditional jump; the JUMP instruction.

## JUSTIFY
(see LEFT-JUSTIFY or RIGHT-JUSTIFY)

# K

## K
(see KILO-)

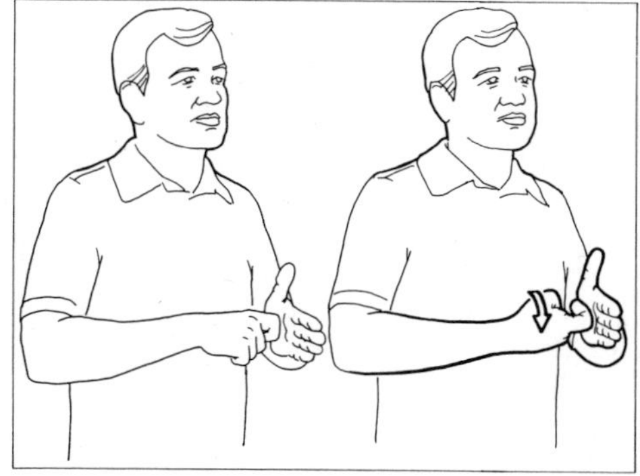

## KEY
(sm)

**Usage:** the sort key; primary and secondary keys; the key field; keyword in context.
**Note:** Like turning a key in a lock.

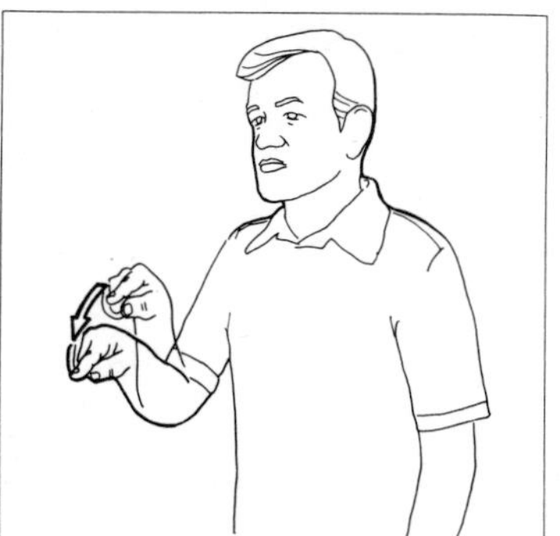

## KEY
(sm)

**Usage:** the SHIFT key; the ATTENTION key; the alphabetic keys on the terminal.
**Note:** Like depressing a key on a keyboard.

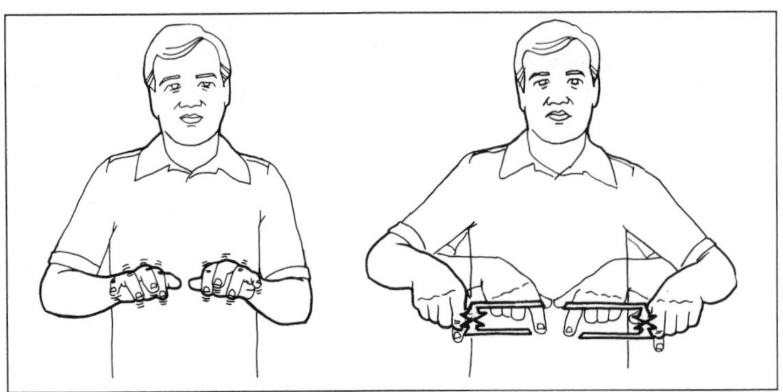

## KEYBOARD

**Usage:** a full alphanumeric keyboard; with a keyboard for data entry.
**Note:** The horizontal "board" is outlined by the thumbs and index fingers.

## KEYPUNCH
(abbr)

**Usage:** a keypunch machine; a keypunch operator; keypunched the data.

## KILO-, KILO-BYTES, K
(abbr)

**Usage:** a signaling frequency of 2.2 kilo-hertz; with 64 kilo-bytes of memory; and 512K of high speed memory.

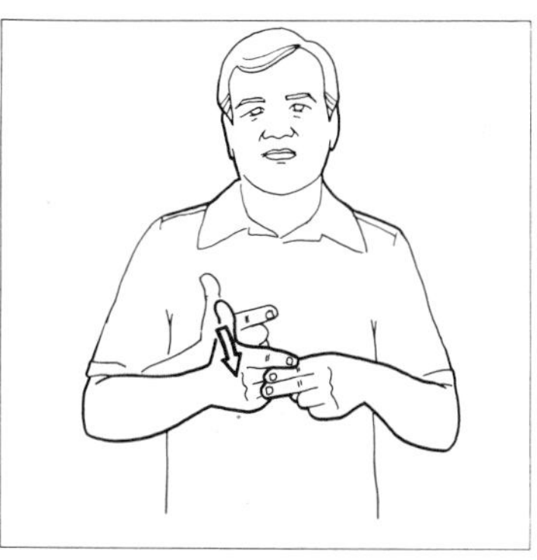

## LABEL

**Initialized form of:** name (L).
**Usage:** a tape label; these instructions should have labels; the data set label.
**Note:** This movement is usually duplicated.

## LANGUAGE

(sm)

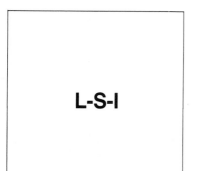

**Usage:** a high-level language; machine language; an application-oriented language.

L-S-I

## LARGE-SCALE INTEGRATION, LSI

(abbr)

**Usage:** made possible by large-scale integration; the manufacture of LSI chips.

L-I-F-O

## LAST-IN-FIRST-OUT, LIFO

(acronym)

**Usage:** a last-in-first-out queuing discipline; using a LIFO rule.
**Note:** The term LIFO is pronounced "life-o."

L-A-Y-O-U-T

## LAYOUT

(fs)

**Usage:** a layout of the output form; file layout; record layout.

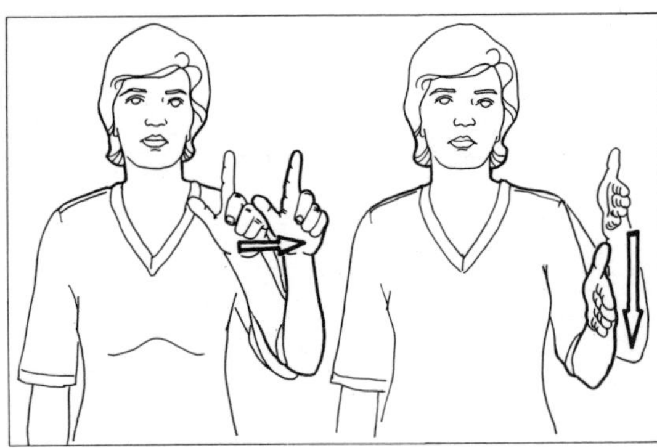

## LEFT-JUSTIFY

(sm)

**Usage:** left-justify the dollar amount; with each line of text left-justified.
**Note:** Should be done with the left hand, even by right-handed persons.

## LENGTH

(sm)

**Same sign for:** long.
**Usage:** block length; record length; word length; a line length of 132 characters.

## LEVEL
(sm)

**Usage:** a different level in the hierarchy; a high-level language; levels of detail in the program design.

## LIBRARIAN*, LIBRARY

**Usage:** secured from the tape librarian; the project librarian; a library program; the program is not in his private library.

## LIGHT

**Usage:** the READY light; a light-pen; the console lights.
**Note:** Middle finger flicks up from under chin.

## LIGHT

**Usage:** the READY light; a light-pen; the console lights.
**Note:** The position and orientation of the hand can be altered to indicate the location of the light and the direction of its rays. Duplicated movement can indicate a blinking light.

## LIFO

(see LAST-IN-FIRST-OUT)

## LIMIT, LIMITED

(sm)

**Same sign for:** restrict.
**Usage:** a limit check; a limited subset of the APL language; to limit output to ten or less pages.

## LINE

(cf. STRING) (sm)

**Usage:** a communication line; a line adapter; a line printer; lines of code.

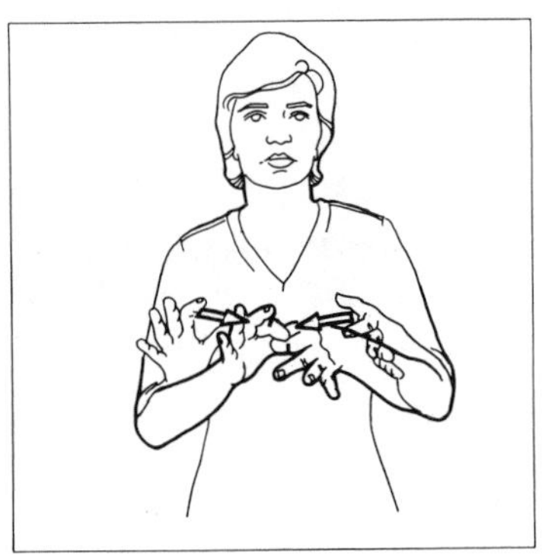

## LINK, LINKAGE

(cf. CONNECT) (sm)

**Same sign for:** attach, belong, join, unite.
**Usage:** to establish a data link; to link to a subroutine; the linkage editor.

L-I-S-P

# LISP

(fs)

**Usage:** using LISP for many problems in artificial intelligence; the LISP language.

**Note:** The term LISP is a contraction of LISt Processing.

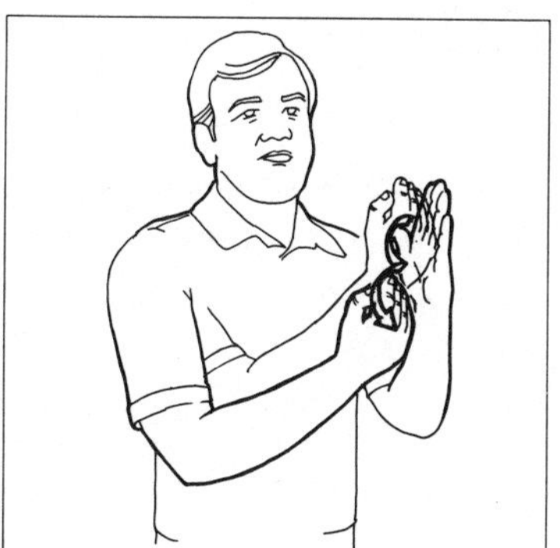

# LIST, LISTING

(cf. CATALOG, INDEX) (sm)

**Usage:** a pushdown list; list processing; a listing of the source program.
**Note:** Bent right hand bumps down left palm.

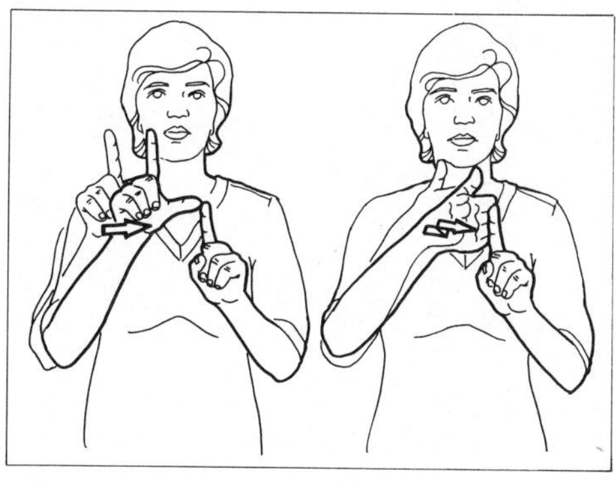

# LITERAL (alphabetic)

(sm)

**Usage:** the use of literals in programming; by enclosing literals in quotes.
**Note:** "letter" + "itself." Also see next entry.

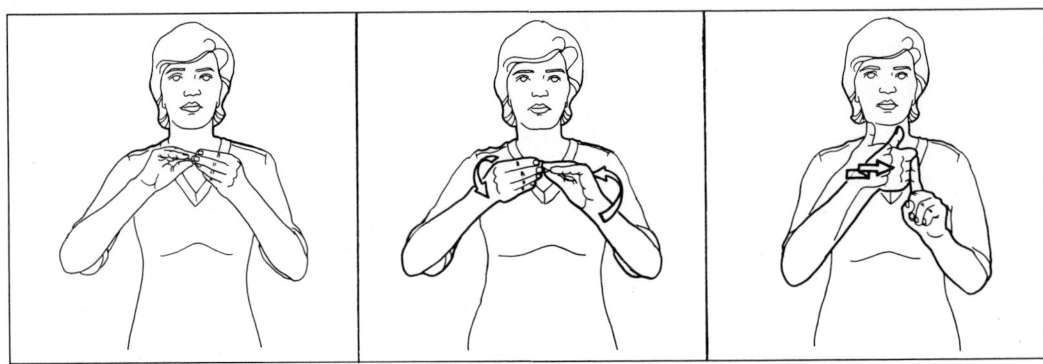

## LITERAL (numeric)

(sm)

**Usage:** the use of literals in programming; a literal value.
**Note:** NUMBER + "itself." Also see previous entry.

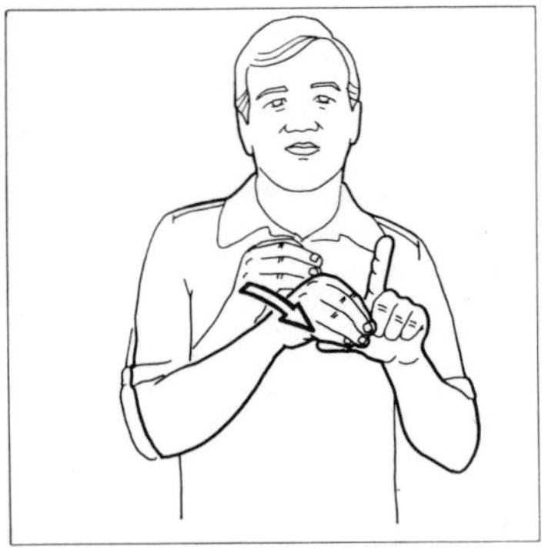

## LOAD, LOADER*

**Usage:** load-and-go; a load module; load leveling; an absolute loader.
**Note:** Right flat-O hand is placed onto thumb of left L-hand.

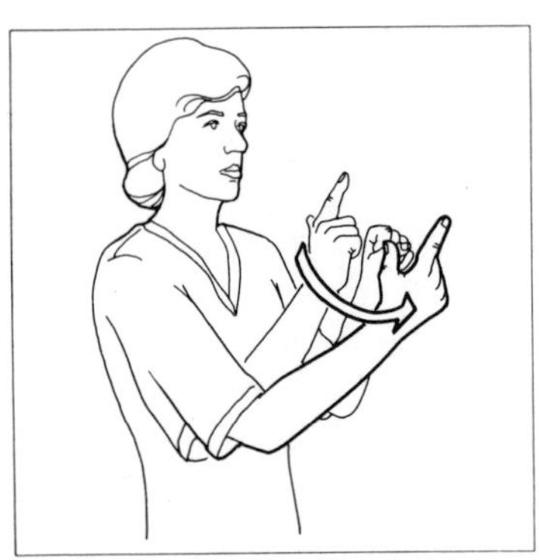

## LOCAL

(sm)

**Usage:** a local variable (not global); a local terminal (not remote).

# LOCATION
(sm)

**Initialized form of:** place (L).
**Usage:** a storage location; the location counter; the location of the buffer.
**Note:** Thumbs of L-hands touch, circle back, and touch again.

# LOGIC, LOGICAL

**Usage:** the design logic; a logic diagram; a logical record; AND and OR are logical operators.

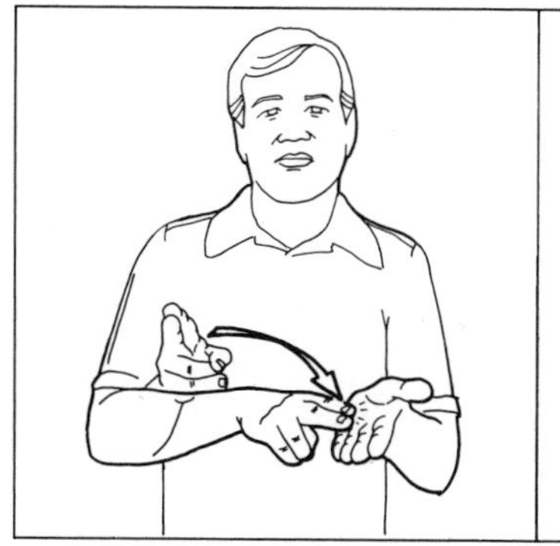

# LOG OFF (verb), LOGOFF (adj.)
(cf. SIGN OFF) (sm)

**Usage:** the logoff procedure; to log off before leaving the terminal unattended.
**Note:** "sign" + DISCONNECT.

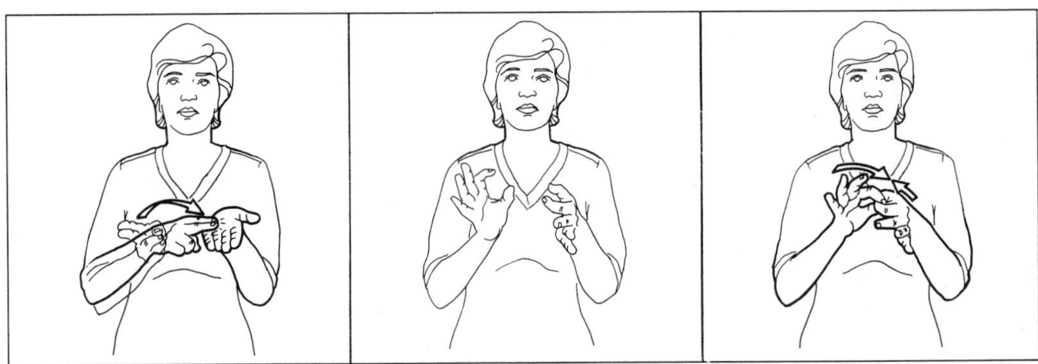

# LOG ON (verb), LOGON (adj.)

(cf. SIGN ON) (sm)

**Usage:** part of the logon message; to log on to the system.
**Note:** "sign" + CONNECT.

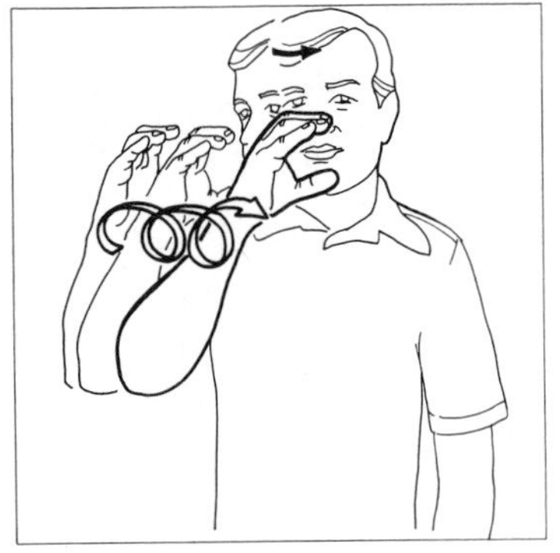

# LOOKUP

(cf. SEARCH, SEEK)

**Usage:** a table lookup procedure; to lookup in the directory.

# LOOP

**Usage:** an endless loop; caught in a loop; a loop counter; a feedback loop; a DO loop.

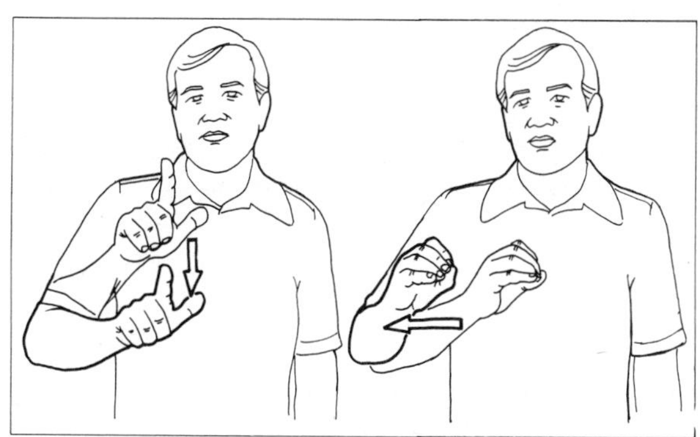

## LOW-ORDER

(sm)

**Usage:** the low-order digit; in the low-order position.

## LSI

(see LARGE-SCALE INTEGRATION)

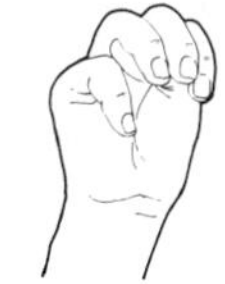

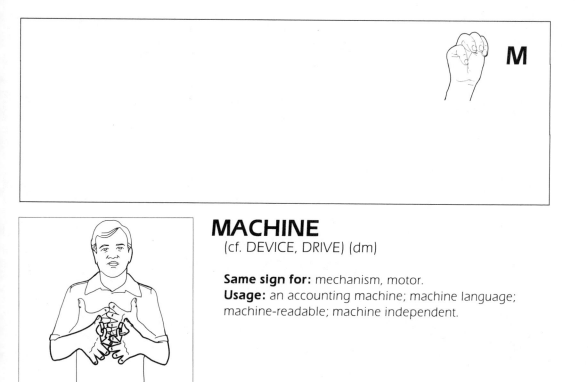

# M

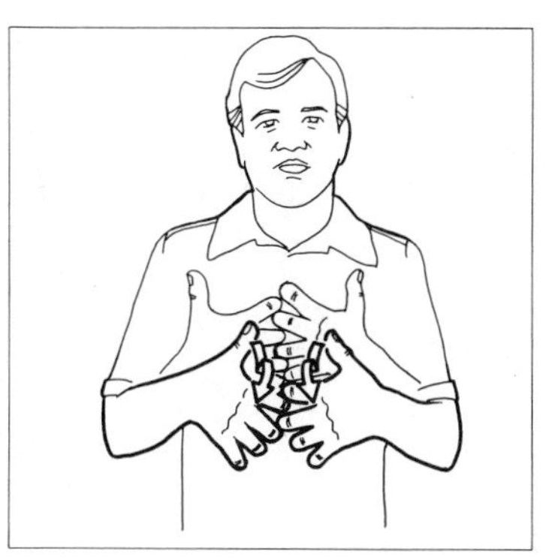

## MACHINE

(cf. DEVICE, DRIVE) (dm)

**Same sign for:** mechanism, motor.
**Usage:** an accounting machine; machine language; machine-readable; machine independent.

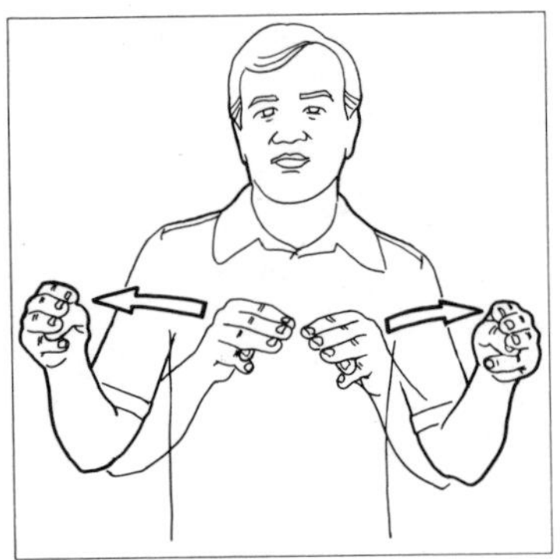

## MACRO
(sm)

**Initialized form of:** large (M).
**Usage:** a macro instruction; a macro language; the macro library.

## MAGNETIC
(sm)

**Usage:** magnetic disk; magnetic ink; magnetic stripe; magnetic tape drive.
**Note:** M-hands pivot toward each other, as if by magnetic attraction.

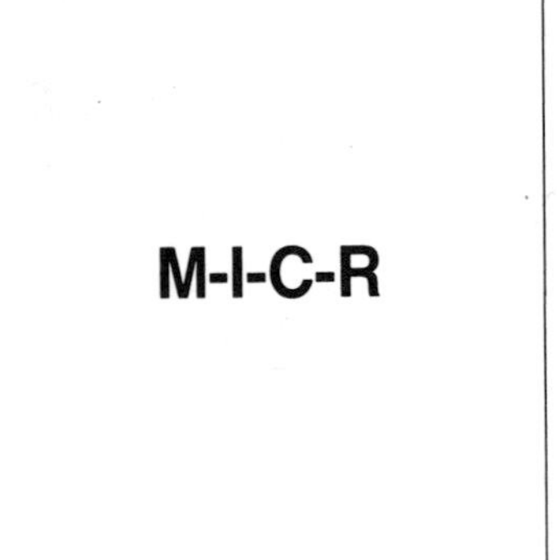


## MAGNETIC INK CHARACTER RECOGNITION, MICR
(acronym)

**Usage:** using magnetic ink character recognition to read the checks; a MICR reader.
**Note:** The term MICR is pronounced "miker."

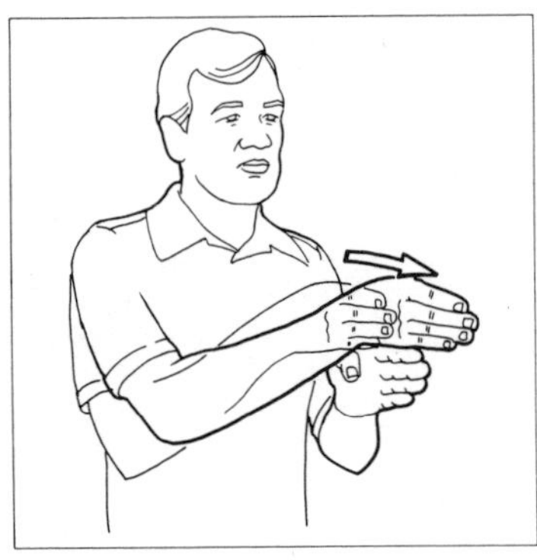

## MAIN
(cf. MAJOR, MASTER) (sm)

**Same sign for:** straight.
**Usage:** the main frame; the main program; main storage; the main path through a program.
**Note:** Right B-hand slides forward on top edge of left B-hand.

## MAINTENANCE

**Same sign for:** keep.
**Usage:** file maintenance; preventive maintenance; maintenance time; the maintenance console.
**Note:** This movement is usually duplicated.

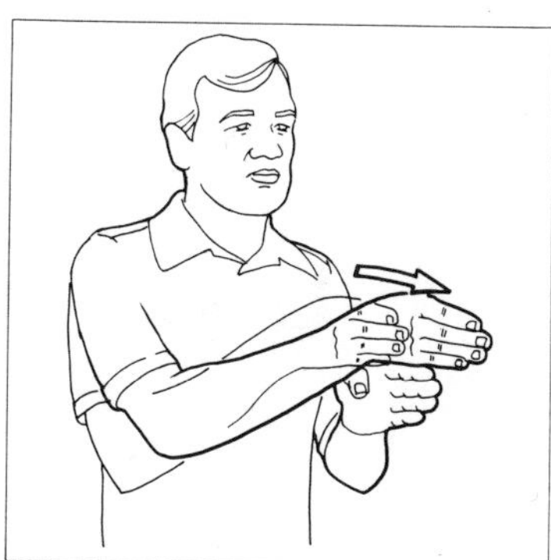

## MAJOR
(cf. MAIN, MASTER) (sm)

**Same sign for:** straight.
**Usage:** the major control field; the major totals; the major task.
**Note:** Right B-hand slides forward on top edge of left B-hand.

## MANAGE, MANAGER*, MANAGEMENT*
(cf. CONTROL)

**Same sign for:** govern, regulate.
**Usage:** to manage resources; the project manager; file managment; installation management.
**Note:** Like holding the reins.

M-I-S

## MANAGEMENT INFORMATION SYSTEM, MIS
(abbr)

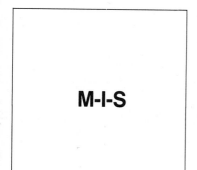

**Usage:** using a management information system for monitoring and control; responsible for MIS design and implementation.

## MARGIN
(sm)

**Usage:** check the right-hand margin; to fit within the column margins.
**Note:** Right thumb slides down little-finger edge of left hand.

## MARK
(sm)

**Usage:** a group mark; the end-of-tape mark; mark sensing.
**Note:** Right hand makes quick pecking movement toward left palm.

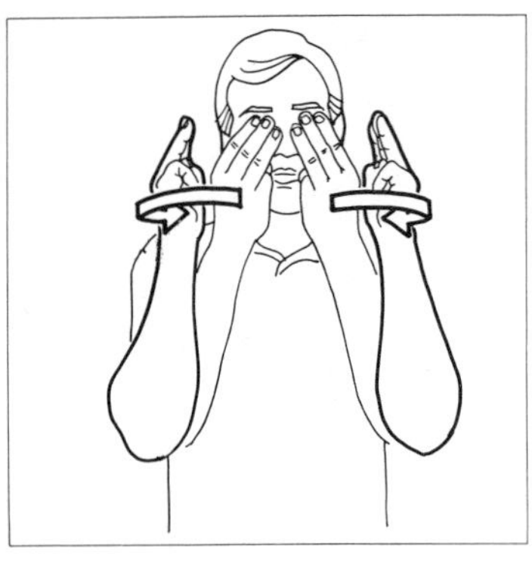

## MASK
(sm)

**Usage:** a half-word mask; to use a bit pattern as a mask; to mask out the low-order bits.

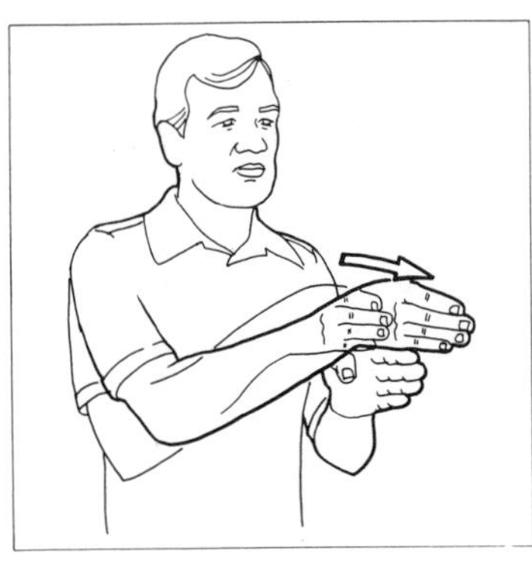

## MASTER
(cf. MAIN, MAJOR) (sm)

**Same sign for:** straight.
**Usage:** the master file; the master console; the master scheduler; the master clock.
**Note:** Right B-hand slides forward on top edge of left B-hand.

## MAXIMUM
(sm)

**Usage:** the maximum delay time; maximum storage capacity.

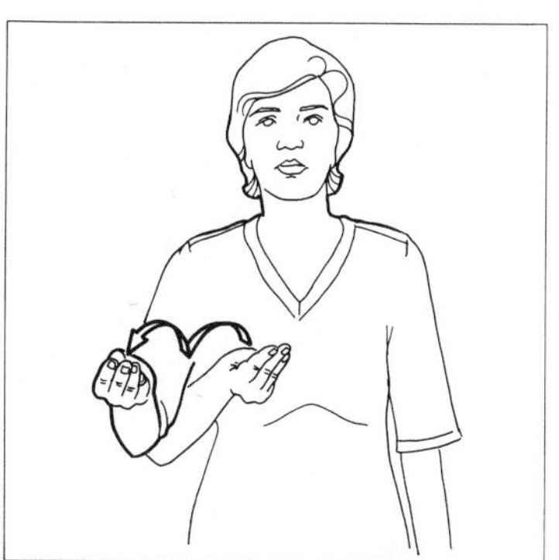

## MEDIA
(sm)

**Initialized form of:** thing (M).
**Usage:** various kinds of storage media; an operator who works only with input/output media.

## MEGA-
(dm)

**Same sign for:** million.
**Usage:** 50 megabytes of disk storage; with a frequency exceeding 1 megahertz.
**Note:** Right M-hand into left palm exactly twice.

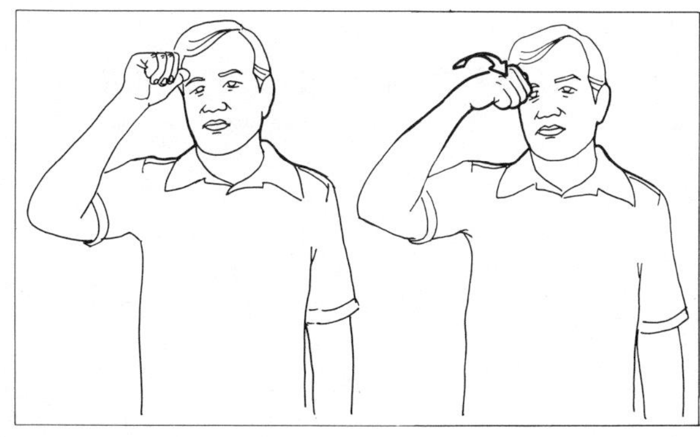

## MEMORY
(sm)

**Usage:** high-speed memory; memory protection; read-only memory.
**Note:** Also see next entry.

## MEMORY
(sm)

**Same sign for:** memorize.
**Usage:** high-speed memory; memory protection; read-only memory.
**Note:** Also see previous entry.

## MERGE
(cf. INTEGRATE) (sm)

**Usage:** a sort/merge routine; to merge two files.

## MESSAGE
(dm)

**Usage:** an error message; message switching; to send a message to the operator; message buffering.
**Note:** F-hands twist back and forth as they separate to the sides; repeat.

## MICR
(see MAGNETIC INK CHARACTER RECOGNITION)

M-I-C-R-O-

## MICRO-
(fs)

**Usage:** microcode; microprocessor; microprogram; microfiche.

M-I-L-L-I-

## MILLI-
(fs)

**Usage:** milliseconds.

M-I-P-S

## MILLION INSTRUCTIONS PER SECOND, MIPS
(acronym)

**Usage:** capable of more than 4 million instructions per second; how many MIPS.
**Note:** The term MIPS rhymes with "tips."

M-I-N-I-

## MINI-
(fs)

**Usage:** a minicomputer; a minidisk.

## MINIMUM
(sm)

**Usage:** the minimum delay time; with a minimum access time of; the minimum execution time; the minimum storage requirement.

## MINOR
(sm)

**Usage:** the minor control field; a minor total.
**Note:** Right B-hand slides forward on bottom edge of left B-hand.

## MIPS
(see MILLION INSTRUCTIONS PER SECOND)

## MIS
(see MANAGEMENT INFORMATION SYSTEM)

## MNEMONIC

**Usage:** mnemonic operation codes; mnemonic symbols; mnemonic names are an aid to the memory.
**Note:** M and then N at forehead.

## MODE
(fs)

M-O-D-E

**Usage:** interpretive mode; conversational mode.

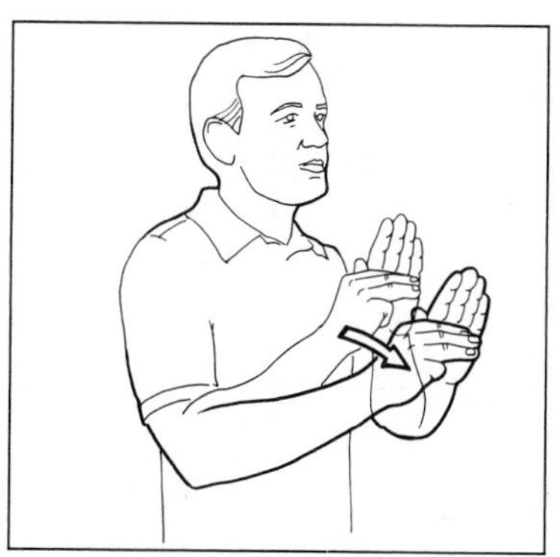

## MODEL, MODELING
(sm)

**Initialized form of:** show (M).
**Usage:** a computer model of the economy; techniques of mathematical modeling.

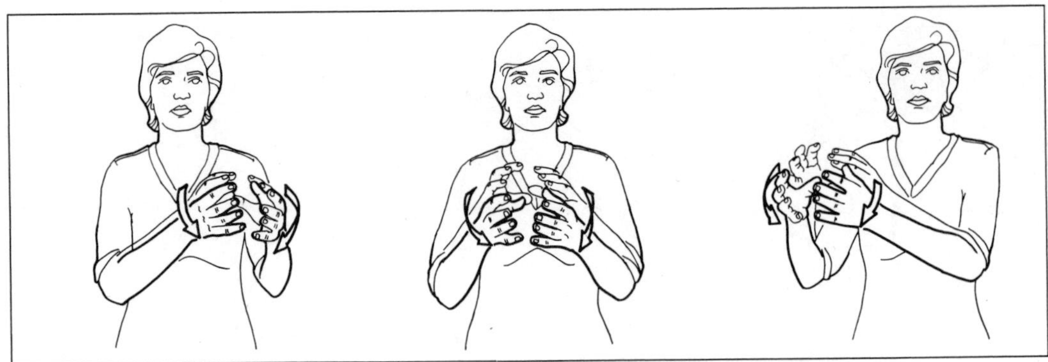

## MODULAR, MODULE

(sm)

**Usage:** modular design; each load module; a control module; the interface between the two modules.

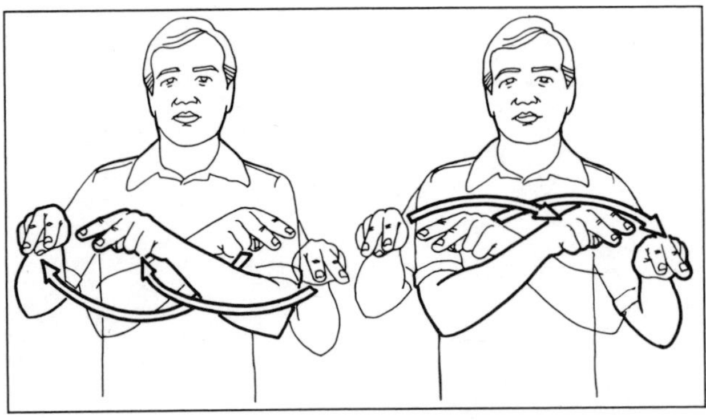

## MONITOR

**Usage:** a monitor program; a hardware monitor.
**Note:** Palm-down V-hands make large horizontal, clockwise circle (looking over a situation).

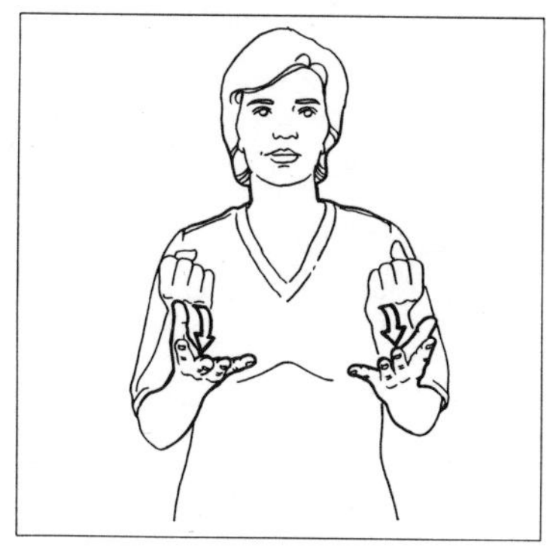

## MULTI-, MULTIPLE-

**Same sign for:** many, multiple, numerous.
**Usage:** a multipass sort; a multiprocessor system; multitasking; multiple-precision; a multiple-address message.
**Note:** This movement is usually duplicated.

## MULTIPLEX, MULTIPLEXER*, MULTIPLEXING

(sm)

**Usage:** to multiplex several inputs onto the same channel; multiplex operation; time-division multiplexing; a multiplexer channel.
**Note:** Several lines into one.

**M-U-X**

## MULTIPLEX, MULTIPLEXER*, MULTIPLEXING

(abbr)

**Usage:** to multiplex several inputs onto the same channel; multiplex operation; time-division multiplexing; a multiplexer channel.

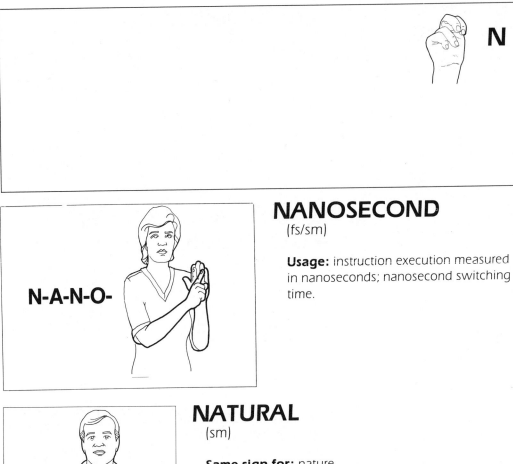

# N

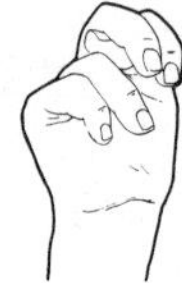

## NANOSECOND
(fs/sm)

**Usage:** instruction execution measured in nanoseconds; nanosecond switching time.

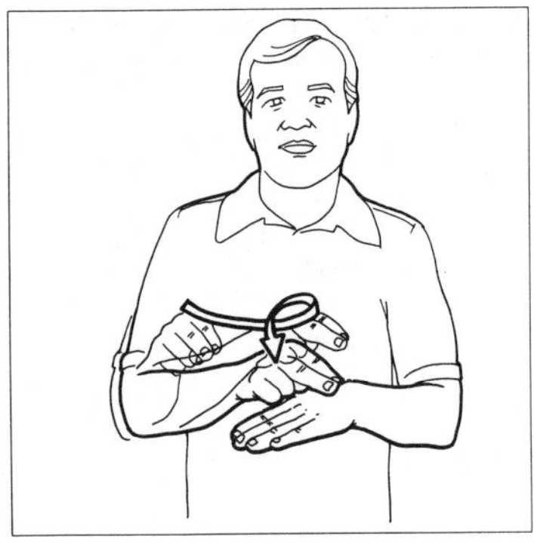

## NATURAL
(sm)

**Same sign for:** nature.
**Usage:** natural language processing; a natural number.

## NC
(see NUMERICAL CONTROL)

## NEST, NESTED

(sm)

**Usage:** to nest one loop within another; nested subroutines.
**Note:** Right G-hand into left C-hand.

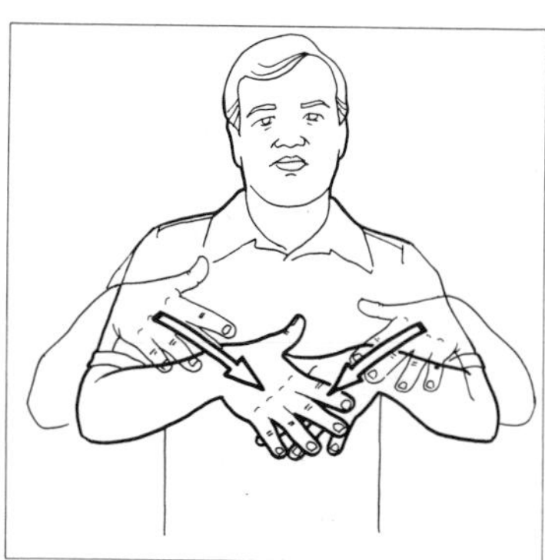

## NETWORK

(sm)

**Usage:** a network analyzer; the network control program; at each node of the network.
**Note:** Represents multiple lines and nodes.

## NODE

(sm)

**Same sign for:** cross, intersect.
**Usage:** at each node of the network; communication links between nodes; major and minor nodes.

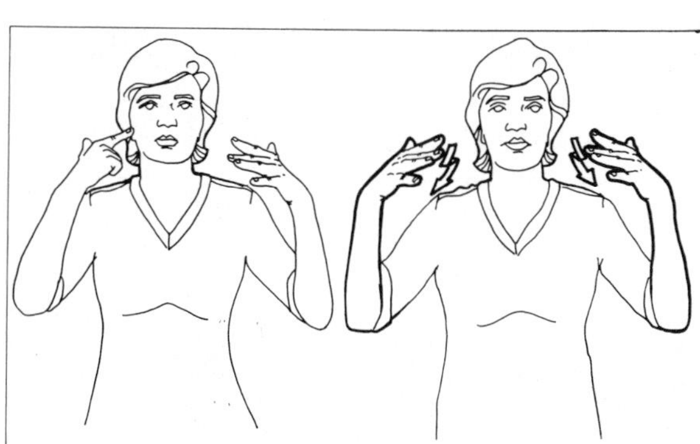

## NOISE, NOISY

**Usage:** signal-to-noise ratio; a noisy line.

# N

## NON-

(cf. IN-, UN-) (sm)

**Same sign for:** doesn't, don't, not.
**Usage:** nondestructive readout; a nonresident program; nonstandard operation; nonlinear programming.
**Note:** Thumb pushes out from under chin.

## NULL

(cf. BLANK, SPACE) (sm)

**Same sign for:** bare, empty, vacant.
**Usage:** a null set; null record; null line; null character.

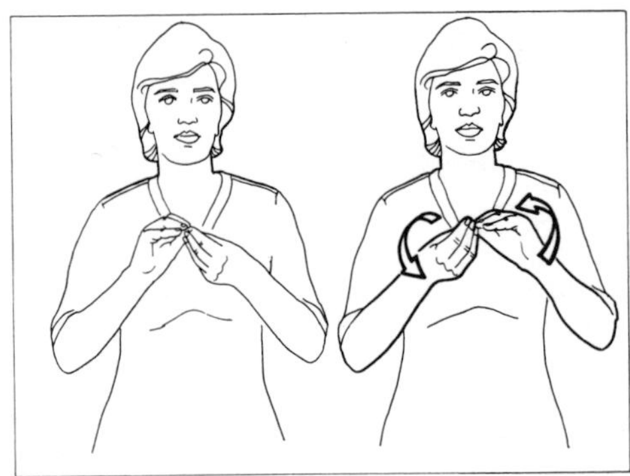

## NUMBER, NUMERIC, NUMERICAL

(cf. DIGIT) (sm)

**Usage:** the number of iterations; numeric data; a numeric keyboard; numerical analysis.

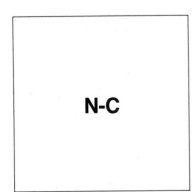

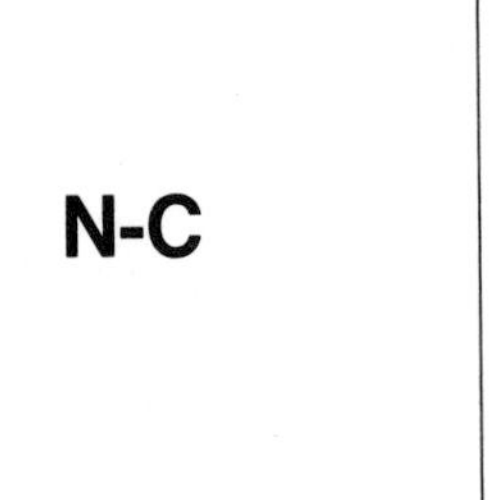


## NUMERICAL CONTROL, NC

(abbr)

**Usage:** part-programming for numerical control; a drafting machine with numerical control; an NC machine tool.

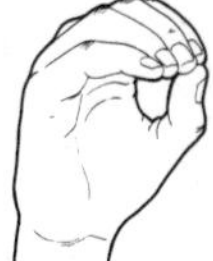


O-B-J

# OBJECT
(abbr)

**Usage:** the object language; the compiler-produced object module.

# OCR
(see OPTICAL CHARACTER RECOGNITION)

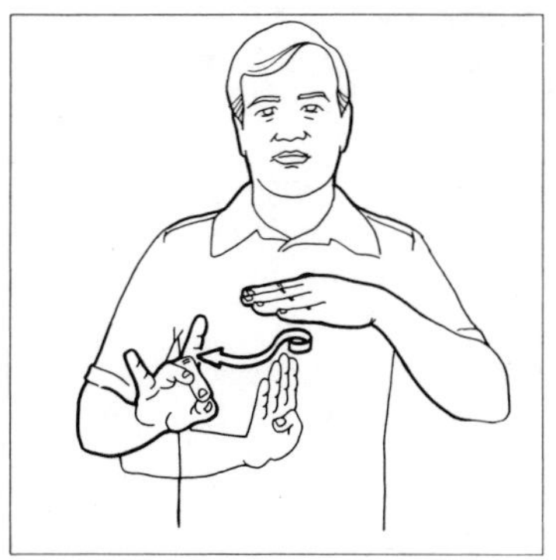

# OCTAL
(sm)

**Same sign for:** base eight.
**Usage:** octal representation; binary-to-octal conversion.

## OEM

(see ORIGINAL EQUIPMENT MANUFACTURER)

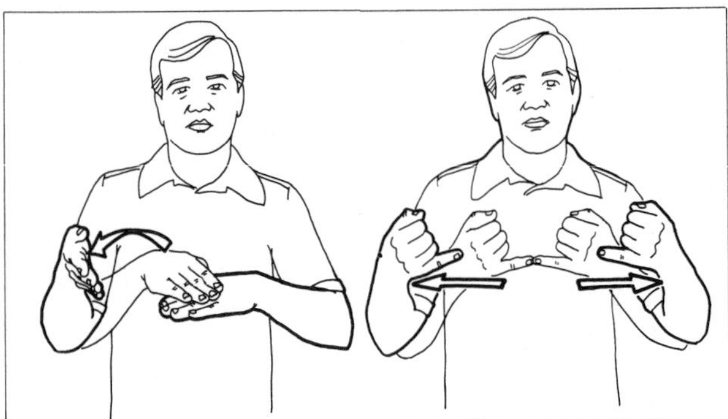

## OFFLINE

(sm)

**Usage:** offline storage; offline data preparation.
**Note:** "off" + LINE.

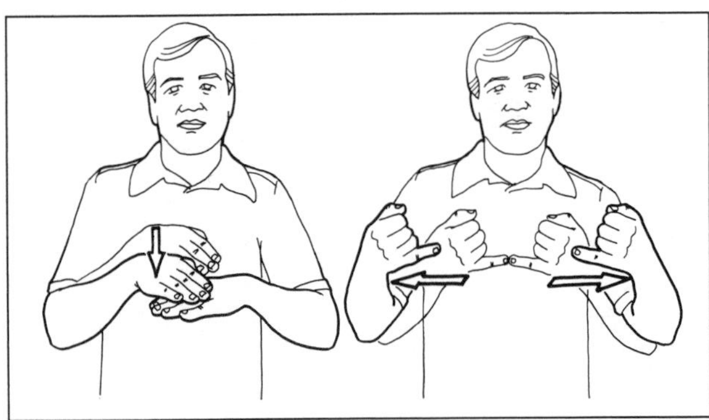

## ONLINE

(sm)

**Usage:** online storage; online processing of analog inputs; an online terminal.
**Note:** "on" + LINE.

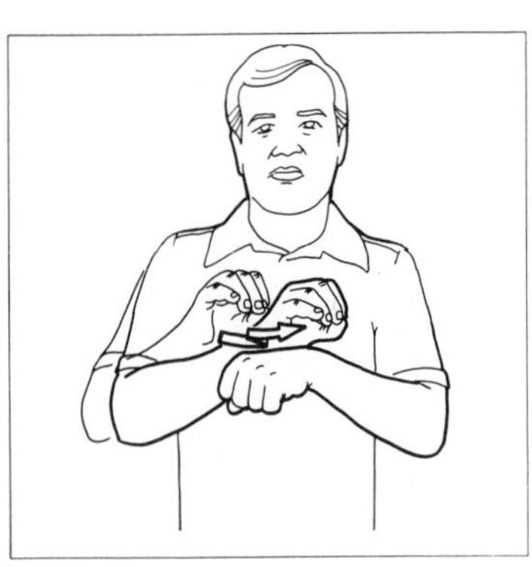

## OPERATE, OPERATION, OPERATIONAL, OPERATOR*

**Usage:** to operate I/O devices; operating environment; concurrent operation; operational procedures; a computer operator.

O-S

## OPERATING SYSTEM, OS

(abbr)

**Usage:** under control of the operating system; a function of the operating system; all handled by OS.

O-P

## OPERATION

(abbr)

**Usage:** each operation code; an arithmetic operation; a logical operation.

O-C-R

## OPTICAL CHARACTER RECOGNITION, OCR

(abbr)

**Usage:** an input form designed for optical character recognition; fonts that the OCR equipment can handle.

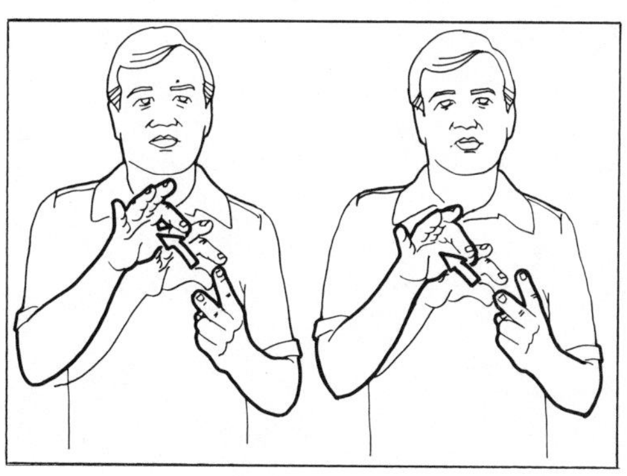

## OPTION

(sm)

**Same sign for:** choice.
**Usage:** specify which option; the default option.
**Note:** Index finger closes on thumb as right hand moves back from left index; repeat right hand movement, but from left middle finger.

O-E-M

## ORIGINAL EQUIPMENT MANUFACTURER, OEM
(abbr)

**Usage:** an OEM interface; an OEM terminal.

## OS
(see OPERATING SYSTEM)

## OUTPUT
(sm)

**Usage:** realtime output; printer output; an output area in storage; an output routine.

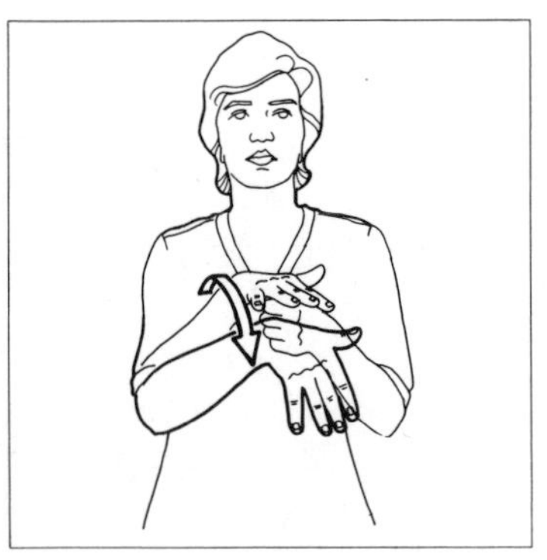

## OVERFLOW
(sm)

**Usage:** the overflow indicator; an overflow position; the overflow record.
**Note:** Right 5-hand maintains contact with left fist as it moves across it and down, like water overflowing.

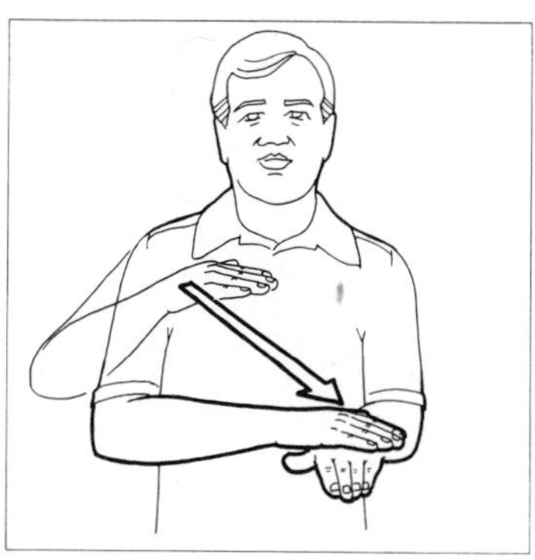

## OVERLAY
(sm)

**Usage:** the overlay structure; divided into multiple overlay segments; to overlay the current program on.
**Note:** Right hand moves down and out from shoulder onto back of left hand.

# P

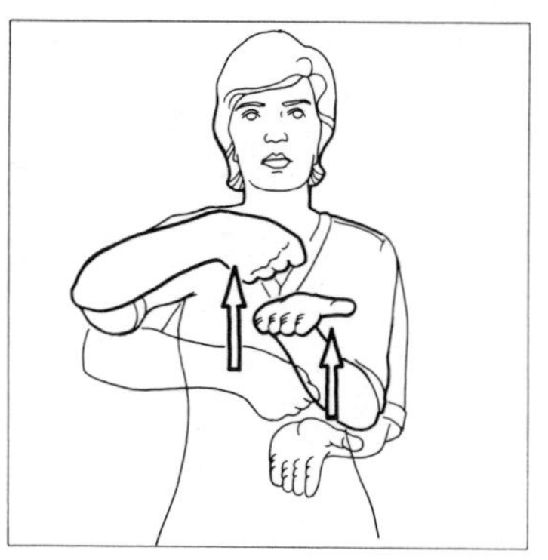

## PACK (noun)
(sm)

**Usage:** a disk pack; to mount the pack on a drive.
**Note:** Like holding a disk pack with the right hand and supporting it with the left.

## PACK, PACKED, PACKING
(sm)

**Usage:** to pack two digits in one byte; packed decimal; packing density; a packing factor of.
**Note:** Wide-C on left palm closes to a narrow-C.

## PACKET
(sm)

**Usage:** to operate a network in packet mode; packet switching.

## PAGE, PAGING

**Usage:** page size; to page in from external storage; page swapping; the paging supervisor.
**Note:** Right P-hand turns over in left palm, like the page of a book.

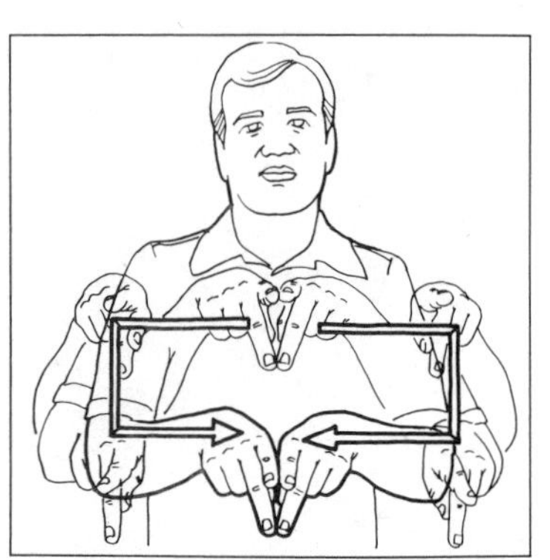

## PANEL
(sm)

**Usage:** the control panel; a display panel; maintenance panel.

## PAPER
(dm)

**Usage:** a paper jam; paper tape; to put paper in the printer.
**Note:** Right palm brushes in and across left palm two or more times.

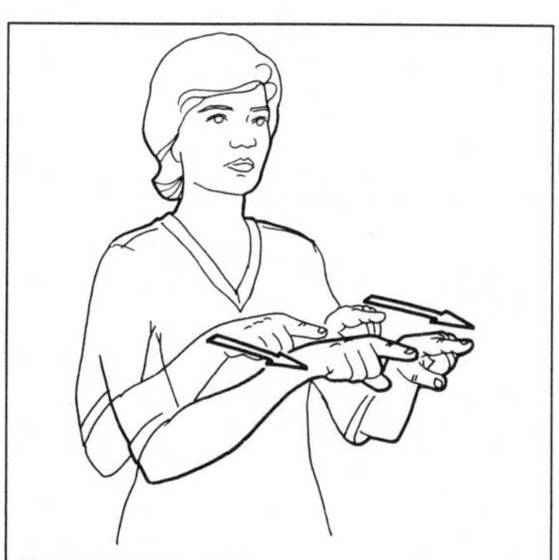

## PARALLEL
(sm)

**Usage:** parallel processing; a parallel adder; parallel transmission.

P-A-R-M

## PARAMETER
(abbr)

**Usage:** a pre-set parameter; a positional parameter; one of the program parameters.

P-A-R-I-T-Y

## PARITY
(fs)

**Usage:** a parity bit; automatic parity check.

## PARTITION, PARTITIONED

(cf. SECTION, SEGMENT) (sm, dm)

**Same sign for:** part, some.
**Usage:** a storage partition; a user partition; a partitioned data set.

P-A-S-C-A-L

## PASCAL

(fs)

**Usage:** using the Pascal language; an experienced Pascal programmer.

## PASS

(sm)

**Usage:** a two-pass procedure; for each sort pass.

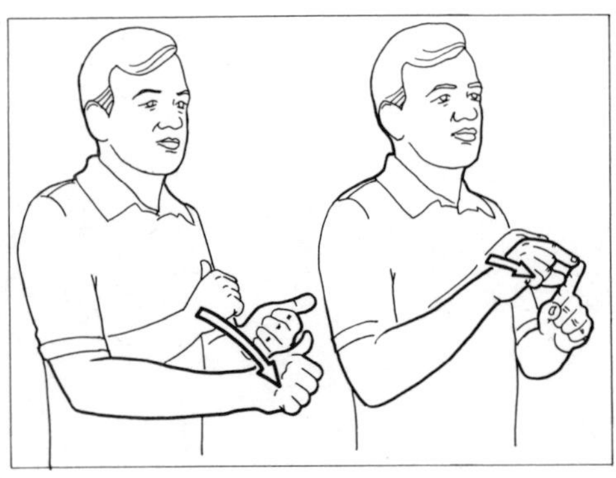

## PASSWORD

(sm)

**Usage:** keep your password confidential; by entering your password when you log on.
**Note:** PASS + WORD. Also see next entry.

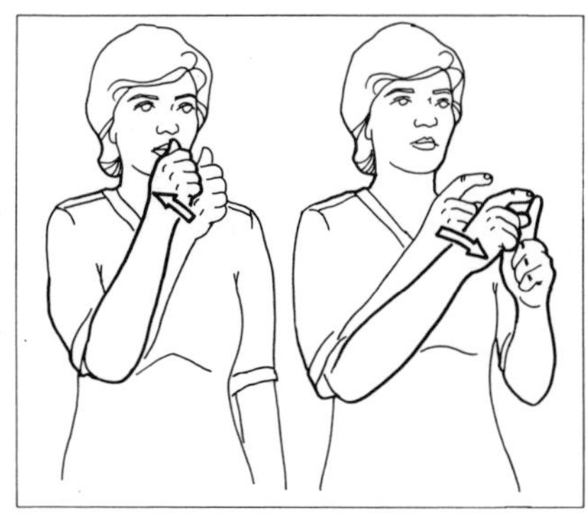

## PASSWORD
(sm)

**Usage:** keep your password confidential; by entering your password when you log on.
**Note:** PRIVATE + WORD. Also see previous entry.

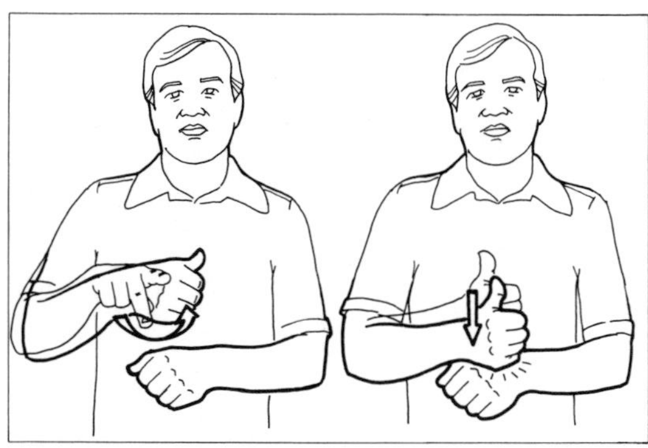

## PATTERN
(sm)

**Usage:** scan the string for that pattern of bits; pattern recognition.
**Note:** P + "establish."

## PERFORMANCE
(cf. ACTION)

**Same sign for:** do.
**Usage:** performance objectives; performance measurement; performance improvement.
**Note:** Palm-down C-hands move to the right and return.

## PERIPHERAL
(sm)

**Usage:** peripheral equipment operator; peripheral units.

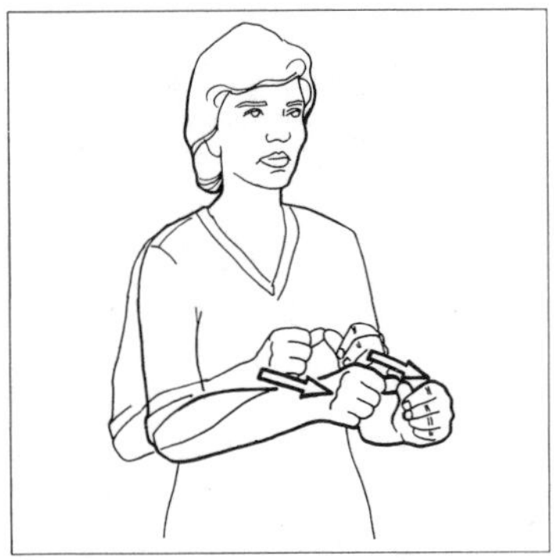

## PERMANENT
(cf. CONSTANT) (sm)

**Same sign for:** continue, persist.
**Usage:** a permanent file; permanent storage; a permanent read/write error.

## PHASE
(sm)

**Usage:** during the merge phase; compile phase; execute phase.

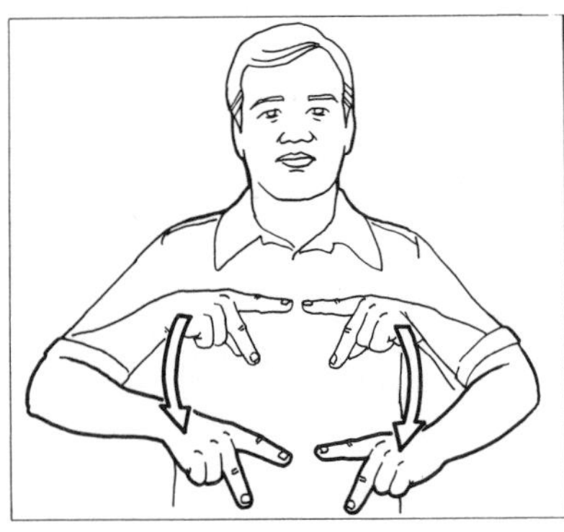

## PHYSICAL
(sm)

**Initialized form of:** body (P).
**Usage:** the physical record; a physical resource.
**Note:** P-hands on chest, then to stomach.

## PICOSECOND
(fs/sm)

**Usage:** picosecond switching time.

P-L-1

## PL/I

(fs)

**Usage:** departments using the PL/I language; the PL/I compiler.
**Note:** The term PL/I is an abbreviation of Programming Language I.

## PLOT, PLOTTER*

(sm)

**Usage:** to plot the output; a flatbed plotter; the plotter step size.
**Note:** Tip of right P-hand plots a graph on left palm.

## PLUG

(sm)

**Usage:** the two units are plug-compatible; a plug board; to plug in the unit.

## PM

(see PREVENTIVE MAINTENANCE)

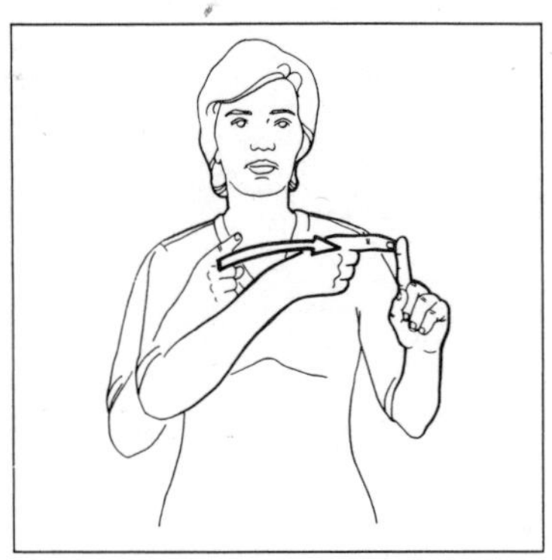

# POINT

(cf. ABSOLUTE) (sm)

**Usage:** branchpoint; restart point; point-to-point transmission.

# POLL, POLLING

**Usage:** to poll each terminal; the polling sequence.
**Note:** The sign for "query" is made two or three times, each time farther to the right.

# POP, POP-UP

(sm)

**Usage:** to pop the stack; to do a pop-up operation on a pushdown list.
**Note:** Right hand moves up quickly.

P-O-R-T

## PORT
(fs)

**Usage:** a dedicated port; the number of ports needed to handle the communication requirement.

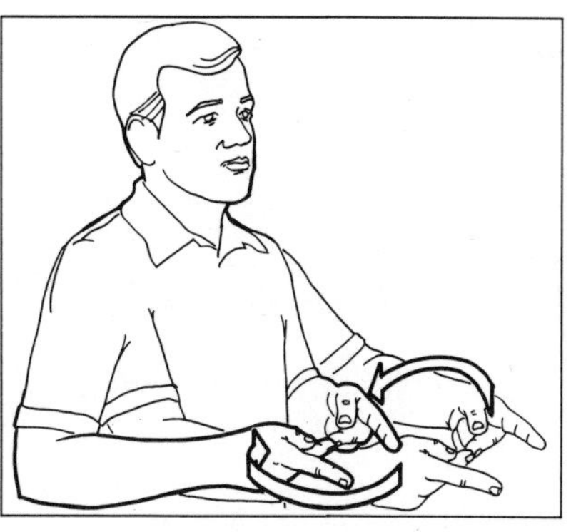

## POSITION
(cf. SHOP) (sm)

**Same sign for:** place.
**Usage:** each character position in the word; the high-order bit position.
**Note:** P-hands touch, circle back, and touch again.

## POST-
(sm)

**Initialized form of:** after (P).
**Usage:** the NC post-processor; a post-installation review; post-recovery procedures.

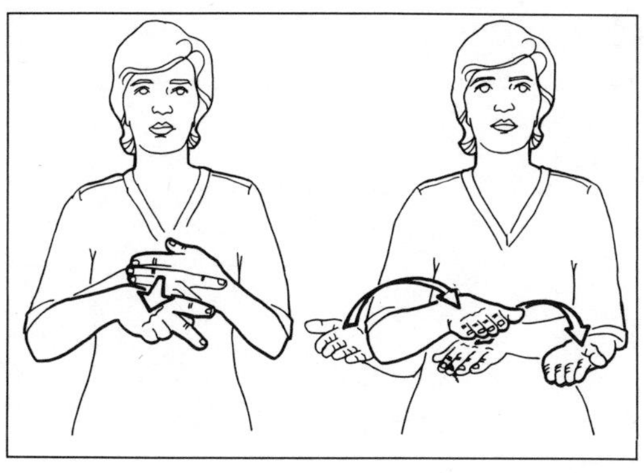

## POSTMORTEM
(sm)

**Usage:** went through a lengthy postmortem; a postmortem dump.
**Note:** POST- + "death."

## PRE-
(sm)

**Initialized form of:** before (P).
**Usage:** a predefined process; a preprocessor; a preset parameter; the data was presorted.

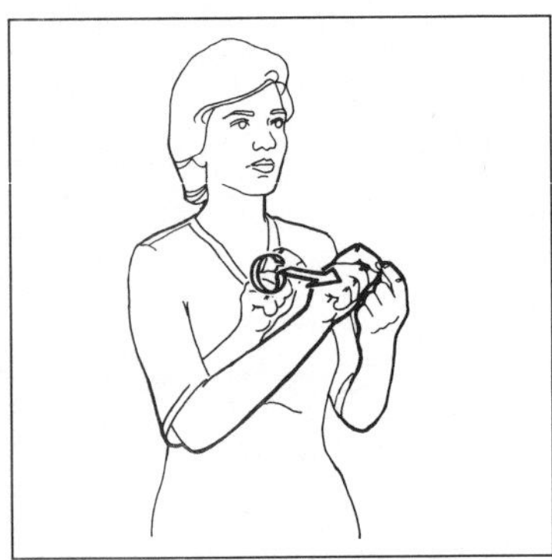

## PRECISE, PRECISELY, PRECISION
(cf. ACCURACY) (sm)

**Same sign for:** exact, exactly.
**Usage:** single-precision arithmetic; double-precision matrix inversion.
**Note:** The small circular motion of the right hand is optional.

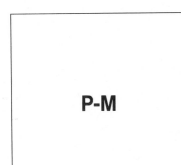

## PREVENTIVE MAINTENANCE, PM
(abbr)

**Usage:** receives preventive maintenance twice a week; the total preventive maintenance time; a machine scheduled for PM.

## PRIMARY
(sm)

**Same sign for:** first.
**Usage:** the primary key; primary file; primary track.

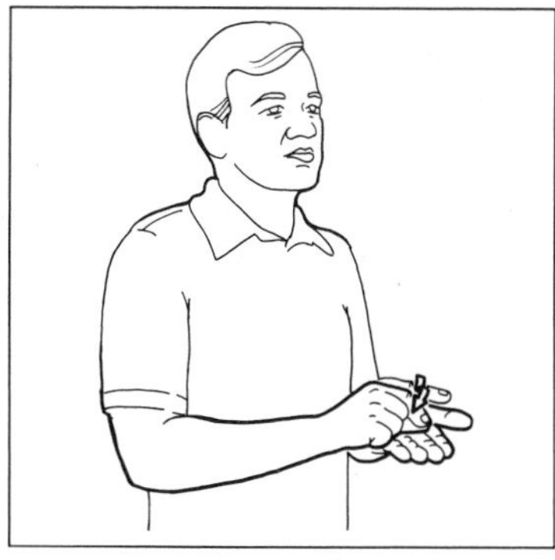

## PRINT, PRINTER*
(dm)

**Usage:** the print control character; to print each record; high-speed printer; a page printer.
**Note:** Index finger of G-hand closes on thumb two or three times.

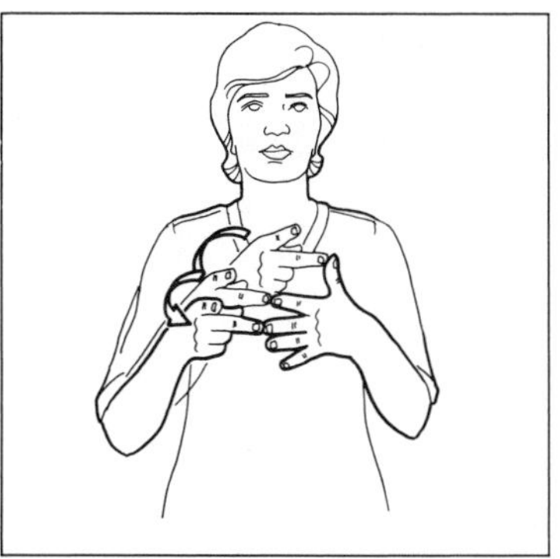

## PRIORITY
(sm)

**Usage:** priority processing; the job's priority; a priority interrupt.

## PRIVACY, PRIVATE
(dm)

**Same sign for:** secret.
**Usage:** data privacy; privacy protection; each user's private library.

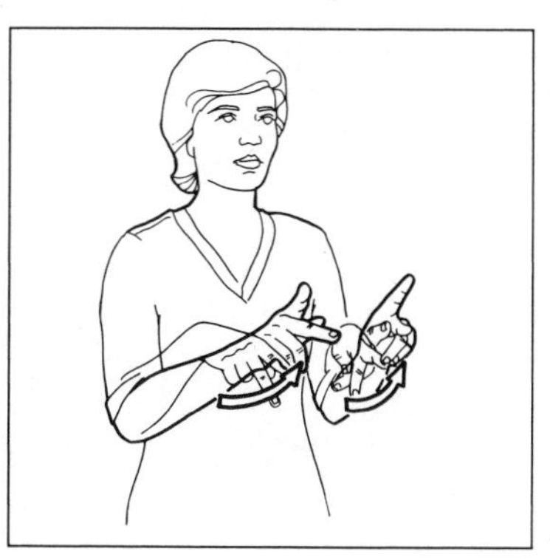

## PRIVILEGED
(sm)

**Initialized form of:** allow, permit (P).
**Usage:** a privileged instruction used only by the supervisory program; privileged users.

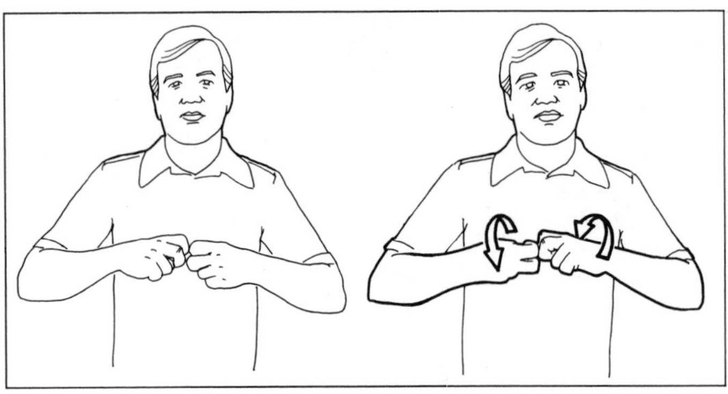

## PROBLEM

**Usage:** problem definition; problem solution; a problem-oriented language.

## PROCEDURAL, PROCEDURE

(cf. PROCESS) (sm)

**Same sign for:** progress.
**Usage:** the procedure division of COBOL; the procedure library; a procedure manual; a procedural language; a procedural abstraction.
**Note:** Bent flat hands move out from body in leapfrogging fashion (right over left, left over right, etc.).

## PROCESS, PROCESSING, PROCESSOR*

(cf. PROCEDURE) (sm)

**Same sign for:** progress.
**Usage:** process control; the development process; batch processing; realtime processing; the host processor.
**Note:** Bent flat hands move out from body in leapfrogging fashion (right over left, left over right, etc.).

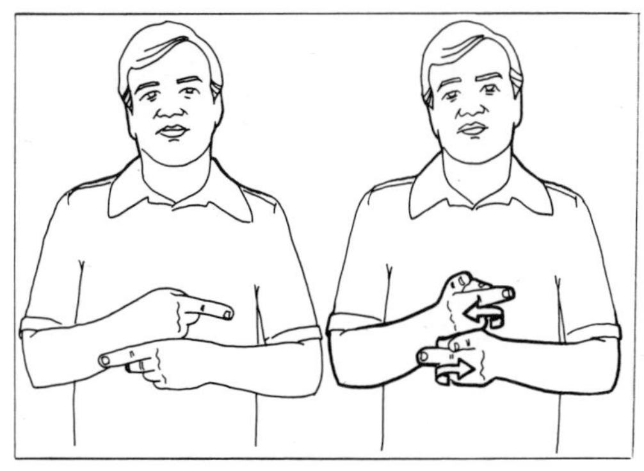

## PRODUCE, PRODUCT

**Initialized form of:** make (P).
**Usage:** to produce high quality code; the end-product; both hardware and software products.

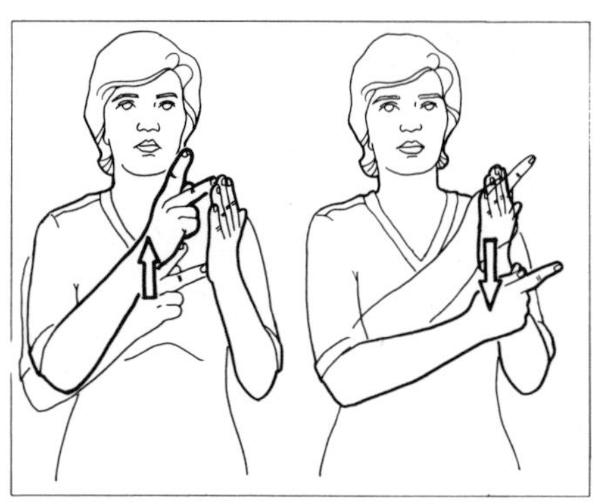

## PROGRAM, PROGRAMMER*, PROGRAMMING

(sm)

**Usage:** a utility program; control program; library program; an APL programmer; programming language; programming standards.
**Note:** Tip of P-hand strokes up the left palm and down the back of it.

**P-R-O-M**

## PROGRAMMABLE READ-ONLY MEMORY, PROM

(acronym)

**Usage:** a routine stored in programmable read-only memory; 8K of PROM.
**Note:** The term PROM is pronounced "prom."

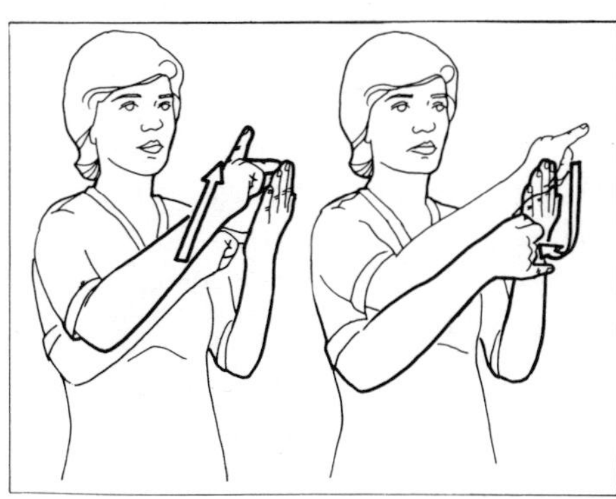

## PROJECT

(sm)

**Usage:** a programming project; project control; the project manager.
**Note:** Tip of P-hand strokes up the left palm, changes to a little finger making a J on the back of the left hand.

## PROM

(see PROGRAMMABLE READ-ONLY MEMORY)

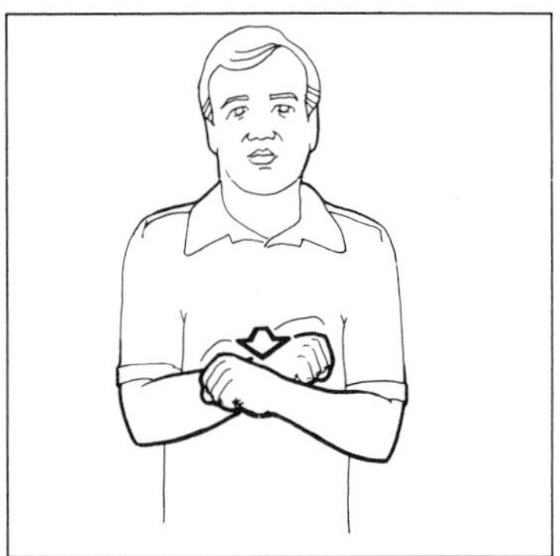

## PROTECT, PROTECTION

(cf. SECURITY)

**Same sign for:** defend.
**Usage:** a protected field; storage protection; file protection.
**Note:** S-hands, crossed at wrists, move forward together.

## PSEUDO-

(cf. ARTIFICIAL, DUMMY) (sm)

**Usage:** pseudo code; a pseudo instruction; a pseudo-random number sequence.
**Note:** Index finger passes in front of lips (perpendicular to direction used in signing REAL).

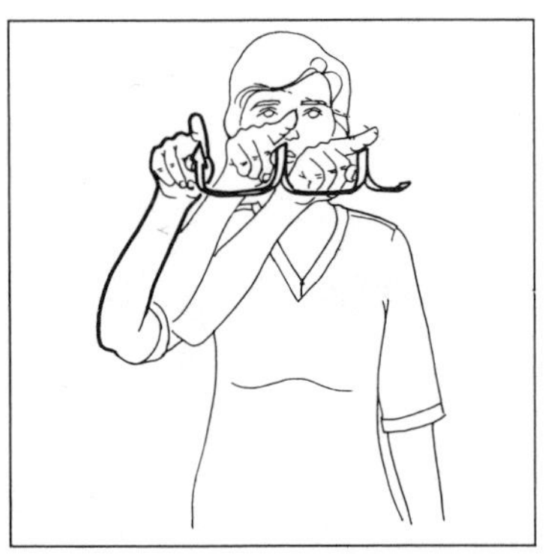

## PULSE

(sm)

**Usage:** a clock pulse; synchronization pulse; pulse width; pulse repetition rate; a pulse train.
**Note:** Index finger indicates a series of pulse spikes.

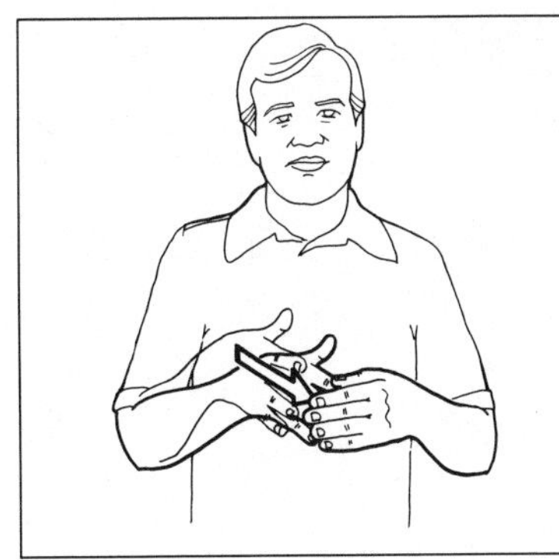

## PUNCH, PUNCHED

**Usage:** a punched card; punched tape; the card punch; in which punch position.
**Note:** Fingertips of right 5-hand punch against left palm.

## PUSHDOWN
(sm)

**Usage:** a pushdown list; pushdown storage; pushdown stack.

# Q

## QUERY
(cf. INQUIRY) (sm)

**Same sign for:** question.
**Usage:** to query a terminal; a query system; a query language.

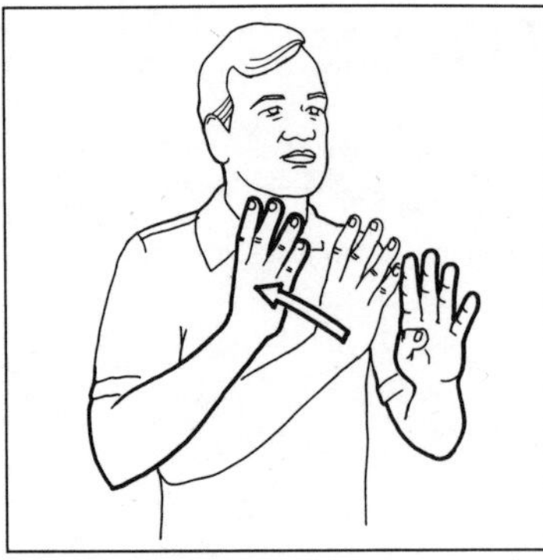

## QUEUE, QUEUING
(sm)

**Same sign for:** line up.
**Usage:** the active page queue; queue management; queuing theory; the average queue length.

R

## RAM
(see RANDOM ACCESS MEMORY)

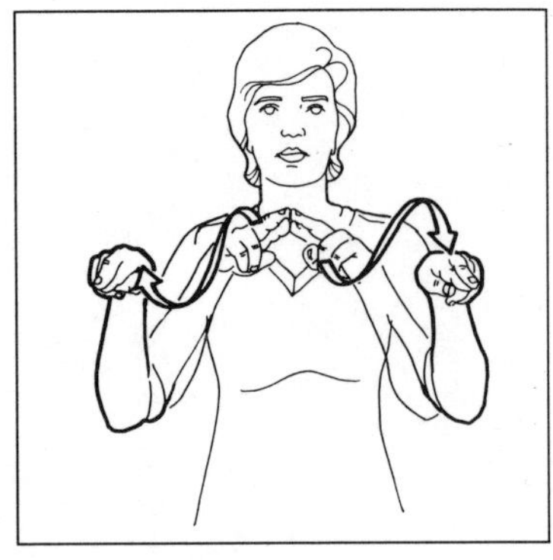

## RANDOM
(sm)

**Usage:** random access storage; random processing; random number generator.
**Note:** Palm-down R-hands separate, moving up and down in random fashion.

R-A-M

## RANDOM ACCESS MEMORY, RAM

(acronym)

**Usage:** a random access memory unit; a large capacity RAM.
**Note:** The term RAM is pronounced "ram."

## RAS

(see RELIABILITY-AVAILABILITY-SERVICEABILITY)

R-A-S-T-E-R

## RASTER

(fs)

**Usage:** at each point of the raster grid; the density of raster lines; a raster scan.

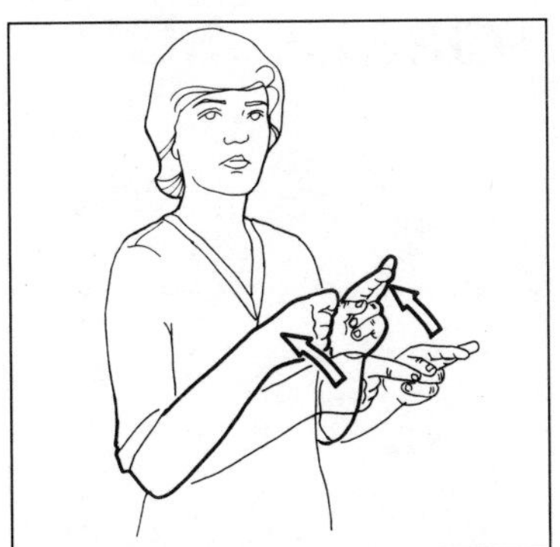

## RATE

**Initialized form of:** fast (R).
**Usage:** the data transfer rate; pulse repetition rate.
**Note:** Left hand R; right hand changes from 1 to X.

# R

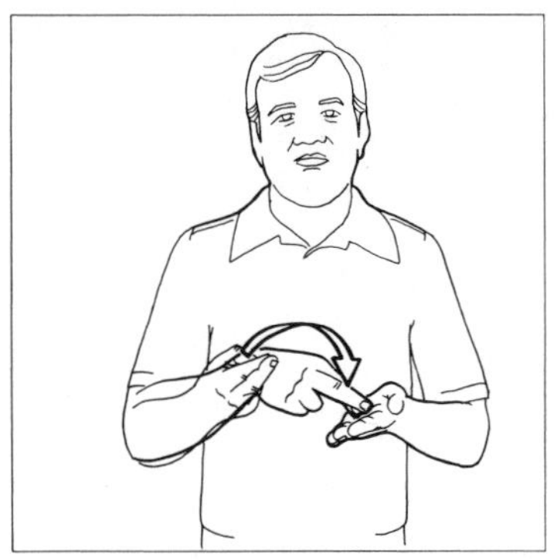

## RE-

(sm)

**Initialized form of:** again (R).
**Usage:** reallocate; restart; reread; reassign; reinitialize.

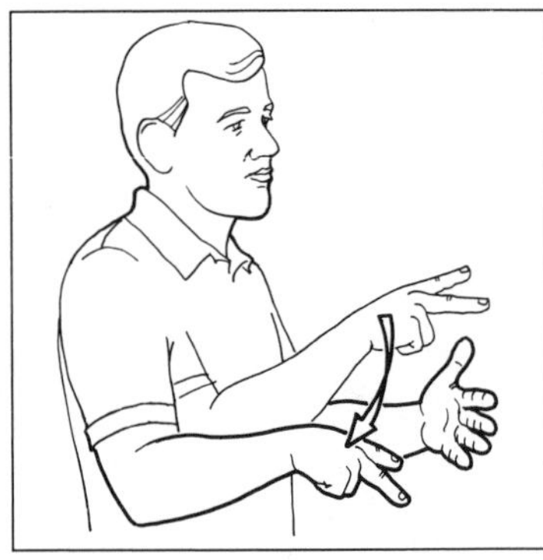

## READ, READER*

**Usage:** to read a record; a read/write head; the card reader.

R-O-M

## READ-ONLY MEMORY, ROM

(acronym)

**Usage:** the computer's read-only memory; how many K of ROM.
**Note:** The term ROM rhymes with "prom."

R-O-S

## READ-ONLY STORAGE, ROS

(acronym)

**Usage:** to modify the read-only storage; protected in ROS.
**Note:** The term ROS rhymes with "boss."

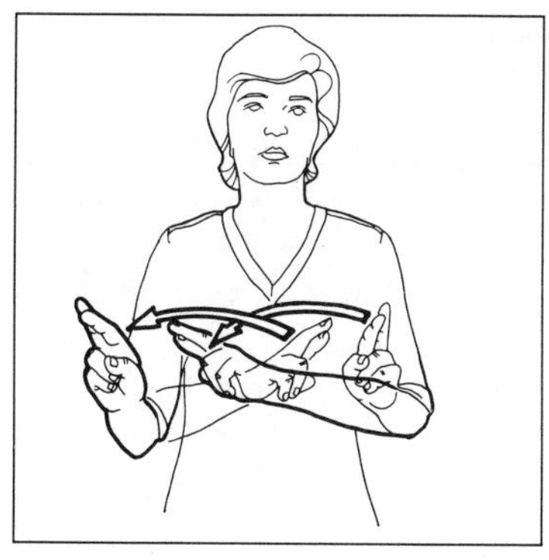

## READY

(sm)

**Usage:** in ready state; the ready queue; ready for execution.

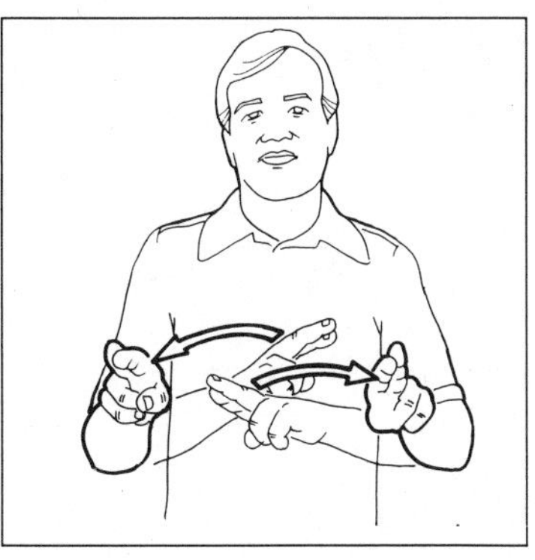

## READY

(sm)

**Usage:** in ready state; the ready queue; ready for execution.

## REAL

(cf. ACTUAL) (sm)

**Same sign for:** really, sure, true.
**Usage:** a real I/O device; the amount of real storage in the virtual system; in realtime simulation.

## RECOGNITION

(sm)

**Initialized form of:** note, notice (R).
**Usage:** pattern recognition; character recognition.
**Note:** Right R-hand from under right eye into left palm.

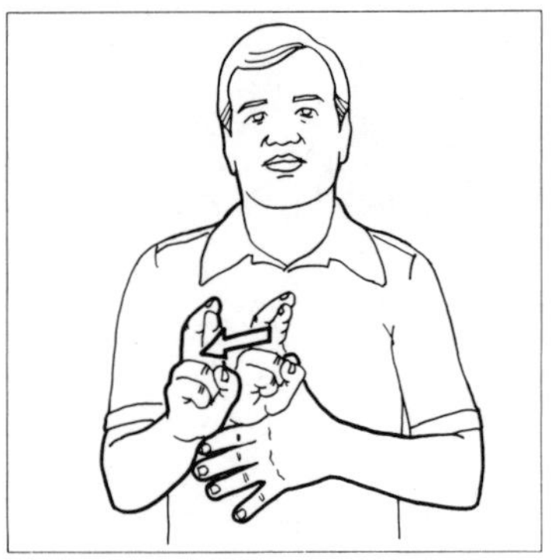

## RECORD (noun)

**Usage:** a logical record; variable-length records; an inventory record; the fields of a record; the record layout.

**Note:** R-hand moves along full length of left index once.

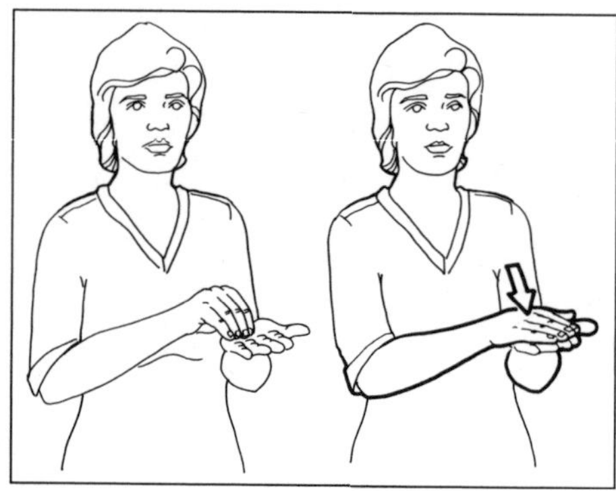

## RECORD (verb), RECORDING

(cf. DOCUMENT) (sm)

**Usage:** to record data on tape; magnetic recording; the recording density.
**Note:** Right thumb and fingertips in left palm; then fingers abruptly open as right hand flattens on left palm.

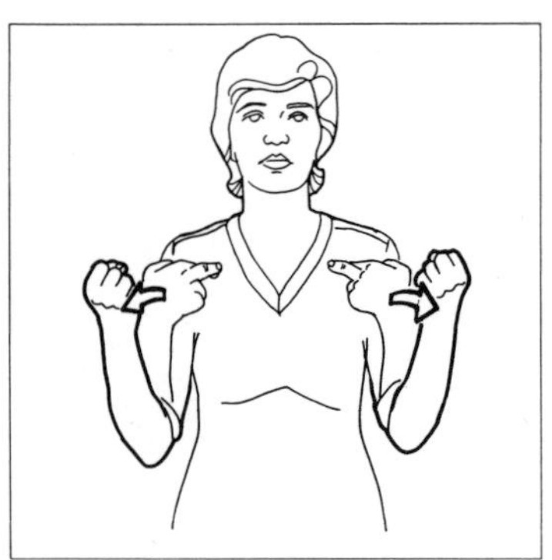

## RECOVER, RECOVERY

(sm)

**Initialized form of:** healthy (R).
**Usage:** to recover from a system malfunction; a recovery routine; the backup and recovery procedure.

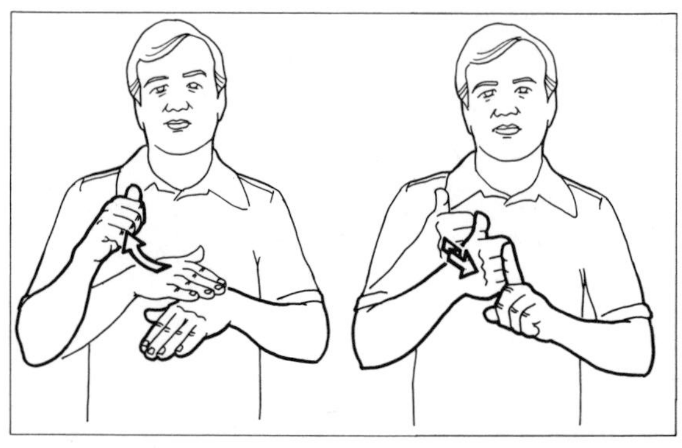

## RECURSIVE, RECURSIVELY

(sm)

**Usage:** a recursive subroutine; a recursively defined sequence.
**Note:** CALL + "itself."

## REEL

**Usage:** a reel of tape; mount the reel on the tape drive.

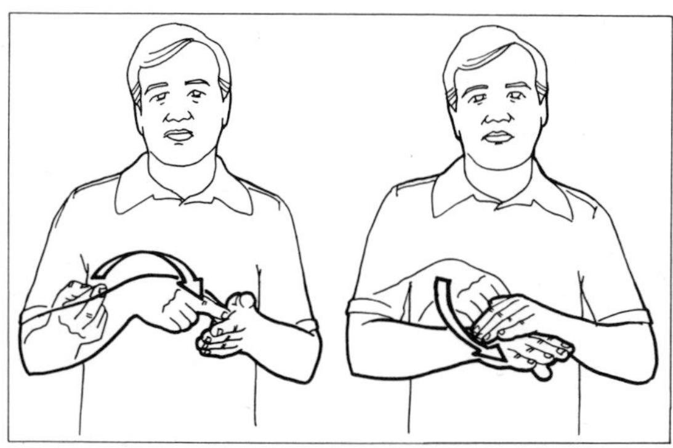

## REENTRANT, REENTRY

(sm)

**Usage:** a reentrant subroutine; the reentry point.
**Note:** RE- + ENTER.

## REGION

(sm)

**Initialized form of:** place (R).
**Usage:** main storage region; an overlay region; a virtual region.
**Note:** R-hands touch, circle back, and touch again.

## REGISTER (noun)

(sm)

**Usage:** the address register; the base register; an index register; the shift register.
**Note:** Right R-hand slides along left palm.

## RELATIONAL

**Usage:** a relational expression; a relational data base; relational operators.
**Note:** F-hands, with interlocked fingers, move out and back.

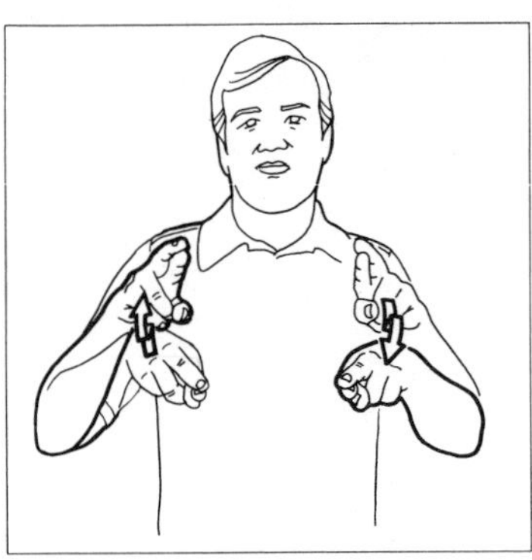

## RELATIVE

**Usage:** relative addressing; relative error; relative vector.

## RELEASE
(sm)

**Usage:** to release the channel; to release pages of storage.

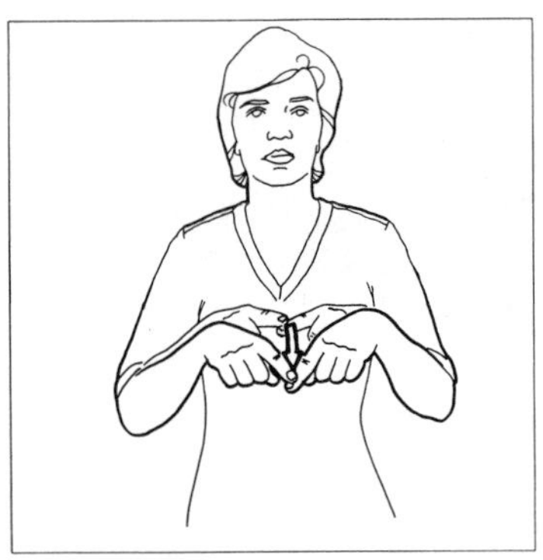

## RELIABILITY*, RELIABLE*, RELY
(cf. DEPEND)

**Usage:** system reliability; an important reliability factor; a reliable unit; to rely on the results.

R-A-S

## RELIABILITY-AVAILABILITY-SERVICEABILITY, RAS
(acronym)

**Usage:** exceeds user expectations for reliability-availability-serviceability; a high priority RAS factor.
**Note:** The term RAS rhymes with "gas."

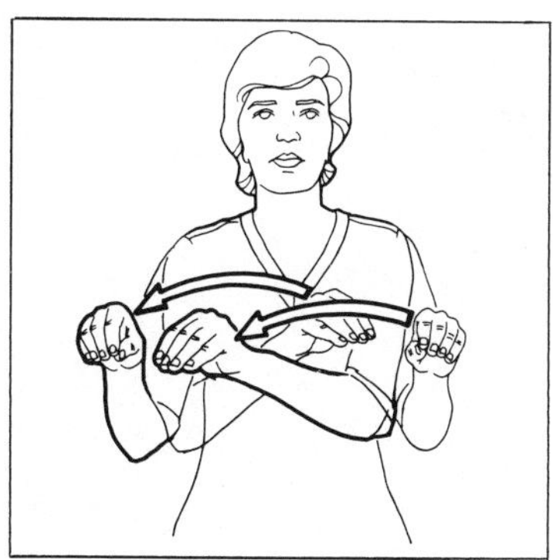

## RELOCATABLE*, RELOCATE, RELOCATION
(sm)

**Same sign for:** move.
**Usage:** relocatable subroutines; to relocate the program; dynamic relocation; relocation factor.

## REMOTE
(sm)

**Same sign for:** distant, far.
**Usage:** remote access to the system; a remote terminal.

R-J-E

## REMOTE JOB ENTRY, RJE
(abbr)

**Usage:** an installation that supports remote job entry; access to the computer via RJE; an RJE terminal.

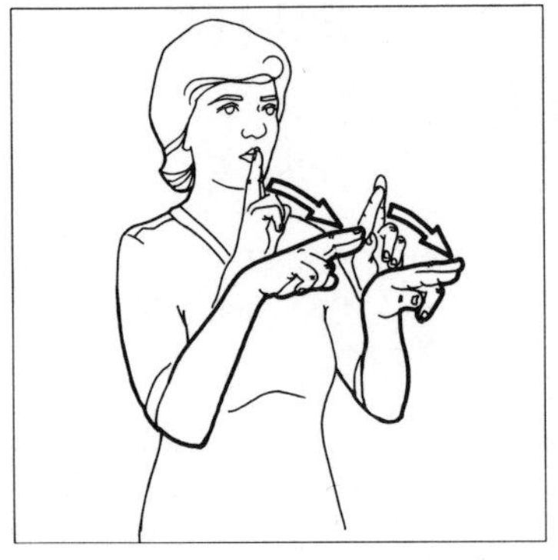

## REPORT

(cf. RESPONSE) (sm)

**Usage:** report generation; the format of the report; the down-time report.

R-P-G

## REPORT PROGRAM GENERATOR, RPG

(abbr)

**Usage:** using the Report Program Generator to create the document; whether to use RPG or COBOL.

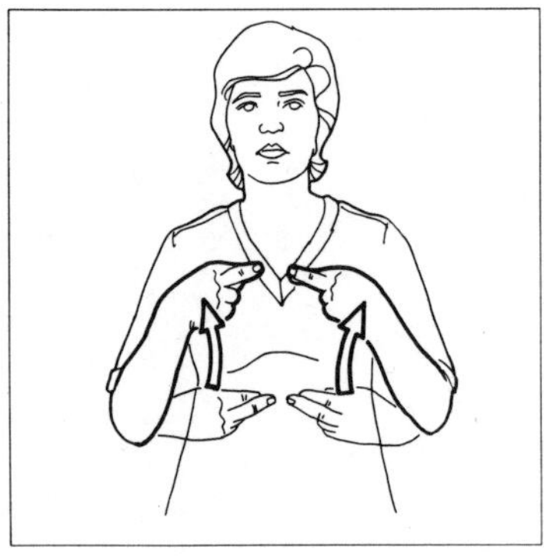

## RESIDENT

(sm)

**Initialized form of:** live (R).
**Usage:** the resident control program; a table of resident segments.
**Note:** R-hands slide up chest.

## RESOURCE

(sm)

**Initialized form of:** thing (R).
**Usage:** resource allocation; resource management.

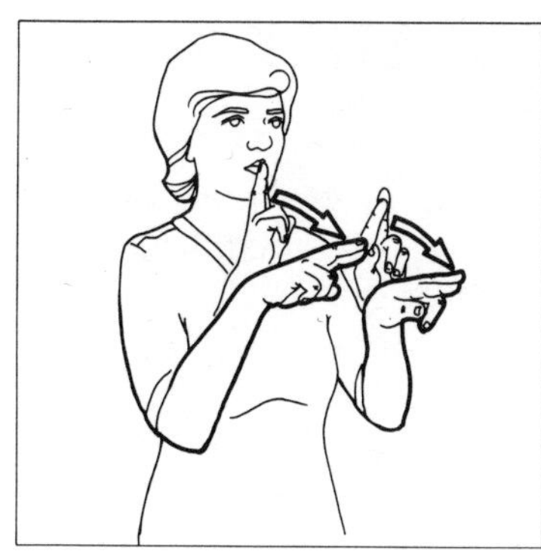

## RESPONSE
(cf. REPORT) (sm)

**Usage:** an inquiry-response system; the average response time; delayed response mode.

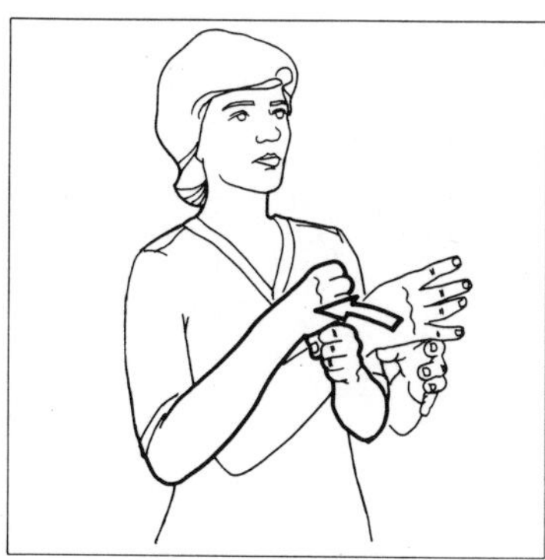

## RETRIEVE, RETRIEVAL
(sm)

**Same sign for:** get, obtain, receive.
**Usage:** to retrieve a record; an information retrieval system.

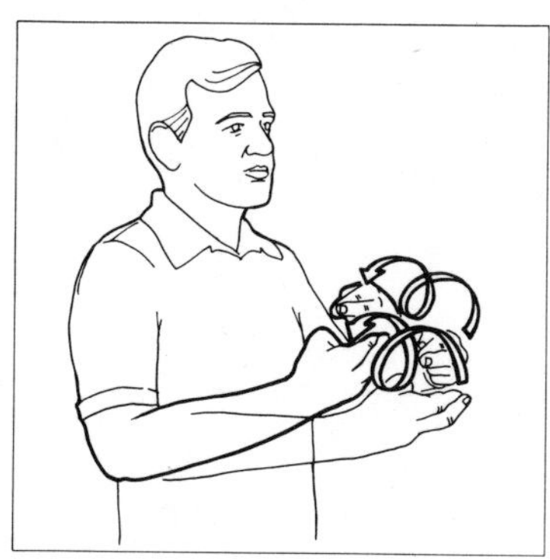

## RETURN
(sm)

**Initialized form of:** come (R).
**Usage:** to establish a return code in the subroutine; to branch and return; a carriage return.
**Note:** R-hands circle each other as they move inward toward body.

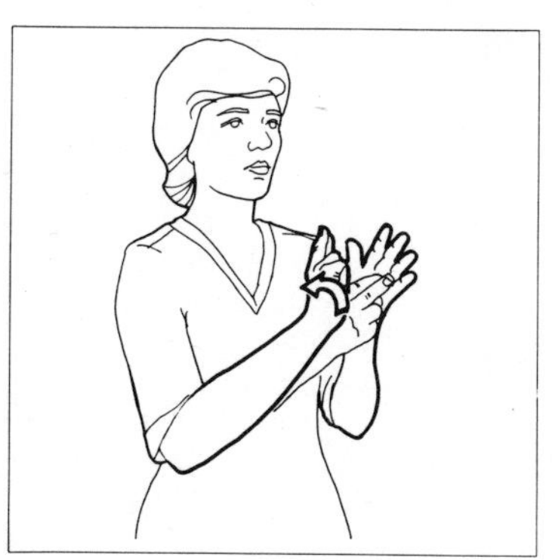

## REVIEW
(sm)

**Usage:** a formal design review; a project review; to review the system specifications.
**Note:** Right R-hand rotates counter-clockwise on left palm (going back over the points).

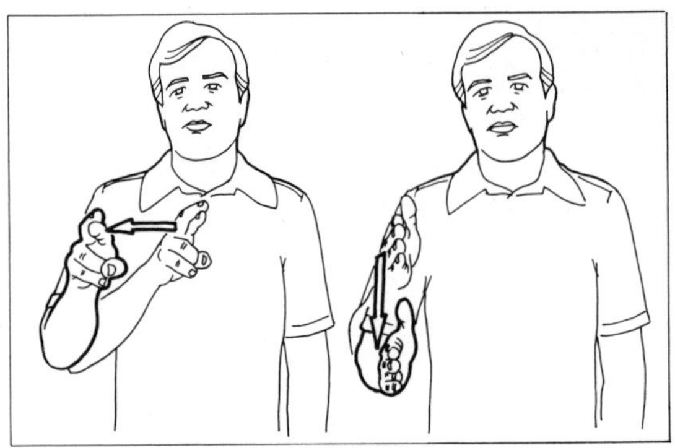

## RIGHT-JUSTIFY
(sm)

**Usage:** right-justify the amount field; to right-justify textual information.
**Note:** Should be done with the right hand, even by left-handed persons.

## RJE
(see REMOTE JOB ENTRY)

## ROM
(see READ-ONLY MEMORY)

## ROS
(see READ-ONLY STORAGE)

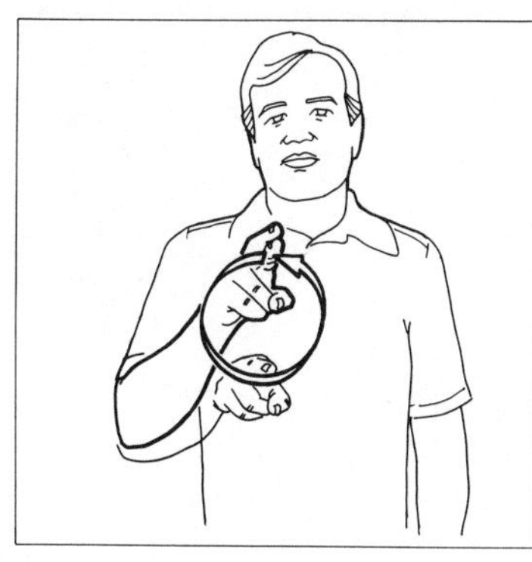

## ROUND
(sm)

**Usage:** to round up; to round down; to round off; a roundoff error.

## ROUTINE
(sm)

**Usage:** a library routine; an output routine; a sort routine.
**Note:** Right R-hand strokes up the left palm and down its back.

## RPG
(see REPORT PROGRAM GENERATOR)

## RUN, RUNNING
(cf. EXECUTE) (dm)

**Usage:** to run a program; a run time of two minutes; ran to completion on the first try; running a job on second shift.

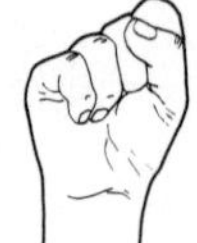

## SATELLITE

(sm)

**Usage:** a satellite computer; three satellite processors connected to the host.
**Note:** Palm-down bent-5 hand to the left, front and right of left index finger.

## SAVE

(cf. STORAGE) (sm)

**Same sign for:** reserve.
**Usage:** to save the contents of the registers; to save a copy for backup; the save area.

## SCAN, SCANNER*, SCANNING

(sm)

**Usage:** to scan the input queue;
a character-by-character scan; an optical scanner;
with a scanning rate of.
**Note:** Instead of a vertical "scan," the sign can be made horizontally along the left palm. The signer's eyes should usually follow the slowly moving hand.

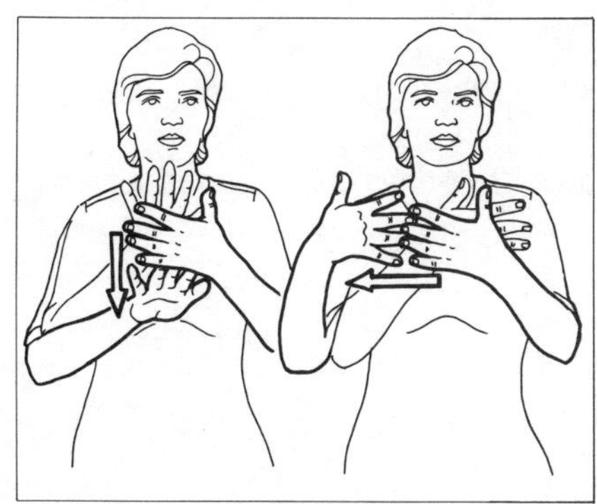

## SCHEDULE, SCHEDULER*

(cf. GRAPH) (sm)

**Usage:** check the schedule; the job scheduler; scheduled maintenance.

## SCIENCE, SCIENTIFIC

**Usage:** a computer science major; scientific application programming.
**Note:** Thumb-down A-hands circle alternately in front of chest.

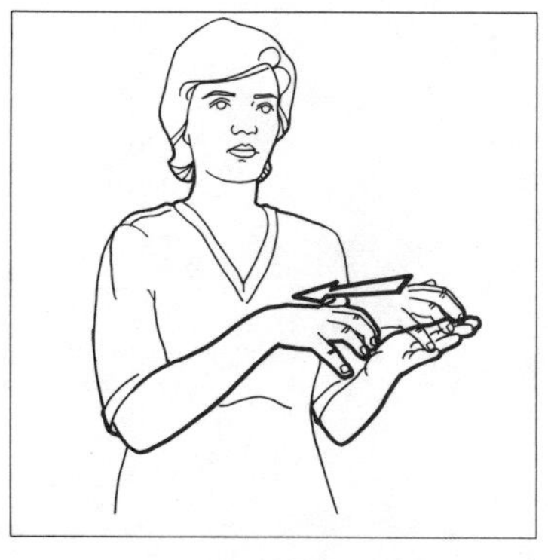

## SCRATCH

(sm)

**Usage:** to scratch a data set; a scratch tape; a scratch pad.

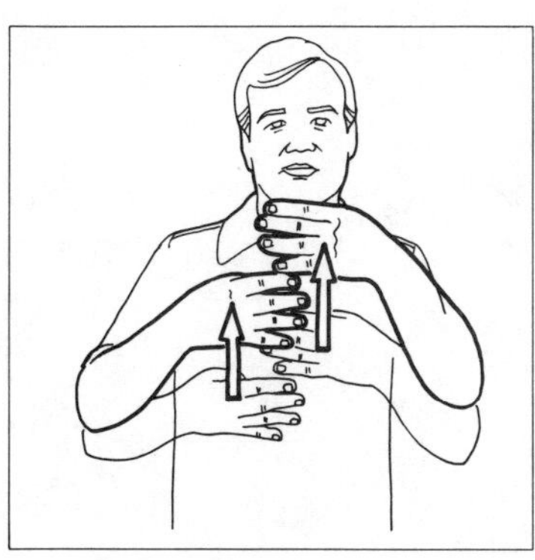

## SCROLL, SCROLLING

**Usage:** the ability to scroll up and down; the scrolling feature.
**Note:** Hands move up together (fingers represent lines of text).

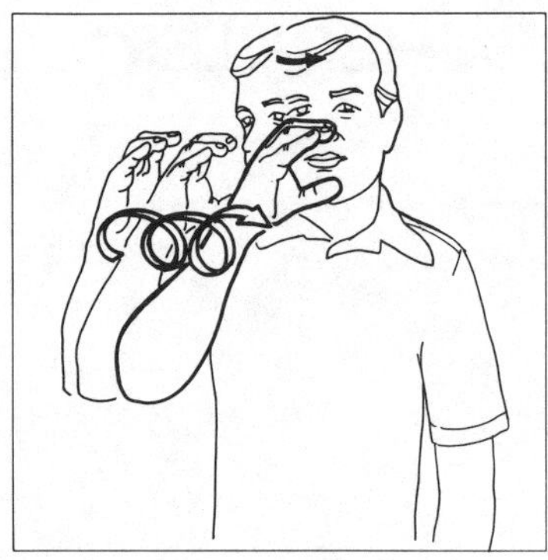

## SEARCH
(cf. LOOKUP, SEEK)

**Usage:** a binary search; the search key; various searching techniques.

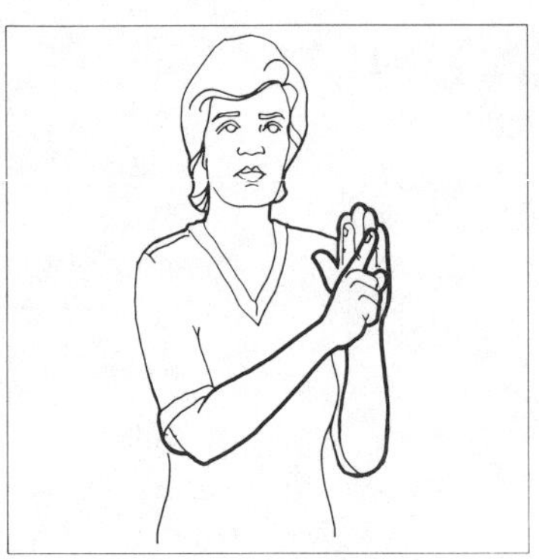

## SECOND (time)
(sm)

**Usage:** a run time of 17 seconds; milliseconds; microseconds; nanoseconds; picoseconds.
**Note:** Right index pivots forward on left palm in quick movement, like ticking of a second hand.

## SECONDARY
(sm)

**Usage:** a secondary file; a secondary key; secondary storage.

## SECTION
(cf. PARTITION, SEGMENT) (sm)

**Same sign for:** part, some.
**Usage:** the control section of the program; the section header; section name.

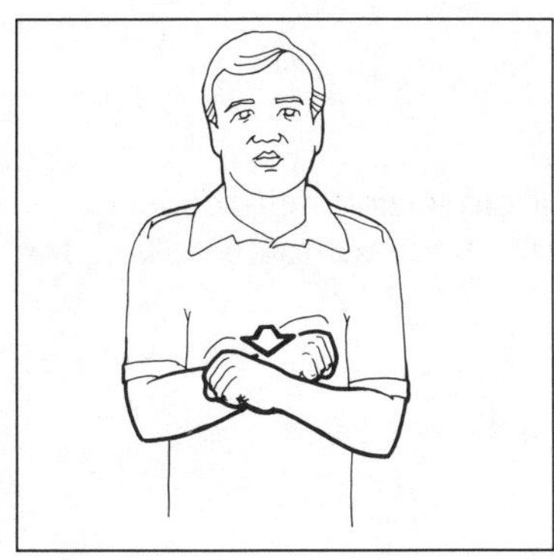

## SECURITY
(cf. PROTECT) (dm)

**Same sign for:** defend.
**Usage:** data security; appropriate security provisions; resource access security.

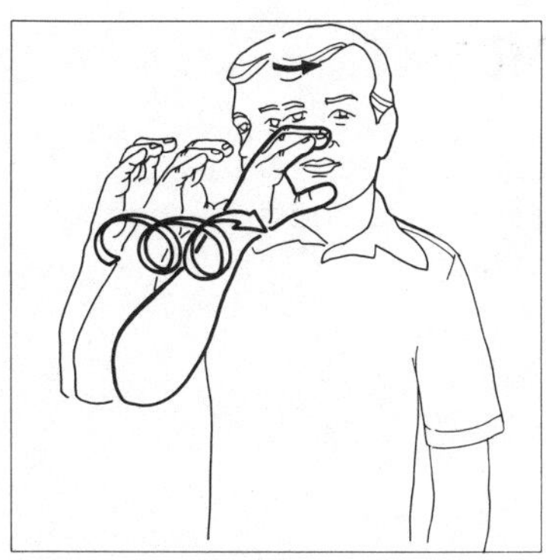

## SEEK
(cf. LOOKUP, SEARCH)

**Usage:** average seek time; to seek a record.

## SEGMENT, SEGMENTED
(cf. PARTITION, SECTION) (sm)

**Same sign for:** part, some.
**Usage:** the segment type; segment number; to divide a program into segments; data segments; a segmented record.

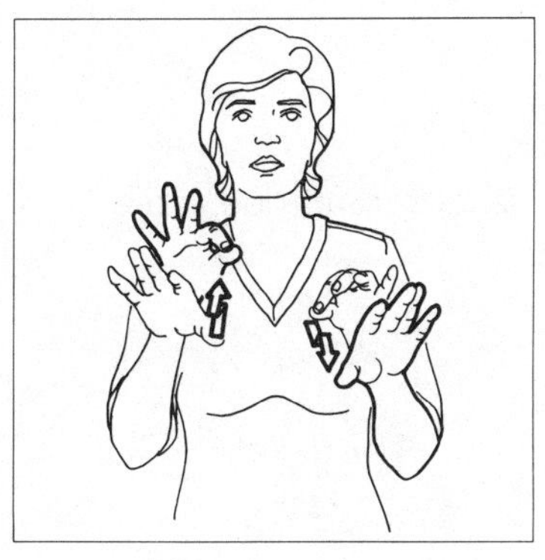

## SELECT, SELECTION, SELECTIVE

**Usage:** to select an algorithm; selection of the polling sequence; a selective dump.

## SELF-
(sm)

**Usage:** self-checking; self-organizing; self-adapting.
**Note:** This sign can also be made without involving the left hand.

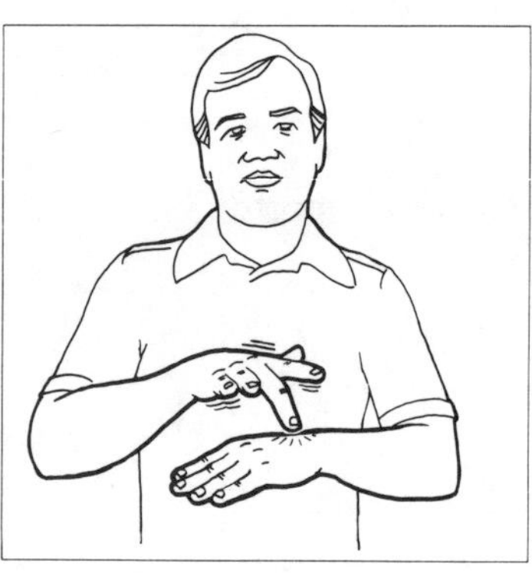

## SENSE, SENSOR*

**Usage:** to sense the holes in the card; sensors to monitor physical processes; a sensor-based system.
**Note:** Contact is light and brief.

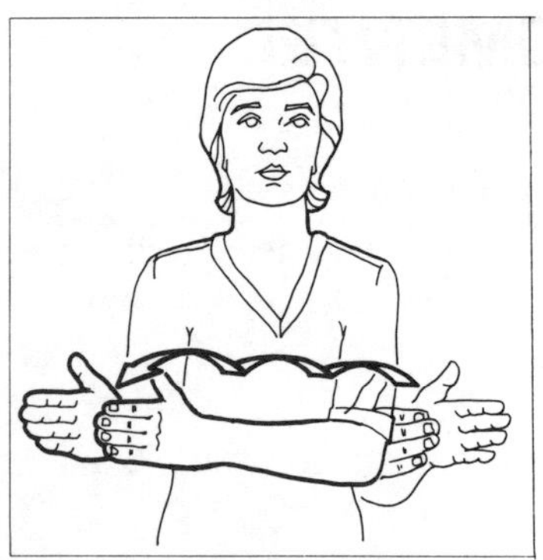

## SEQUENCE, SEQUENTIAL
(cf. SERIAL, SORT) (sm)

**Usage:** the calling sequence; collating sequence; sequential processing; sequential access method.

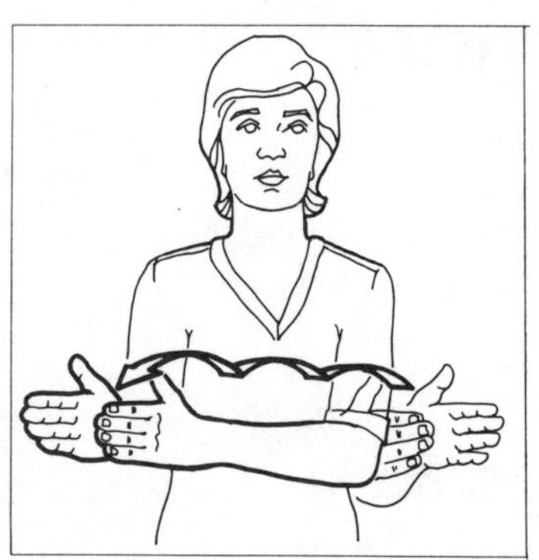

## SERIAL
(cf. SEQUENCE, SORT) (sm)

**Usage:** serial processing; serial transmission; a serial adder.

## SERVICE
(cf. UTILITY)

**Usage:** quick turnaround service; telephone service; a service routine.

## SET
(sm)

**Initialized form of:** class (S).
**Usage:** the instruction set; a data set; an alphanumeric character set; a set of values.

## SETUP
(cf. INITIALIZE, INSTALL) (sm)

**Same sign for:** establish.
**Usage:** setup time; any tapes required for the setup.

## SHARE, SHARED, SHARING
(cf. COMMON)

**Usage:** to share a channel; a shared resource; a shared file; a time sharing system.
**Note:** Lower edge of right hand sweeps back and forth in angle formed by left thumb and fingers.

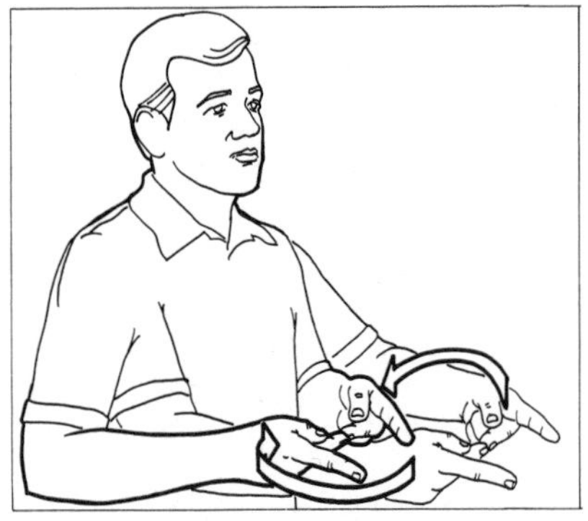

## SHOP
(cf. POSITION) (sm)

**Same sign for:** place.
**Usage:** to operate a closed shop; a completely open shop.

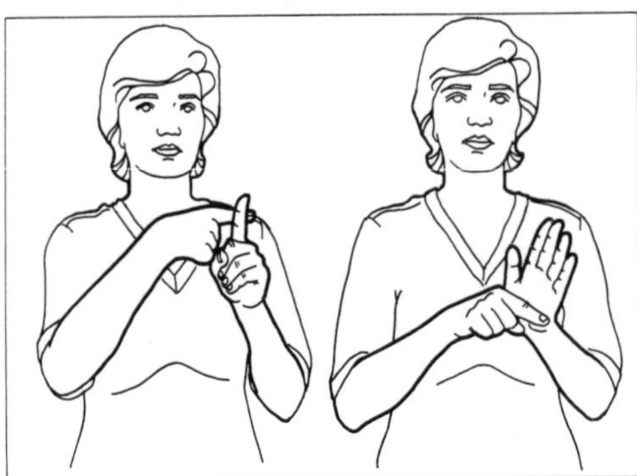

## SIGN, SIGNED
(sm)

**Usage:** a sign bit; the sign position; a signed field.
**Note:** "plus" + "minus."

## SIGN OFF (verb), SIGN-OFF (adj.)
(cf. LOG OFF) (sm)

**Usage:** the proper sign-off procedure; to save the updated file before signing off.
**Note:** SIGN + DISCONNECT.

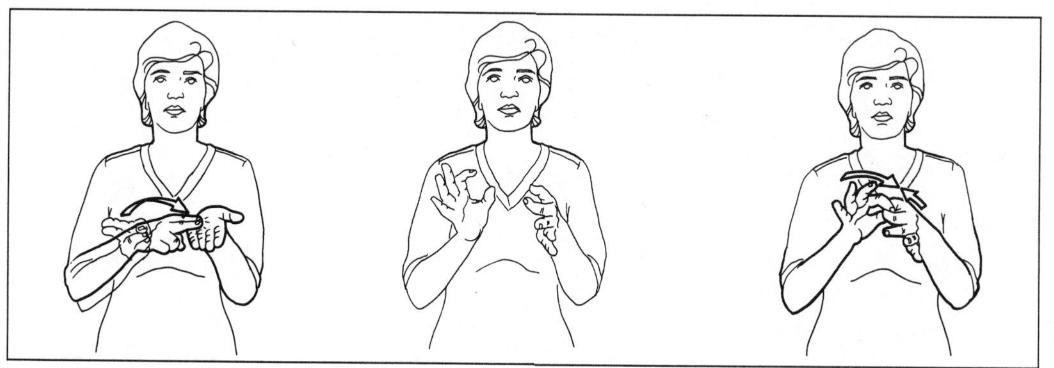

## SIGN ON (verb), SIGN-ON (adj.)

(cf. LOG ON) (sm)

**Usage:** your sign-on password; to sign on the system; the number of users that are signed on.
**Note:** SIGN + CONNECT.

S-I-G-N-A-L

## SIGNAL

(fs)

**Usage:** signal-to-noise ratio; the start signal; signal transformation.

## SIMULATE, SIMULATION, SIMULATOR*

**Usage:** to simulate the economy; realtime simulation; simulation techniques; a flight simulator.
**Note:** "do" + "same."

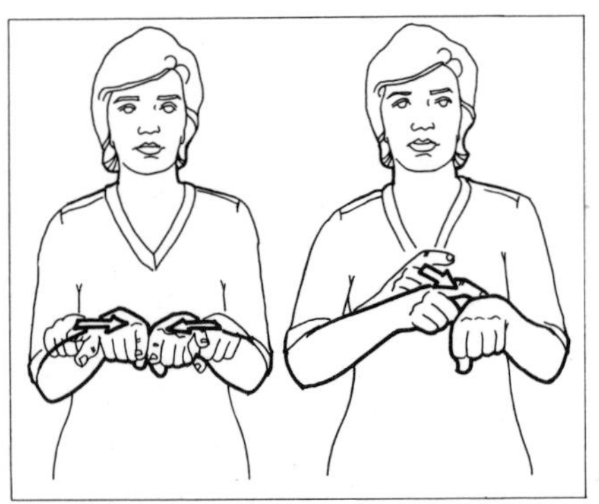

## SIMULTANEOUS

(cf. CONCURRENT) (sm)

**Usage:** simultaneous operation; simultaneous transmission.
**Note:** "same" + TIME.

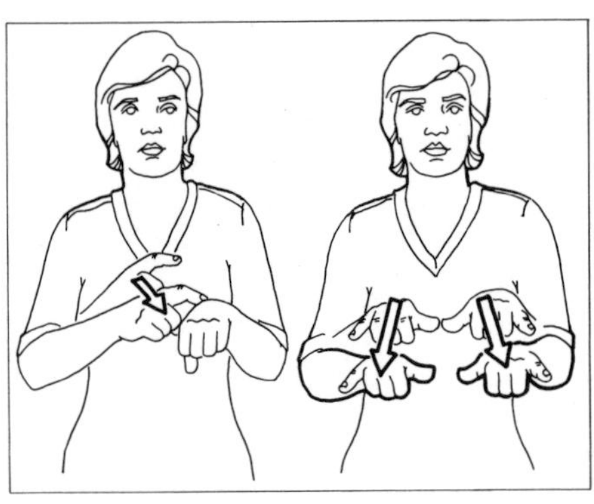

## SIMULTANEOUS

(cf. CONCURRENT) (sm)

**Usage:** simultaneous operation; simultaneous transmission.

## SINGLE-
(sm)

**Usage:** a single-address instruction; single-precision arithmetic; to single-step through a program.

## SKIP
(sm)

**Usage:** to skip the next instruction; skip three records.
**Note:** Bent-U from fingers to heel of left palm.

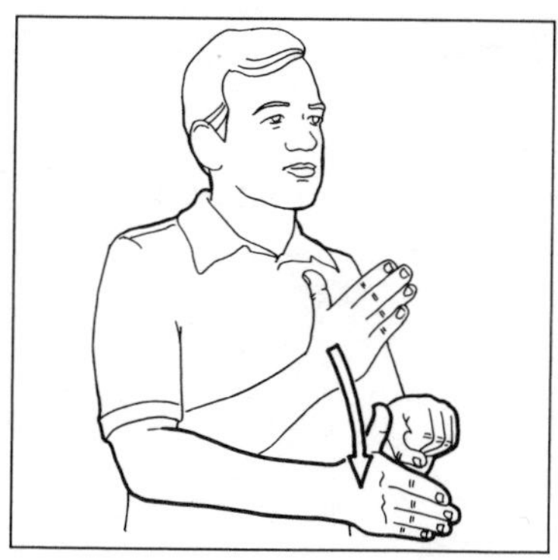

## SLICE
(sm)

**Usage:** in each time slice.
**Note:** Right hand brushes down past left fist.

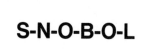

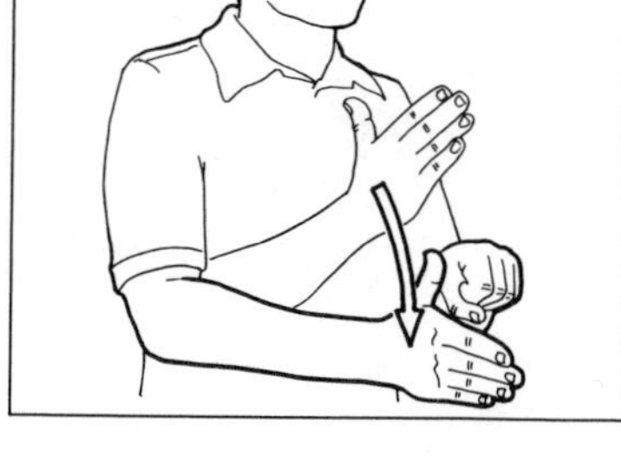


## SNOBOL
(fs)

**Usage:** the SNOBOL language; a SNOBOL program.
**Note:** The term SNOBOL is pronounced "snowball."

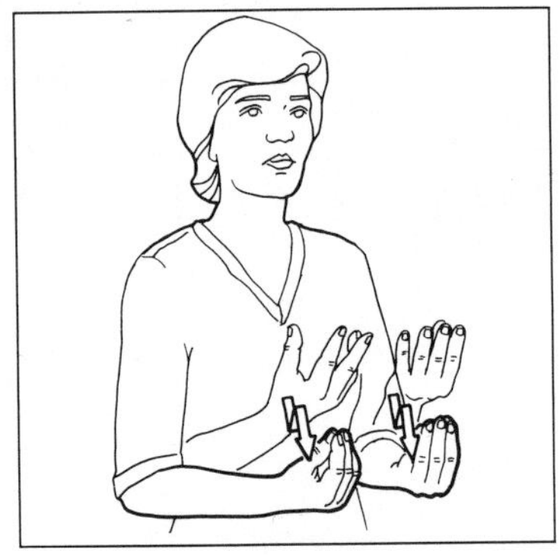

## SOFT

(dm)

**Usage:** a soft error; a soft-copy terminal.

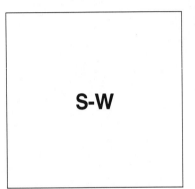

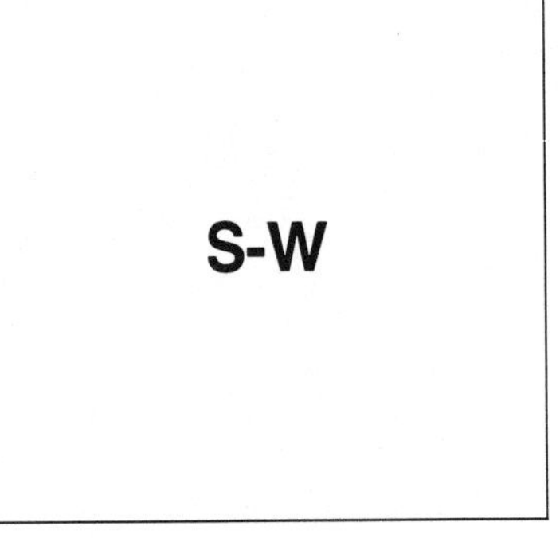


## SOFTWARE

(abbr)

**Usage:** software design; software engineering; software support.

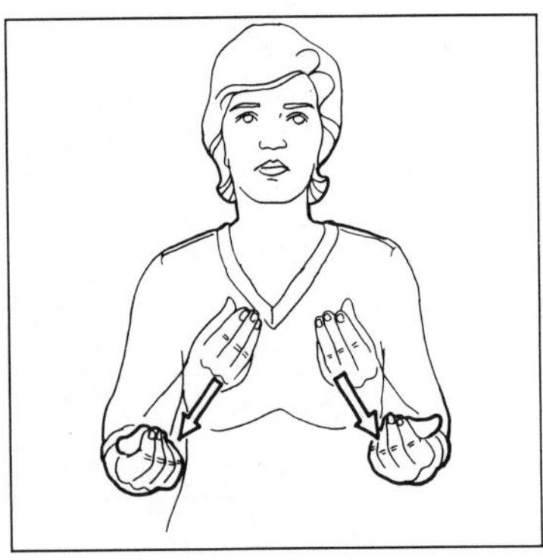

## SOLUTION, SOLVE

**Same sign for:** dissolve, melt.
**Usage:** the problem solution; heuristic solutions; to solve the equations.
**Note:** Thumbs slide out as fingers close.

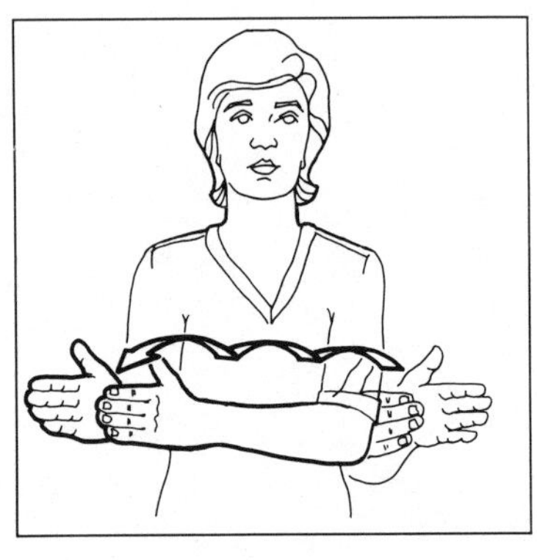

## SORT

(cf. SEQUENCE, SERIAL) (sm)

**Usage:** to sort the file by part number; the field used for the sort key; a bubble sort; a sort program.

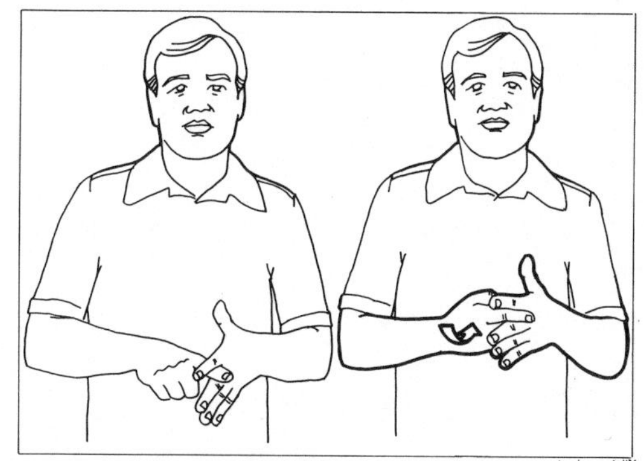

## SOURCE

(cf. INITIATE, START) (sm)

**Same sign for:** begin.
**Usage:** the source language; a source module; the source program.

## SPACE

(cf. BLANK, NULL) (sm)

**Same sign for:** bare, empty, vacant.
**Usage:** a space character; leave three spaces; the space bar.

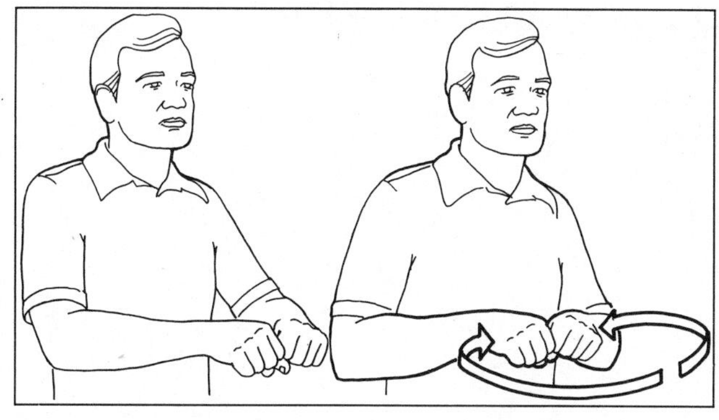

## SPACE

(sm)

**Initialized form of:** place (S).
**Usage:** working space in memory; the total space requirements.

## SPEC
(see SPECIFICATION)

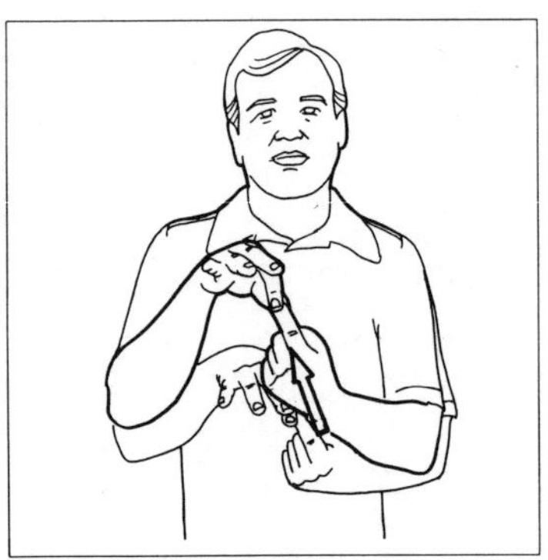

## SPECIAL
(cf: EXCEPT) (sm)

**Usage:** special characters; a special-purpose computer; a special-purpose language.

S-P-E-C

## SPECIFICATION, SPEC
(abbr)

**Usage:** a design specification; functional specifications; performance specs.
**Note:** The term SPEC is pronounced "speck."

## SPEECH

**Same sign for:** oral.
**Usage:** a speech synthesizer; a speech recognition system.
**Note:** Bent-V circles in front of mouth.

## SPOOL, SPOOLING

**Usage:** to spool the data; a spooling operation; virtual spooling devices.
**Note:** The term SPOOL is an acronym for Simultaneous Peripheral Operations On-Line.

## STAGE, STAGING

**Usage:** to stage the data; a staging device.

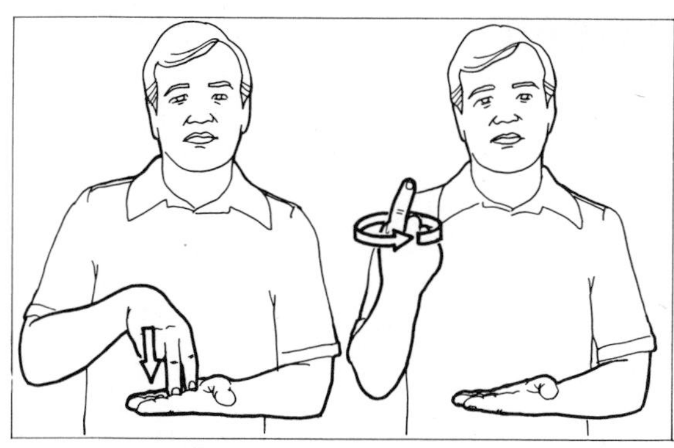

## STAND-ALONE

**Usage:** a stand-alone system; stand-alone word processing equipment.
**Note:** "stand" + "alone."

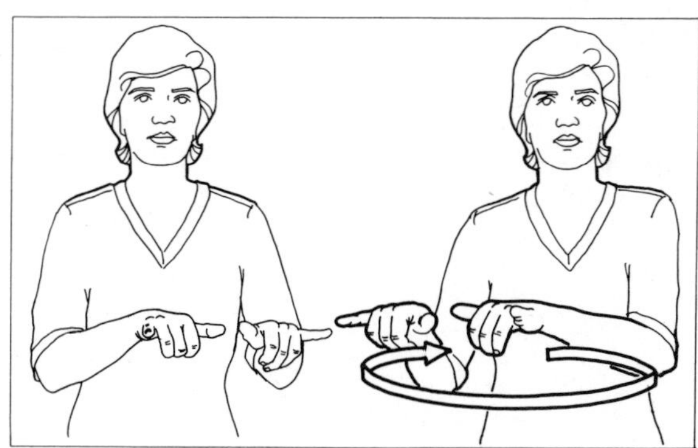

## STANDARD

**Usage:** a standard interface; standard procedure; documentation standards.
**Note:** Palm-down Y-hands circle together.

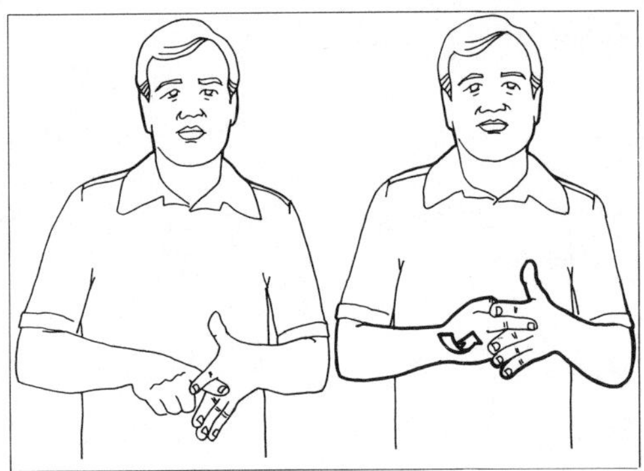

## START

(cf. INITIATE, SOURCE) (sm)

**Same sign for:** begin.
**Usage:** a start signal; the start key; start/stop operation; a cold start.

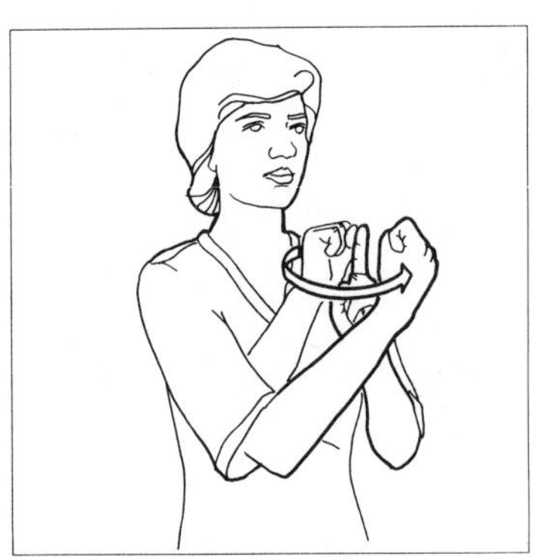

## STATE, STATUS

(sm)

**Same sign for:** situation.
**Usage:** in a wait state; a finite-state machine; system status; status code.

## STATEMENT

(sm)

**Same sign for:** sentence.
**Usage:** a source statement; control statement; the statement number; a conditional statement.

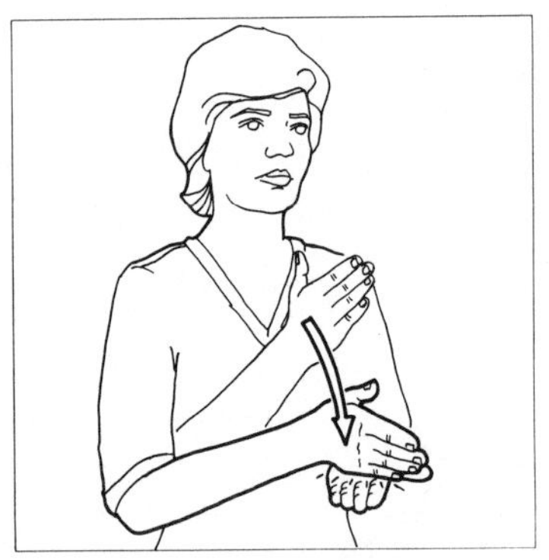

## STOP

(sm)

**Same sign for:** cease.
**Usage:** start/stop transmission; the stop code.

## STORAGE
(cf. SAVE)

**Same sign for:** reserve.
**Usage:** auxiliary storage; buffer storage; storage capacity.

## STORE, STORED
(cf. BANK)

**Usage:** store-and-forward mode; to store the personnel data; a stored program.

## STREAM
(dm)

**Usage:** the input job stream; parallel instruction streams.

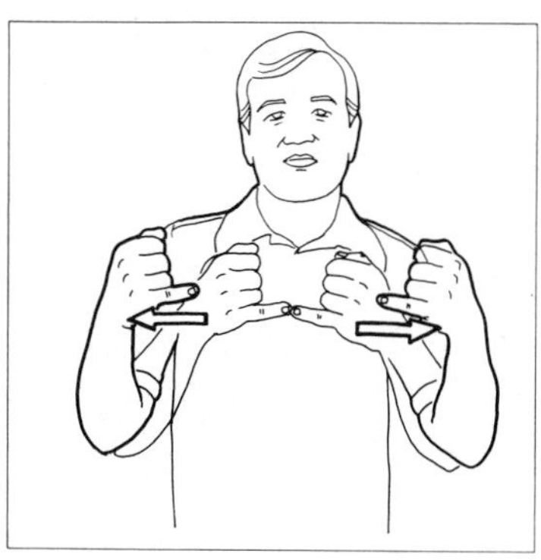

## STRING
(cf. LINE) (sm)

**Usage:** to scan a character string; a bit string.

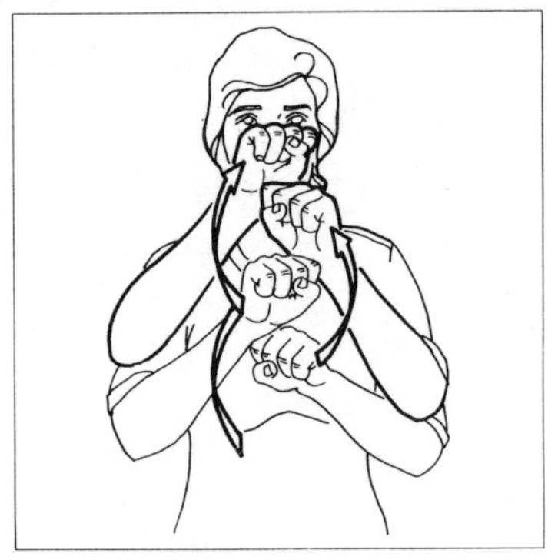

## STRUCTURE, STRUCTURED
(sm)

**Usage:** data structure; block structure; structured programming.
**Note:** Each S-hand is placed alternatively atop the other.

## SUB-

**Usage:** subsystem; subset; subchannel; subfield; subtask.

## SUBROUTINE
(sm)

**Usage:** a subroutine call; a recursive subroutine; each subroutine of the program.
**Note:** S-hand up the left palm and R-hand down its back.

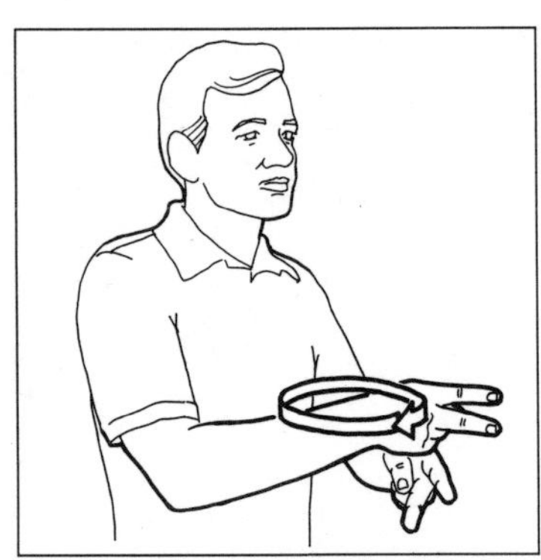

## SUPERVISOR*, SUPERVISORY

**Usage:** the system supervisor; the overlay supervisor; a supervisory program.

## SWAP
(sm)

**Same sign for:** exchange, substitute.
**Usage:** page swapping; at each swap-in and swap-out cycle.

## SWITCH, SWITCHABLE*, SWITCHED, SWITCHING
(cf. VARY) (sm)

**Usage:** a program switch; switchable channels; a switched network; a switching function.
**Note:** V-hands turn from palm down to palm up to palm down again.

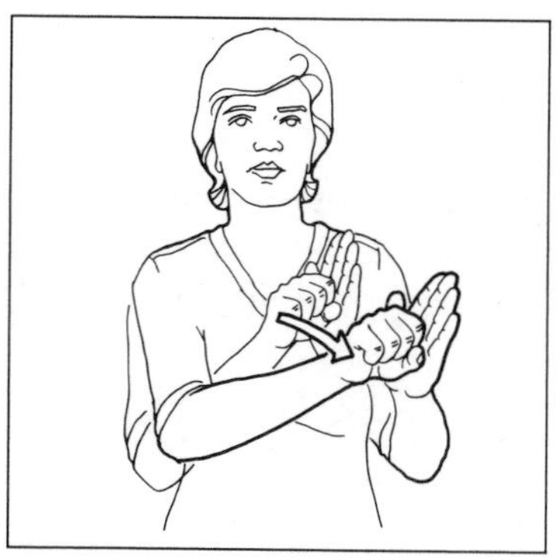

## SYMBOL, SYMBOLIC
(sm)

**Initialized form of:** show (S).
**Usage:** a flowchart symbol; symbol manipulation; symbolic addressing; symbolic language.

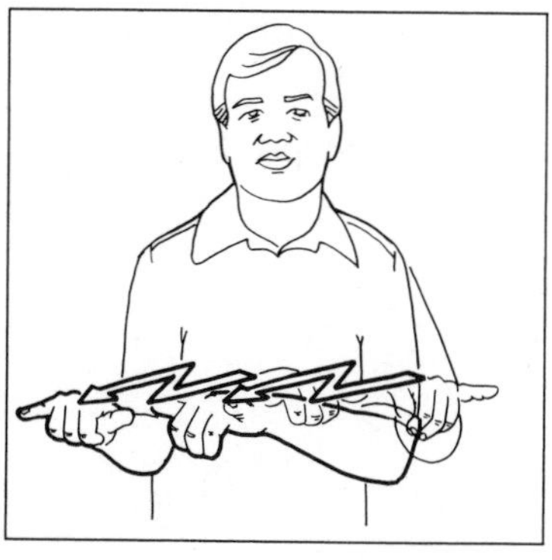

## SYNCHRONOUS
(sm)

**Usage:** synchronous operation; synchronous data transfer.
**Note:** Palm-down Y-hands move out and to the right in a Z pattern.

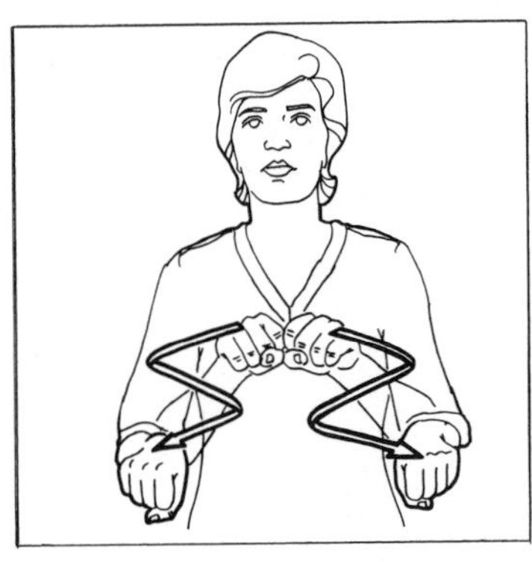

## SYSTEM
(sm)

**Usage:** a system analyst; a system programmer; system definition; an NC system.

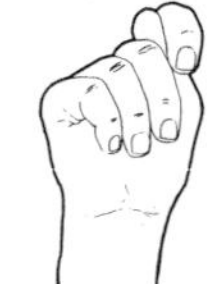

# T

## TABLE
(sm)

**Usage:** table lookup; truth table; decision tables; a table-driven procedure.

## TAPE

**Usage:** a tape drive; paper tape; the tape librarian.

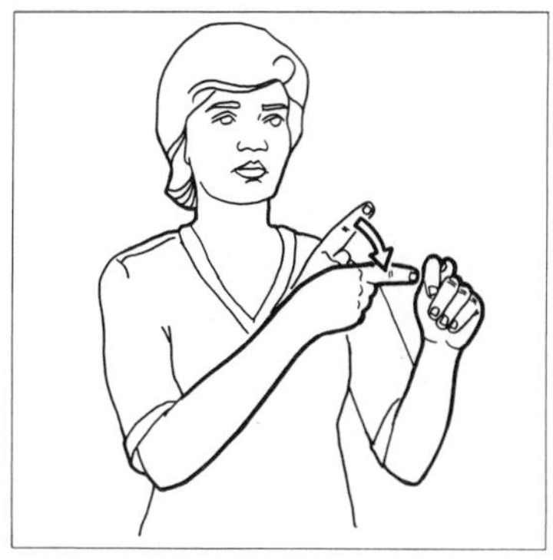

## TARGET
(sm)

**Usage:** converted to the target language; the target machine; target representation.
**Note:** Right index pivots down to point at left T-hand.

## TASK
(cf. WORK)

**Usage:** task management; the scheduling of task executions; a change in the task status.

## TECHNICAL
(dm)

**Usage:** the technical requirements; a technical writer; a good technical background.
**Note:** Bent right middle finger touches lower edge of left palm twice.

## TECHNIQUE
(sm)

**Initialized form of:** way (T).
**Usage:** good programming techniques; a technique for generating random numbers; a sorting technique.

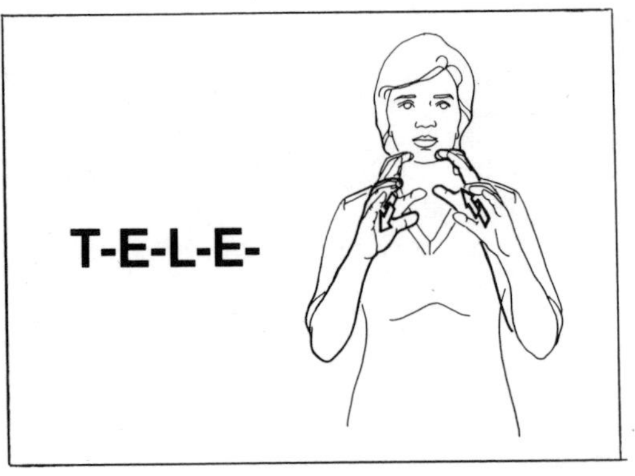


## TELECOMMUNICATION

(fs/dm)

**Usage:** a telecommunication network; telecommunication systems.

## TELETYPEWRITER, TTY

(abbr)

**Usage:** a terminal compatible with teletypewriters; a TTY exchange service.

## TEMPORARY

(dm)

**Same sign for:** brief, short.
**Usage:** temporary storage; a temporary data set; a temporary file.
**Note:** Right H slides back and forth on left H.

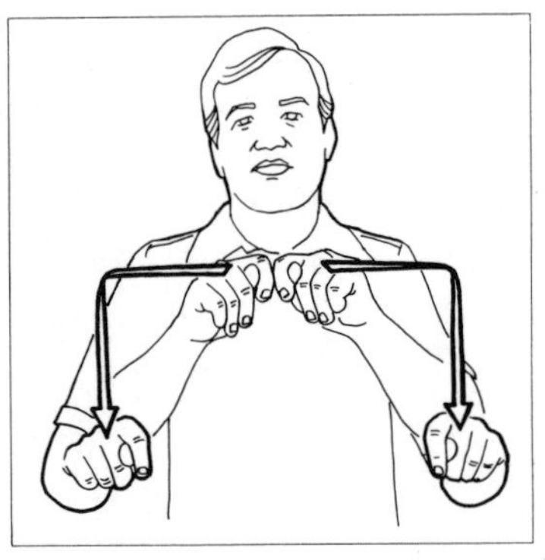

## TERMINAL

(sm)

**Usage:** terminal entry; from a remote terminal; a hard-copy terminal; a CRT terminal.

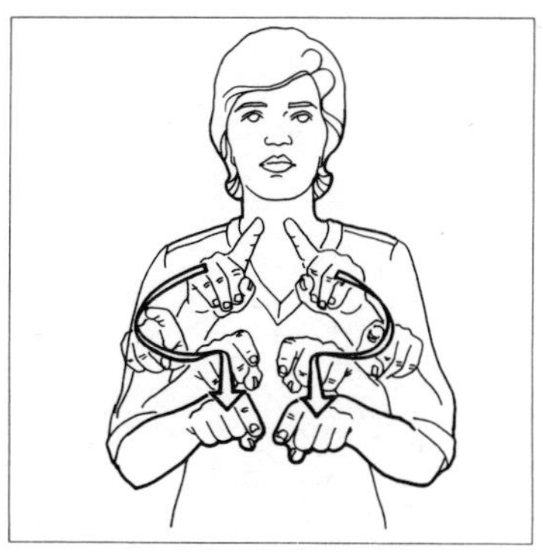

## TEST
(sm)

**Usage:** passed its performance test; unit test; system test; test cases; test data.
**Note:** Right and left hands sign QUERY together.

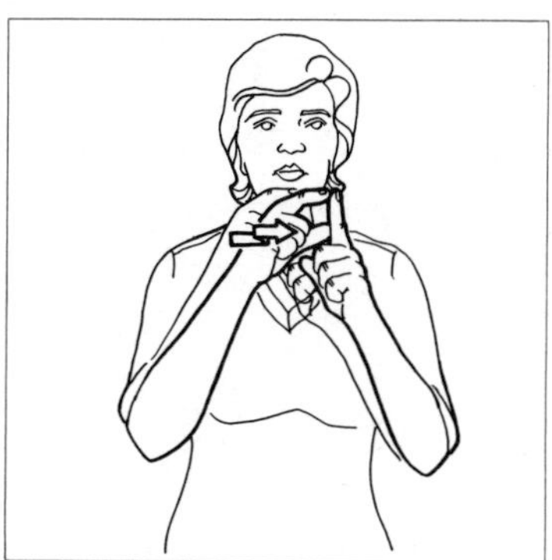

## TEXT

**Usage:** text editing; text processing; two columns of text.
**Note:** Make sign for WORD; move hands to the left and sign WORD again.

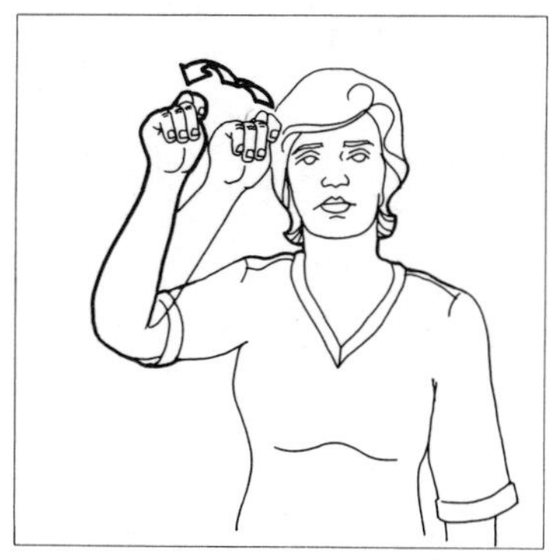

## THEORY

**Initialized form of:** imagine (T).
**Usage:** information theory; game theory; graph theory.

## THROUGHPUT
(sm)

**Usage:** throughput in terms of jobs per day; improved throughput.
**Note:** "through" + "put."

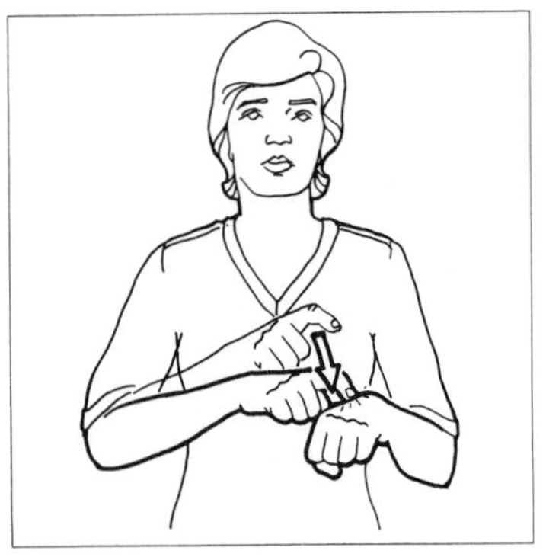

## TIME

**Usage:** time sharing; realtime applications; 3 millisecond access time; 30 minutes of down time.

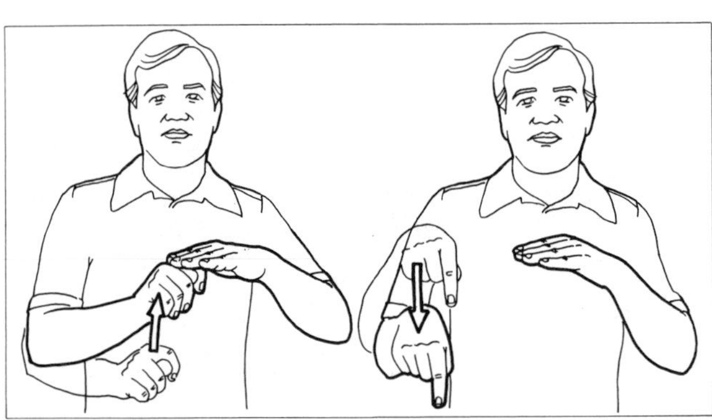

## TOP-DOWN
(sm)

**Usage:** top-down programming; top-down design.

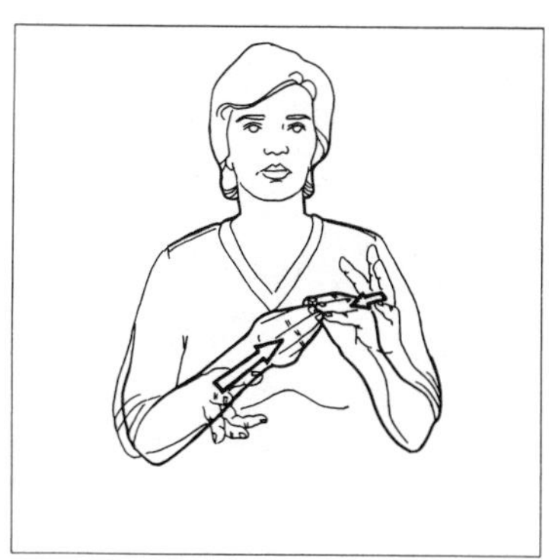

## TOTAL

(cf. ADD) (sm)

**Same sign for:** sum.
**Usage:** the final total; the hash total; intermediate totals.

## TRACE

(sm)

**Usage:** an address trace; a trace routine; to trace the flow of control.
**Note:** Right T-hand moves from fingers to heel of left palm in wavy movement.

## TRACK

**Usage:** a read/write head for each track; tracks per disk surface; 8-track tape.
**Note:** Palm-down T-hand makes horizontal circle.

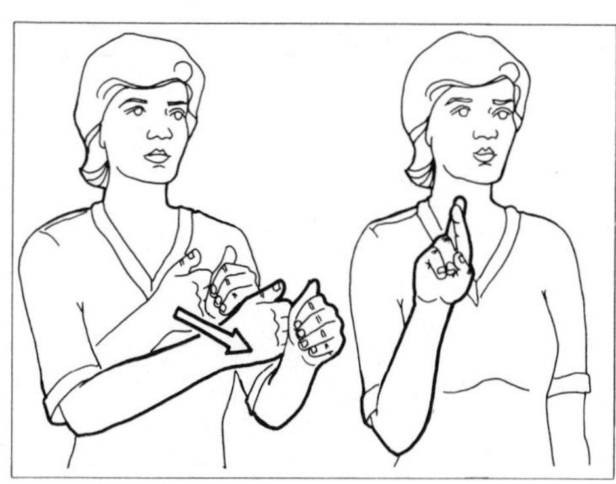

## TRAILER

(sm)

**Usage:** a trailer label; a trailer record.
**Note:** "follow" + -ER.

# TRANSACTION
(sm)

**Initialized form of:** happen (T).
**Usage:** the transaction file; a transaction code; to process a transaction.

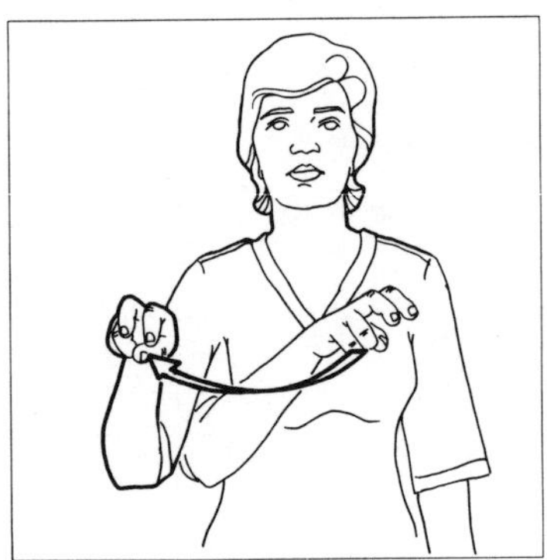

# TRANSFER, TRANSFERABILITY*
(sm)

**Usage:** data transfer rate; a block transfer; the total transfer time; the transferability of programs among systems.

# TRANSIENT

**Usage:** a transient error; a transient routine.
**Note:** "appear" + "disappear."

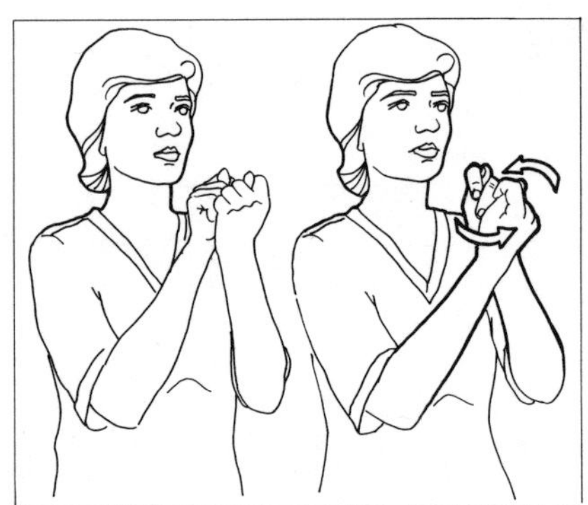

# TRANSLATE, TRANSLATION
(sm)

**Initialized form of:** change (T).
**Usage:** translates the program into assembly language; by using translation tables.

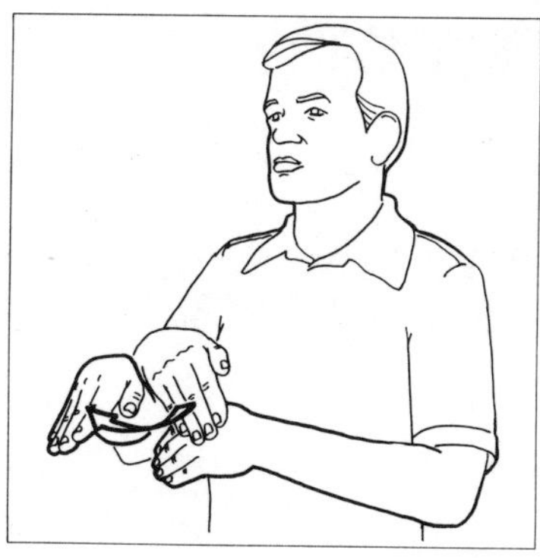

## TRANSMISSION, TRANSMIT

(sm)

**Same sign for:** send.
**Usage:** to transmit data; transmission code; transmission line.
**Note:** Right hand on back of left swings out.

## TTY

(see TELETYPEWRITER)

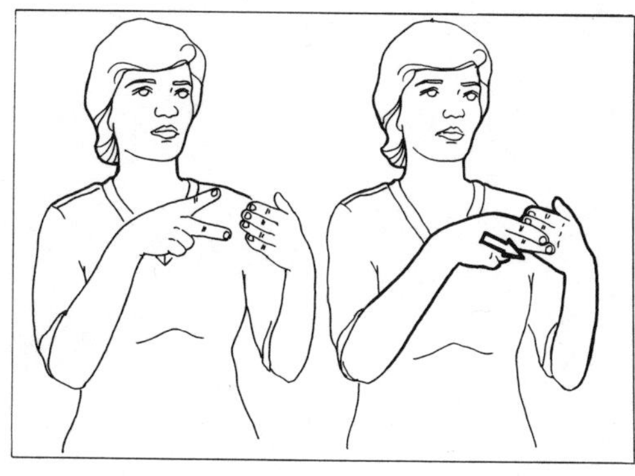

## TRUNCATE, TRUNCATION

**Same sign for:** cut off.
**Usage:** to truncate the low-order digits; with labels longer than 10 characters being truncated; a truncation error.

## TURNAROUND

(sm)

**Usage:** the average turnaround time; can expect quick turnaround for batch jobs.

## TYPE, TYPING, TYPIST*

(cf. CONSOLE)

**Same sign for:** typewriter.
**Usage:** required to type in your password; data entry requires typing skills; word processing allows a typist to make changes easily.
**Note:** Imitate typing movements.

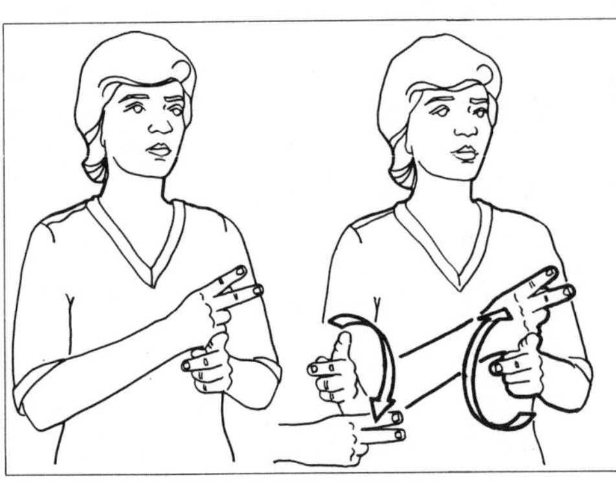

## TYPE

(sm)

**Same sign for:** kind.
**Usage:** the data type is "character"; type declaration.
**Note:** Right-V on left-V; hands circle each other and return to starting position.

# U

## UN-

(cf. IN-, NON-)

**Same sign for:** doesn't, don't, not.
**Usage:** unformatted; unprotected; unrecoverable; unassigned; unscheduled; unpacked.
**Note:** Thumb pushes out from under chin.

U-N-I-T

## UNIT
(fs)

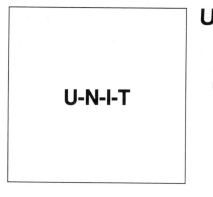

**Usage:** a control unit; a tape unit; unit addressing; unit record; unit testing.

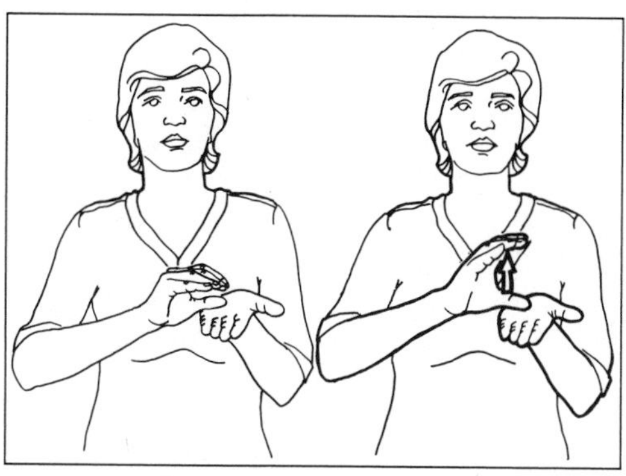

## UNPACK
(sm)

**Usage:** to unpack a field.
**Note:** Right narrow-C on left palm opens to wide-C; opposite of PACK.

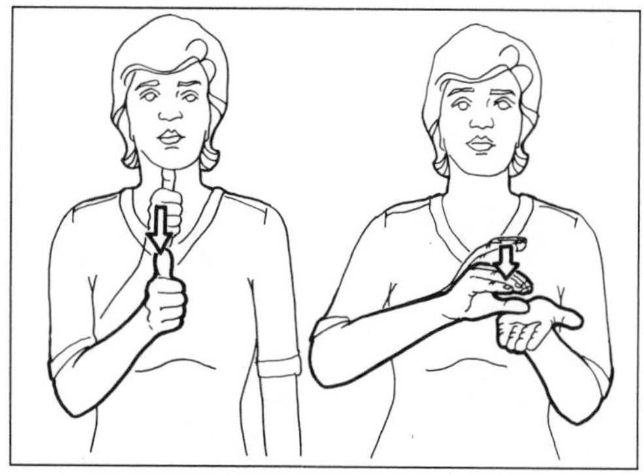

## UNPACKED (adj)
(sm)

**Usage:** unpacked data.
**Note:** UN- PACKED.

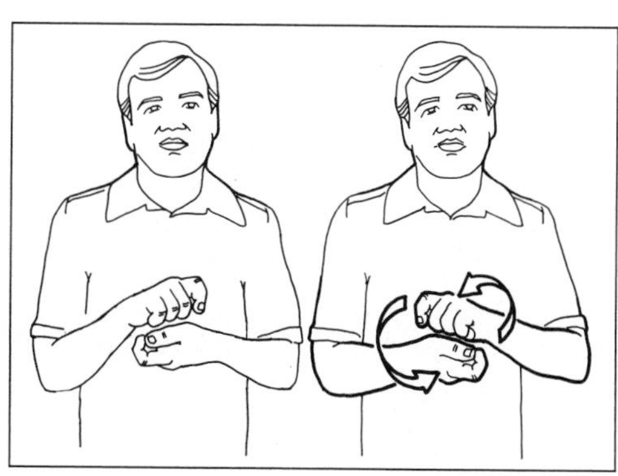

## UPDATE, UPDATED
(cf. CONVERSION) (sm)

**Same sign for:** change.
**Usage:** to update the master record; a copy of the updated file.

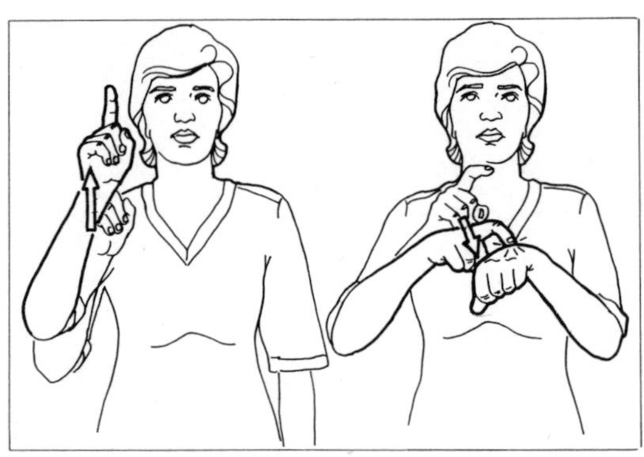

# UPTIME

**Usage:** the percentage of uptime; system uptime.
**Note:** "up" + TIME.

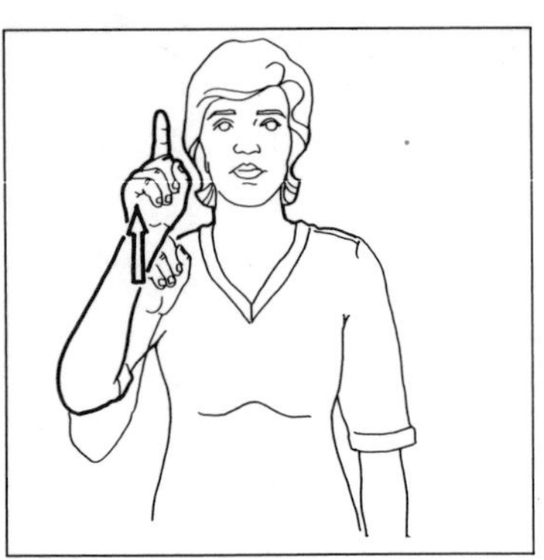

# UPWARD
(sm)

**Same sign for:** up.
**Usage:** is upward compatible with the other system.

# USE, USER*

**Usage:** to use good documentation principles; the user ID; a user terminal.

# UTILITY
(cf. SERVICE)

**Usage:** a utility program; various utility routines.

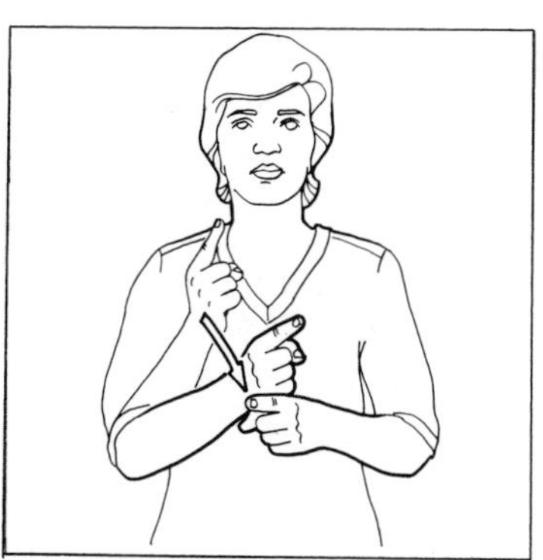

## VALID, VALIDATION, VALIDITY
(sm)

**Same sign for:** correct, right.
**Usage:** a valid character; a validation procedure; performs a validity check.

## VALUE
(sm)

**Usage:** the initial value of the parameter; to assign values.
**Note:** V-hands arc upward.

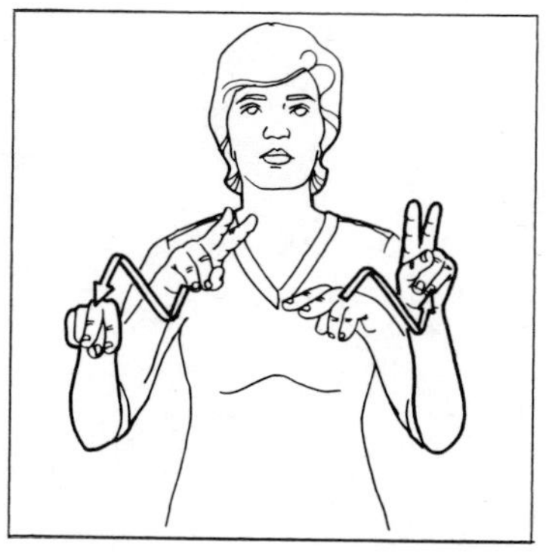

## VARIABLE
(sm)

**Initialized form of:** various (V).
**Usage:** variable-length records; a subscripted variable.

# V

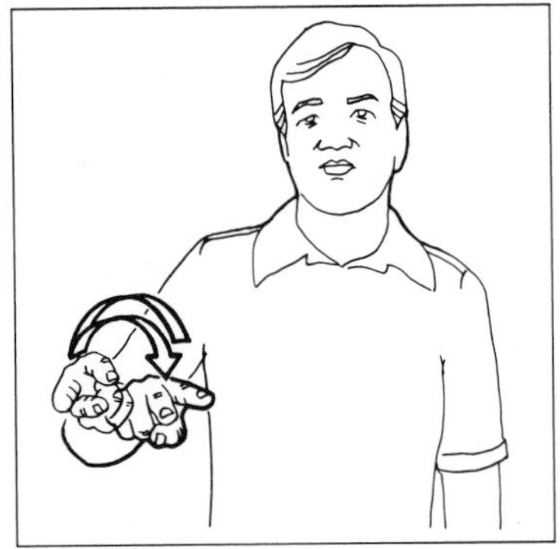

## VARY

(cf. SWITCH) (sm)

**Usage:** to vary the device offline; to vary online.
**Note:** V-hand turns from palm down to palm up to palm down again.

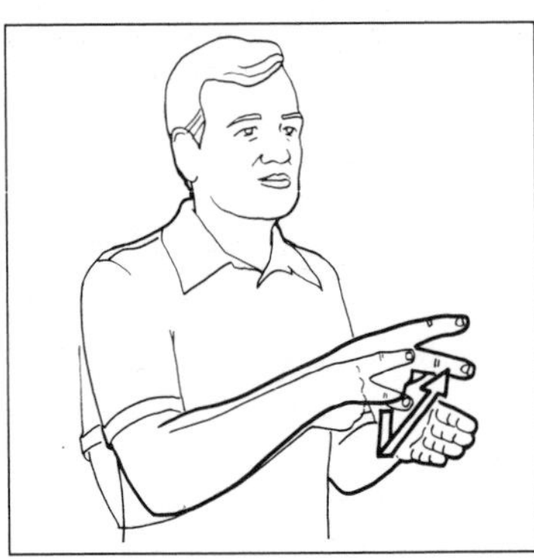

## VERIFICATION, VERIFIER*, VERIFY

(sm)

**Initialized form of:** check (V).
**Usage:** displayed for visual verification; card punch and verifier; to verify the data; program design verification.
**Note:** Middle finger of V-hand makes a check mark in left palm.

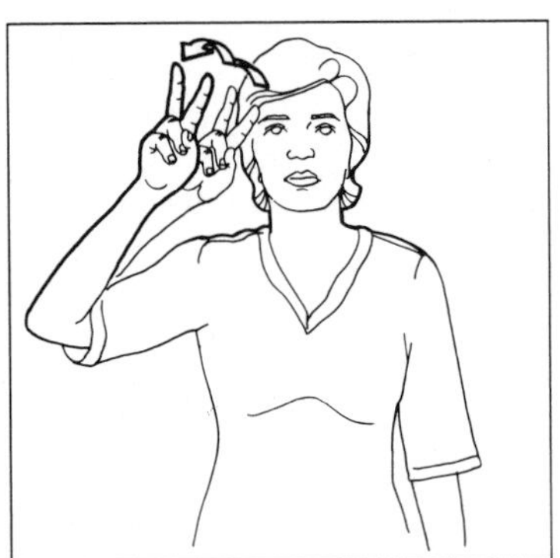

## VIRTUAL

(sm)

**Initialized form of:** imagine (V).
**Usage:** a virtual address; a virtual disk; virtual memory.

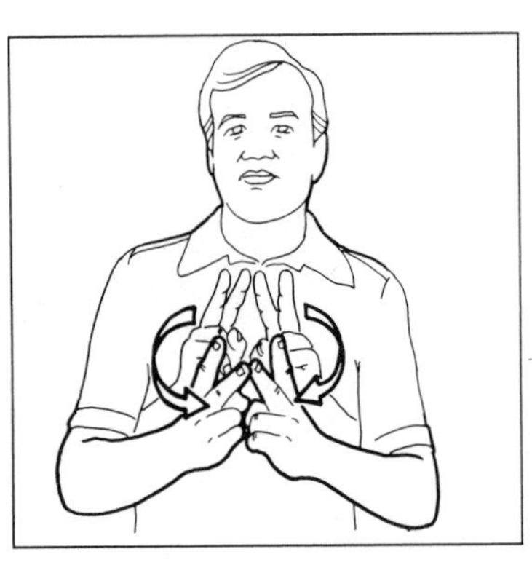

## VOLUME

(sm)

**Initialized form of:** class (V).
**Usage:** a virtual volume; a multiple-volume file; the volume serial number; a tape or disk volume.

V-T-O-C

## VOLUME TABLE OF CONTENTS, VTOC

(acronym)

**Usage:** to update the volume table of contents; to reference the VTOC.
**Note:** The term VTOC is pronounced "vee-talk."

W

## WAIT

**Same sign for:** pending.
**Usage:** in a wait state; the total waiting time.
**Note:** Twiddle fingers.

## WALK-THROUGH
(sm)

**Usage:** a design walk-through; to review the code by holding a walk-through.
**Note:** "walk" + "through."

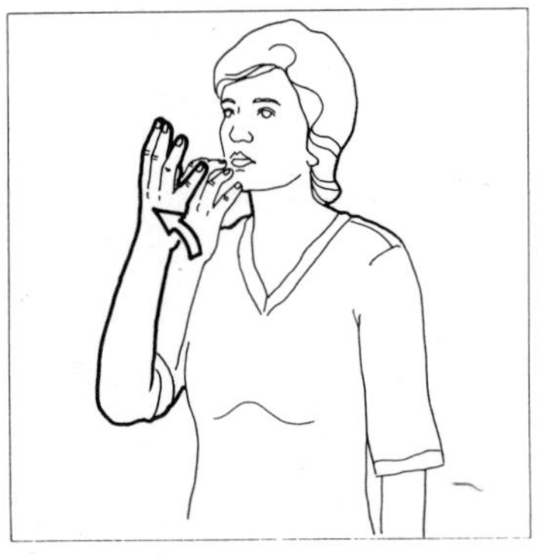

## WARM
(sm)

**Usage:** a warm start.
**Note:** Right hand slowly opens in front of mouth.

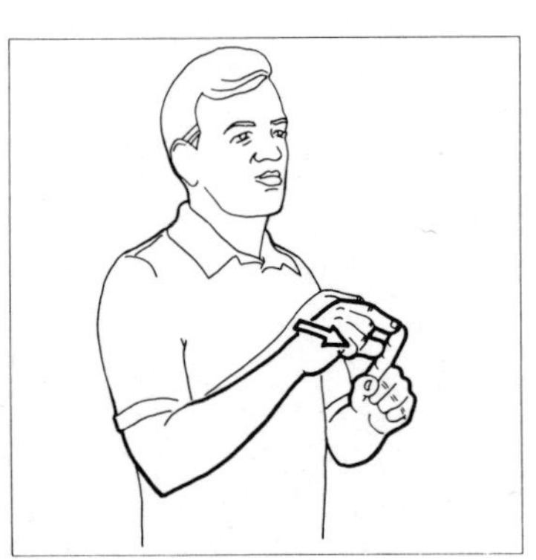

## WORD
(sm)

**Usage:** word length; an instruction word; bits per word; word processing.

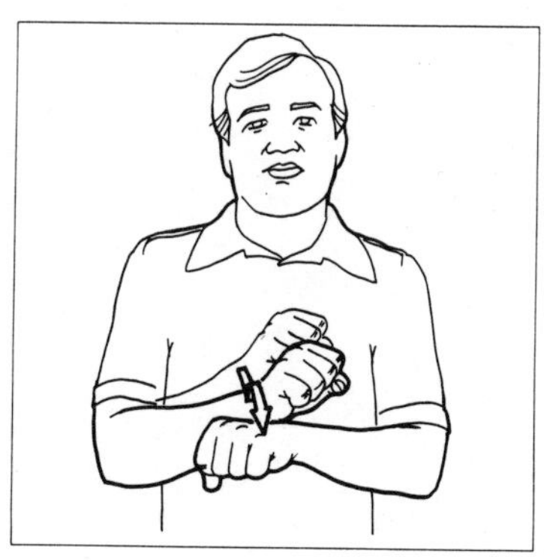

## WORK, WORKING

(cf. TASK)

**Usage:** a work station; a work file; working storage; APL workspaces.

## WRITE

(cf. CODE)

**Usage:** to write a record; a read/write head; to write a program.

# Appendix

## Additional Vocabulary

The following uncapitalized terms are not entries in this book, but the sign for each (in some context) is the same as the capitalized entry to its right. For example, the sign for "abbreviate" (which is not an entry) is the same as for "ACRONYM" (which is an entry).

abbreviate ACRONYM
ability -ABILITY
able -ABLE
again ITERATE
allow ENABLE
another ALTERNATE
associate INTERACTIVE
assume DEFAULT
attach CONNECT

bare BLANK
base two BINARY
base eight OCTAL
base ten DECIMAL
base sixteen HEXADECIMAL
begin START
belong CONNECT
below BASED
block DISABLE
breakdown BOMB
brief TEMPORARY
brilliant INTELLIGENT

can -ABLE
cancel CORRECT
capable -ABLE
cave in BOMB
cease STOP
change CONVERT
chilly COLD
choice OPTION
clean CLEAR
collapse BOMB
concentrate ATTENTION
condense ACRONYM
continue CONSTANT
converse CONVERSATIONAL
correct VALID
criticize CORRECT
cross NODE
cut off TRUNCATE

defend PROTECT
detach DISCONNECT
deteriorate DEGRADE
deviate BRANCH
disrupt INTERRUPT
dissolve SOLVE
distant REMOTE
divert BRANCH
do ACTION
doesn't NON-
don't NON-

eliminate DELETE
else ALTERNATE
empty BLANK
entrance ENTRY
establish SETUP
exact ACCURATE
exactly ACCURATE
exchange SWAP

fake ARTIFICIAL
false ARTIFICIAL
far REMOTE
fast IMMEDIATE
figure CALCULATE
first PRIMARY
flexible FLOPPY

gather ACCUMULATE
get RETRIEVE
govern CONTROL

impede INTERRUPT
in INTERNAL
increase INCREMENT
inform INFORMATION
insect BUG
interfere INTERRUPT
intersect NODE
into ENTER
investigate INSPECTION

join CONNECT

keep MAINTENANCE
kick BUMP
kind TYPE

| | |
|---|---|
| last | F |
| let | E |
| line up | O |
| long | LE |
| many | M |
| measure | BE |
| mechanism | DE |
| melt | SO |
| memorize | ME |
| middle | CE |
| million | ME |
| mingle | INT |
| mistake | ERR |
| motor | MA |
| move | REL |
| multiple | MUL |
| multiply | CAL |
| nature | NAT |
| nice | CLEA |
| not | NON- |
| notify | INFO |
| now | CURR |
| numerous | MULTI |
| obtain | RETRIEVE |
| order | COMMAND |
| other | ALTERNATE |
| part | SECTION |
| pending | WAIT |
| period | DECIMAL POINT |
| persist | CONSTANT |
| place | POSITION |
| possible | -ABILITY |
| postpone | DEFERRED |
| prevent | DISABLE |
| progress | PROCEDURE |
| promote | ADVANCED |
| promotion | ADVANCED |
| put off | DEFERRED |

| | |
|---|---|
| question | QUIRY |
| | MEDIATE |
| | AL |
| | RIEVE |
| | NTROL |
| | E |
| | T |
| | D |
| | RIBUTE |
| | ATE |
| | SMIT |
| | EMENT |
| | ORARY |
| | LIGENT |
| | ON |
| | BUTE |
| | H |
| | ACRONYM |
| summary | ACRONYM |
| summon | CALL |
| sure | REAL |
| take up | DEFAULT |
| talk | CONVERSATIONAL |
| there | AVAILABLE |
| true | REAL |
| twice | DOUBLE |
| typewriter | TYPE |
| underlying | BASED |
| unite | CONNECT |
| up | UPWARD |
| vacant | BLANK |
| winter | COLD |
| wrong | ERROR |

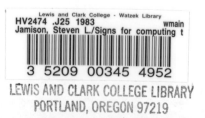